JEFF HOLMES

A SEASON
— TO BE —
CHEERFUL

GLASGOW RANGERS 1992/93

First published by Pitch Publishing, 2017

Pitch Publishing
A2 Yeoman Gate
Yeoman Way
Worthing
Sussex
BN13 3QZ
www.pitchpublishing.co.uk
info@pitchpublishing.co.uk

A CIP catalogue record is available for this book
from the British Library.

ISBN 978-1-78531-325-7

Typesetting and origination by Pitch Publishing

Printed in the UK by Bell & Bain, Glasgow, Scotland

Contents

For my dad, John Holmes.
Forever in my thoughts

Acknowledgements

W RITING about this season in particular brought back an awful lot of great memories. They may have taken place 25 years ago, but the moment I started my research, back they came. The treble, Leeds United, Marseille, Ally McCoist's golden boot, the 44-game unbeaten run, and so many more. I was present at just about every game: I lived it and it was a wonderful time to be a Rangers supporter. But you take the good with the bad, they say!

The guys I interviewed for the book were all first class. I met some in restaurants, others at Ibrox, and we did a couple by e-mail and telephone. It all adds up to a massive thank you to Archie Knox, John 'Bomber' Brown, Dale Gordon, David Robertson, Ally Maxwell, Ian Durrant, Gary McSwegan, Dave McPherson, Stuart McCall and Pieter Huistra for agreeing to participate in this book.

It's always a great pleasure for me to interview those who were fortunate enough to pull on the famous blue jersey. I've watched them from the terracing and the stand for more years than I care to remember, so to share a coffee and their insight into our club is a wonderful privilege.

And to former Rangers director John Gilligan, who was kind enough to pen the foreword. His memories of 1992/93 were a joy to read and I thank him very much. John is a real bluenose at heart and exactly the type of person the club needed at the time to get back on its feet.

A special thanks also to Cheryl Fleming for tracking down and interviewing Dale Gordon. My meagre expenses would never have extended to an overnight stay in Dubai!

As always, it's impossible to undertake a book such as this without the help of many individuals. Among them are David Mason, Alex Boyd, Stephen Docherty and Andy McInnes, who all lent a hand, while Stephen Rothwell came up with the tickets I wanted to feature at the head of each chapter.

However, Davie Lambie was arguably the man of the match. His individual caricatures made me smile, and were the perfect way to introduce each interviewee. But just like the squad of 1992/93, it's a team game here!

And finally to Paul Camillin, Jane Camillin and all the team at Pitch Publishing. If there is a better sports publisher out there then I've yet to find it. Once again they were on top of everything and open to new suggestions and ideas. Salute!

Foreword

RANGERS FC has been with me all my life. My family were all bluenoses and I can't remember a single day when Rangers hasn't been part of my conversation, wherever I am in the world.

I first met the author Jeff a couple of years ago when he contacted me on behalf of Big Jock Wallace's grandson John, who was coming over from Spain for a game. Young John wasn't looking for special treatment and wanted to sit in the Broomloan Front with his mates. Jeff gave me a call and we invited John up to The Blue Room after the match. We've been friends ever since and we also had his gran and dad over for a game last season.

Tradition and history is what matters, and it must be protected. Having Big Jock's family back at the club was as it should be; it felt right. Growing up in a Church of Scotland family, and being a member of the Boys' Brigade, the values given to me have stood me in great stead and shaped my life. Rangers FC was always an extension of those values.

We have been tested like no other support and have stood loyal and true to our club and its values, but without our phenomenal backing we would be just another team. The day we won our club back is one of the best days of my life. Being a director of Rangers was very special and I'll continue to support the club in any way I can from outside the boardroom.

Now on to 1992/93; an amazing season in so many ways. We won the treble and continued our run towards nine in a row. We had an amazing squad dominated by Scottish and English players. It included Goram, Nisbet, Robertson, Gough, McPherson, Brown, Durrant, McCall, McCoist, McSwegan, Ferguson, Hateley, Steven, Stevens and Gordon. Our team was British with a Scottish backbone.

In a season full of highlights, the best for me was beating a wonderful Leeds United side in the Battle of Britain. We were all stunned when Leeds scored first at a packed and raucous Ibrox; it was met with a weird silence that had me doubting it was even a goal! Then that fantastic comeback to win 2-1 after an own goal by Lukic and a winner from guess who ... Mr McCoist himself.

I couldn't get to Leeds as I had just started a new job with McEwan's Lager based in – wait for it – Aberdeen. So I watched the match with some fellow bluenoses and other fans in a pub called Cocky Hunters. When Big Hateley smashed in the opener I went absolutely mental and got no hassle from anyone, as all the Gers fans were going nuts!

We were battered for a while before getting that amazing second goal: Bomber wins a tackle and the ball breaks to Fergie, who passes it forward to Durrant. He plays it out to Hateley, who has come wide left. The big man whips over a brilliant cross that is met by the onrushing Super Ally and he guides a fabulous header into the back of the net.

History will show we were denied our chance of a place in the final by questionable means, but the run remains our best and we should have been in that final, where we would have stood a real chance of winning.

Since then we've had the 'Lovenkrands Final', the last-day win against Dunfermline to clinch the title and of course Helicopter Sunday.

The last five years have been tough, but we're a tough support; we bend to no one and we will be there for 55 – that's for sure.

Yours aye,
John Gilligan
Former Rangers Director

Introduction

WEDNESDAY, 21 October 1992; not a date that rolls easily off the tongue, but one which presented me with a dilemma. I knew I would be asked to work late that afternoon, and that was the problem. A big problem.

At the time I was employed by Scottish Television as a stagehand/prop man. It was a good job, my first job actually. I had started in the Cowcaddens television programme factory in January 1977. I was an extremely loyal employee, but that day I would have to introduce a little cunning.

I was working on the latest episode of the cop drama *Taggart*, and we were filming in Airth, a little village close to Falkirk. The one-off special was called 'Fatal Inheritance' and starred Hannah Gordon as the proprietor of an upmarket country club-cum-spa. The show was due to air on New Year's Day. Detective Chief Inspector Jim Taggart books into a health farm to keep an eye on the good doctor, after she receives a Not Proven verdict in the court case relating to the murder of her husband's lover. The usual Taggart fare.

That was all good and well, but I had a more pressing problem; how to get out of working late that Wednesday. Due to the nature of the filming, a string of night shoots were necessary, although the only place I wanted to be that evening was Ibrox as Leeds United visited in the second round, first leg of the European Cup.

I had a ticket, of course, and the only thing left for me to do was convince the production designer (my boss) that I had to be elsewhere from around 6pm until around 10pm. He wasn't a football man, and it would have been unprofessional to have asked for time off, especially as half the crew were Rangers supporters and were desperate to be at the match. No problem. A future location required some finishing touches and as I drove off in the rented Transit van, he waved with a mixture of friendliness and suspicion. I had convinced him the job only required the services of one man for a couple of hours. He would never know, would he?

I motored towards Glasgow and the traffic was heavy. After all, 43,250 others had the same idea; maybe not to bunk off work, but to get to the game on time. I had left Airth with time to spare so I had little to worry about.

Arriving at the ground, I searched for a parking space in the pot-holed streets surrounding Ibrox and eventually paid a couple of mini Goodfellas to 'watch my van' and walked the short distance to the ground.

Striding towards the Broomloan Road stand I could feel a real sense of anticipation within my fellow supporters. There was a real sense that this could be our night. Of course, Leeds were a top team and had some fantastic players but our collective spirit, I felt, could see my team prevail over two legs and qualify for the group stages of the first ever Champions League.

That was the hope as I filed into the stadium, grabbed a pie and soft drink and took my seat a dozen rows from the front in BF2, just to the right of the goal, as you look on to the lush green grass of home.

I was in 20 minutes early and began squinting through my programme as the Leeds players were put through their paces 20 yards in front of me. Some did a series of little stretches, others practised heading, and half-a-dozen took shots in at John Lukic.

The guy next to me, a middle-aged man with a Fife twang, supped on his coffee while telling me exactly why we would put three or four past the big Serbian. I was (half) listening but the poor sod wouldn't be around much longer as the moment he raised his paper cup to his mouth, a wayward Gary McAllister shot missed the goal completely but struck Mr Fifer perfectly on the nose, sending a mixture of coffee, glasses, the pages of my programme and blood up into the air and back down again in slow motion as my buddy-for-the-evening bit the dust. He was out of it. McAllister was completely unaware of the pandemonium his rotten attempt on goal had caused as the very minute the ball left his boot, the Leeds players were summoned to leave the field and head back to the dressing room for one final pre-match pep talk.

The paramedics attended to Mr Fifer and he was taken off on a wee stretcher never to return. The incident left a strange feeling in the moments before the big game, but sadly Mr Fifer was all but forgotten as the teams made their way on to the park amid a crescendo of noise. No away supporters (allegedly); just Rangers fans willing their team on to a famous victory with cheering, screaming, singing and roaring. Would it be enough? We were only seconds away from finding out. Let the long-awaited Battle of Britain commence.

The game started and we settled down for the evening. The weeks leading up to this vital European Cup tie had dragged but it was finally here. Now to enjoy. Whoops, here comes Leeds straight away. WOAH! That Gary McAllister has the ball on the edge of the area. Duck everyone, we don't wanna end up like Mr Fifer! We breathed a huge sigh of relief as the net saved us from a fate similar to that of Mr Fifer. The downside? We were 1-0 down inside the first minute!

Okay, the goal was scored at the opposite end of the ground, but have you never heard of dramatic licence?

Well. I didn't see that coming, if you know what I mean. Thankfully, though, John Lukic threw one into his own net and Ally McCoist bagged a second to give us a slight advantage to take down to Elland Road a fortnight later. The final whistle blew and there was a surreal cloud of apprehension hanging over the stadium as we filed out into the night; perhaps we all reckoned the 2-1 lead wouldn't be enough to get us through to the promised land of the Champions League.

Anyway, I had more pressing matters to hand. Like would my hired Transit van still be in one piece; would it be on bricks – or empty? I needn't have worried as the Ant Hill Mob proved very able custodians, and I sped (not illegally) back to Airth to re-join the crew. On entering the expansive grounds of Airth Castle, the first person I encountered was our production designer, who greeted me with a warm smile and asked if I had enjoyed the game! I was about to put on my best 'confused face' when he added, 'We seen you on the TV,' when Ally McCoist scored, and with that he flashed another smile and walked off. He knew how much I loved Rangers.

Rumbled. It had been an eventful evening and I joined in the night's filming and not another word was spoken. Oh, and 2-1 proved more than enough for us to progress in the competition and collect our 'Fatal Inheritance'.

The 1992/93 season was certainly proving eventful, and as it wore on, we would come to discover just how successful it would be.

Jeff Holmes
September 2017

1

McCoist makes it to Tuscan Paradise

P RE-SEASON started belatedly for eight members of Walter
Smith's squad as they were given extra time off following
their participation in the European Championships in Sweden,
although eyebrows were raised when goal king Ally McCoist insisted
on returning to training early!

The wily gaffer added three new faces to his group, with two of
them – Trevor Steven and Dave McPherson – returning to Ibrox after
spells away. Former Motherwell goalkeeper Ally Maxwell, who had
spent the previous season in dispute with the Fir Park club, also signed
as back-up to Scotland's number one Andy Goram.

The new arrivals aroused speculation that Smith would have to
offload players to balance the books but he insisted that wasn't the
case, saying, 'There is no way we are actively trying to sell anyone.
We used 27 players in our first team last season, so this year will be
every bit as difficult. If you take that into consideration nobody can
say we have too many players.

'Demands on players in the modern game are far greater than
they have ever been, so it's important to have a large squad to cover
injuries and suspensions.

'Transfer speculation will always follow a club the size of Rangers
but we just have to put up with it. I don't want to sell anyone, but if

a club is interested in a player who is not featuring for the first team then we will consider it.'

Smith reckoned he had assembled his strongest squad since joining six years previous, and while that was naturally seen as a positive, the flip side meant some players would be left disappointed at not getting regular first team football in the coming season. However, the boyhood Gers fan insisted he wouldn't flinch at making the kind of decisions that would keep Rangers at the forefront of Scottish football. Smith's side had won four titles in a row and players like Trevor Steven had been acquired to ensure competition for places would remain as keen as ever.

The players returned for pre-season training buoyed by the prospect of a tilt at a brand new European competition – the Champions League. The new initiative did exactly what it said on the tin, unlike the present day when as many as four clubs from some countries take part. It would begin life as the European Cup, with 36 teams battling to get into a group stage called the Champions League. The winner from each group of four would meet in a winner-takes-all final.

The draw for the first round – which was made while Rangers were at their pre-season training camp in Italy – paired the Light Blues with Danish champions Lyngby, a tie Smith had been keen to avoid. The Danes had provided their national squad with four players, and each played their part in the Scandinavian country's unlikely Euro Championship success in Sweden.

Smith said, 'Last season you wouldn't have wanted to face Sparta Prague as a non-seeded side and I think this year you would have picked Lyngby as one to avoid. That was my immediate reaction and I think it will be an awkward tie.'

Lyngby had won the Danish championship for only the second time in their history and were something of an unknown quantity. With this in mind, Smith planned to watch them in action at least twice.

But while the top-team players were just getting down to some serious work in readiness of a tough season ahead, two under-age representative teams had just returned from Northern Ireland after taking part in the prestigious Milk Cup competition for youth teams.

Rangers' under-16s and under-14s had been to Coleraine for the event and the older age group beat Nottingham Forest 2-1 in the final in front of 10,000 fans at The Showground.

The under-14s were desperately unlucky as they fell to Norwich City at the semi-final stages, losing 3-2 with a goal conceded in the final minute of extra time. Norwich went on to beat Hearts in the final.

Rangers' goal hero in the final of the under-16 competition was none other than Charlie Miller, who bagged a double and earned himself the Golden Boot as the tournament's top scorer. Young Ger Andy O'Brien picked up the top goalscorer award in the under-14 section and Rangers were named most successful club.

Ibrox youth coach Alistair Stevenson said, 'The standard of play at the Milk Cup is very high so we were delighted with the showing of both our teams. We were given fantastic backing by Rangers supporters in Ulster and received many presentations.'

On their way to winning the competition, Rangers' under-16s beat Londonderry Select 3-2, IDV, from Iceland 5-0, Austrian side Steyr Wels 13-1, and Priory County, from England, 4-0 in their sectional games. In the quarter-finals they thumped Grasshoppers Zurich 9-1 before edging Crewe – widely acknowledged as having one of the best youth policies in Britain – 1-0 in the last four.

With assistant manager Archie Knox looking on, Rangers led Forest 1-0 at half-time in the final but conceded an equaliser. Roared on by a partisan crowd, though, Miller scored a sensational winner to earn Gers the gold medals.

The under-14s scored 30 goals in their three sectional games, which included a 20-0 rout of an Icelandic side.

Meanwhile, one player who was hoping to put his own personal nightmare behind him was Dutch winger Pieter Huistra, who admitted he had felt really down after being left out of the previous campaign's Scottish Cup Final win over Airdrie. It was the second season in succession that Huistra had brought down the curtain on a campaign with a scowl on his face rather than a smile.

At the end of 1990/91, Huistra missed out on the deciding league match with Aberdeen. Twelve months later, and after a starring role in the Scottish Cup semi-final, the Dutchman failed to make the squad for the final against Airdrie – which he felt contributed to him being omitted from the Holland squad for the European Championship finals.

The then 25-year-old moaned, 'After injuries, that fortnight has been the worst experience in my career. The same thing happened the previous year when I was involved in every match of the season except the league decider against Aberdeen.

'Last season, I was involved in most of the games before the cup final, and with a place in the European Championships also at stake, it was even more disappointing to miss out. I think my chances of playing in Sweden would have been better had I played in the cup final. I was part of the preliminary squad of 25, and when two pulled out, I thought I would have been in contention for a place but the coach picked Rob Witschge, who wasn't even involved in the original 25!'

Despite being involved in all the earlier rounds of the Scottish Cup, Huistra didn't get a winner's medal – and insisted he didn't know why he was being left out of the Hampden 13. He said, 'Only the manager can answer that. It was his decision and he will have his reasons. To be fair, it was a hard decision for him to make, but it was also a tough one for me to accept. It is something I will be reminded of even after my career is over, just because it was such a huge moment.'

However, the Dutchman was ready to knuckle down, work hard and fight for a regular first-team place. And there was one more man he wanted to impress, new Dutch coach Dick Advocaat!

He said, 'If I am playing well for my club, I hope to be involved with the national team again. It's a big honour to play for your country, but my main consideration is playing for Rangers. After all, it is the club who pay my wages.'

The month of July saw the Light Blues head for the luxurious Il Ciocco resort in Tuscany, where coaches Archie Knox and Davie Dodds put the players through their paces. Mind you, there was still time for some light-hearted banter – which would always be the case with players such as Ally McCoist and Ian Durrant in the squad. In fact, 'Coisty' came away with arguably the line of the trip when he quipped, 'I'm so sharp I could open a tin of peas with my foot!'

Mind you, Durrant wasn't too far behind, and when he saw no-nonsense striker Paul Rideout warming up he said, 'Paul is taking the bounce games seriously. I caught him sandpapering his elbows!'

But even before the squad departed for Italy, there was a shock in store for everyone. McCoist had been on a family holiday in the Seychelles and was due to hook up with Smith, Knox and co. at Heathrow. Knox wagered that legendary latecomer McCoist would live up to his reputation but it was Durrant who pocketed the cash when McCoist was on time, and at the airport long BEFORE the rest of the squad! It was perhaps the first, and last time it would happen.

Mind you, when the players clapped eyes on Coisty's luggage, the banter was soon flowing again. He had a 'Hilda Ogden' trolley with him, and inside was a couple of t-shirts and shorts, a pair of boots and two CDs – Guns 'n Roses and Bruce Springsteen. Thankfully, kitman Jimmy Bell had packed his training gear and clothes before leaving Glasgow.

Full-back David Robertson hopped aboard the flight as a first-time dad, with his wife Kym giving birth to daughter Chelsea just a fortnight beforehand.

The flight to Pisa took two hours and after arriving at Il Ciocco just after 4pm, the players had a short training session to loosen up before returning to the hotel about 8pm and eating, which was followed by a game of cards and then bed. The schedule for the week-long training camp was: a light breakfast at 9am, meet at the hotel entrance for 10am and the five-minute drive up the mountain to the pitches, which are set at an altitude of 700 metres. Training until noon, and then back down for lunch and an 'everyman' break from 1pm until 2pm. That was followed by a two-hour siesta and then another session between 4pm and 6pm.

The morning session was definitely the toughest, and consisted mostly of running, interspersed with games of Torro to re-establish the first touch. The work was hard for the players, but even harder for Steven Pressley and David Hagen, who were responsible for helping Archie Knox set up training exercises, move goals, collect balls and assist Jimmy Bell with training gear and fridge coolers full of water and ice.

However, Hagen said, 'We're the youngest here so it's only right we help out. Besides, we're used to it from our time on the groundstaff. It was an unbelievable bonus when we were told we would be making the trip a few days beforehand. The training has been difficult, but you only pick up good habits from the more experienced players. They are full of encouragement and point out if you are doing anything wrong. The trip is all about experience and it can only help us for the season ahead.'

Rangers were the first of three teams to use Il Ciocco that summer. The week after, Liverpool were scheduled to arrive, and a further seven days later, AS Roma were due. Quite incredibly, staff at the training complex were expecting 5,000-6,000 Roma fans to arrive just to watch their favourites train.

Assistant boss Knox was adamant there would be no slacking, and said, 'If the players try to get fly, we've got to be equally as fly,

21

if not flyer.' But he added, 'There is only so much you can get out of people and we've got it – and a little bit extra.'

One man who was hoping for a quiet week was club doctor Donald Cruickshank, who had been at Ibrox for 20 years prior to the trip. He said, 'In the past, pre-season tended to be very haphazard. We used to go to Sweden and play a few games and it was more like training during the season than intensive pre-season work.

'The training conditions in Italy are ideal with one exception – the pitch can sometimes be a bit hard, but they've had a lot of rain recently so it should be perfect. The type of food is also a great benefit as it is high carbohydrate with plenty of fruit – ideal for athletes.'

But he added, 'In my opinion, players who return to pre-season training vastly unfit very rarely ever catch up with their team-mates. These days, most players learn to look after themselves on their holiday and I reckon fitness at this stage is much better than in previous seasons.'

And it would have to be as there was a long and gruelling season ahead. Each top-flight team was scheduled to play an energy-sapping 44 league games, and if the Light Blues were to be successful in both domestic cups and Europe, they were looking at a 65-game campaign!

Mind you, one of the most overworked staff members at Il Ciocco was kitman Jimmy Bell, whose equipment list read like an inventory of the Ibrox boot room – and more. Some of the items he was asked to take included; three sets of training gear for each player (t-shirt, slip, shorts, socks, training shoes, flip-flops and moulded kangaroo-skin adidas Copa Mundial boots – although those with individual boot deals could wear whatever they chose). His trunk also included 20 adidas footballs, spare boots, laces, insoles, boot stretchers, polish and 48 packs of Gatorade juice.

The players would also go through around 20 two-litre bottles of water a day at training sessions, although that was provided by the centre. It was originally hoped that Jimmy would drive to Il Ciocco with the five hampers of kit plus mountain bikes before the players' arrival but the French drivers' dispute put paid to those plans.

The gruelling sessions were intended to build up sharpness, not just physically but mentally too. At one point, a Davie Dodds thunderbolt in a training game cracked the bar and fell at an awkward height for Ally McCoist, who managed to control it with one touch and thunder it past Ally Maxwell. As soon as the ball hit the back of the net, Coisty walked over to John Spencer and said, 'Spenny, I want your comments on that piece of finishing.' Quick as a flash, Spenny replied, 'Ally, there are only two players in Scottish football who could have scored that type of goal – and I'm the other one!'

But despite the razor sharp reflexes that helped him score the goal, Coisty let slip that he was considering a change of position. 'Did you see me there?' he asked his team-mates after an impressive display in the middle of the park. 'I was like Ray Wilkins, picking up passes from the back four and spraying them about the park. I fancy moving to that position in my mid-30s!'

The highlight of the final day at Il Ciocco was a friendly seven-a-side match between a Rangers staff line-up and a waiters' select. However, the staff side was dealt a pre-match blow when Archie Knox was forced to call off with an injury, although his place was ably filled by a female Italian gynaecologist who was staying at the hotel on holiday and had wandered up to watch training. She proved a more than adequate replacement as the Gers turned in a fighting performance to win 8-5. Physio Bill Collins played a blinder in goals, while Walter Smith and Davie Dodds held the defence together. The watching crowd – made up of excess players and waiters – enjoyed the spectacle!

It was soon time to leave Il Ciocco but when the squad arrived at Pisa Airport, they learned of an hour's delay to their flight. While waiting, the Liverpool squad arrived and there were handshakes all around as Graeme Souness – looking fit and healthy after a heart operation – met up with his former colleagues.

John Brown would be a key participant in the forthcoming campaign, and he went into the season having taken strides towards completing his UEFA A Licence qualification at the SFA's Inverclyde coaching centre. He said, 'Players tend to take coaching for granted but I find the courses really open your eyes to the job coaches do and the preparation they undertake. It was rewarding to speak to other players, coaches and managers, even from the amateur levels. Everyone can learn from each other.

'There was a lot of group work, which was very rewarding, with other players and coaches such as Murdo MacLeod, Keith Wright, Gerry Collins, Ray Farningham, Ally Dawson and Davie Irons participating. Stuart Munro was also there attempting to get the "A" advanced certificate, which is the third qualification, and I think he was successful. These courses set you up for later life, but in the short term they are also worthwhile as they get you in good shape for the season ahead.'

Off the field there was plenty of praise for Rangers supporters from Chief Superintendent Jim Kay of Govan Police Office. Mr Kay was complimenting fans on their good behaviour inside and outside Ibrox during the previous season. The number of arrests was reduced by 50 per cent from the campaign before, with the majority for drink-related offences.

He said, 'Rangers supporters have established an enviable record of good behaviour over recent years. I am looking forward to the new season and I am sure the supporters will continue to show that their behaviour is an example for others to follow.'

During the 1991/92 season, Ally McCoist scored 39 goals in 49 matches, which led to a clutch of awards coming his way, and none were as welcome as the adidas Golden Boot, with Super Ally reinforcing his reputation as one of the best finishers in Europe.

But as he entered his tenth season with the club since John Greig signed him from Sunderland, he had a message of caution for his very own follow-follow brigade and said, 'I don't think I can score as many goals or as many important goals as I did last season. I know I say it myself, but last season the important and spectacular goals I scored were a dream. Hearts at Tynecastle, Hibs at Ibrox, Celtic in the Scottish Cup and the two against Aberdeen on the last day of the season – they were all vital goals and it will be difficult to match that.

'I also don't think it's getting any easier to score in the Premier League, but if there's one thing I've picked up in my time it's experience, so I'll be doing my best to match those past achievements.'

McCoist was quick to praise strike partner Mark Hateley for his role in their smash 'n' grab partnership, which contributed 62 goals to the Rangers cause in 1991/92, and with comeback king Ian Durrant also looking to fully reintroduce himself to the team, there was no way McCoist would fail to reach a personal target of 200 career Rangers goals (he was sitting on 179) through a lack of ammunition.

He said, 'There seems to be some sort of telepathy between Ian and myself. He always seems to know the runs I make and the passes to play. We saw some of that towards the end of last season – although I'm not happy about him getting the man of the match award against Falkirk when I scored a hat-trick!

'Seriously, the wee man has had a very thorough pre-season. He's been looking good and that will make him sharper for the year ahead, and that's great news for Rangers.'

Meanwhile, one player who couldn't wait for the action to begin for real was 24-year-old Scott Nisbet – despite the Edinburgh-born defender knowing he was facing a real scrap to win a starting place.

Nisbet's favoured position was central defence, and the close-season signing of Dave McPherson – his main rival for the berth alongside Richard Gough – certainly didn't scare big Nissy, but with Gary Stevens out injured, the right-back berth was also up for grabs.

Nisbet said, 'Just because we've signed Davie doesn't mean my best chance of a game is at right-back. There's nothing to stop me aiming for a game in the middle of the defence.'

Nisbet had starred for Rangers in the first half of 1991/92 in central defence before injury forced him on to the sidelines and allowed Oleg Kuznetzov and then John Brown to take over. But right-back was also a position the versatile Nissy had filled on numerous occasions.

He said, 'I played at right-back for just about the whole season when Terry Butcher broke his leg and I've covered for Gary [Stevens] quite a few times, but it's up to the manager to make the decisions on where I'll play.

'To be honest, I don't mind competing for any position, no matter where it is. I have no preference for either full-back or central defence, just as long as I get a game. Full-back is definitely the harder position to play. You must watch the line more carefully for offside and physically it is more difficult as you have to constantly be in support. David Robertson and Gary Stevens both fill the role very well because they are excellent athletes as well as very good players.'

Nisbet added, 'I didn't miss a day's pre-season training and now it's up to me to win my way into the team. If I achieve that, I then need to put pressure on Walter Smith with my performances so he can't drop me. It's up to me to make his job much harder.'

Brian Reid was two years younger than Nisbet, but his aims and objectives were exactly the same: he was gunning for an elusive defensive role. The talented youngster had just endured a nightmare eight-month spell on the sidelines and was desperate to get back playing regularly. He had managed a couple of comeback games at the tail end of the previous season – but that was for the Ibrox second and third strings.

He said, 'I surprised even myself by just how well pre-season training went. I thought I would struggle, but I kept up with the front pack, although I probably helped myself by doing two weeks' work before the trip to Italy. Hopefully I impressed the coaches in training. I don't know if they thought I would be a bit behind, but I feel I've been holding my own.

'I also feel I have to work harder than the other players as they have last season under their belts, so it has been a challenge to get to their level of fitness. Now I'm ready to start afresh, just like everyone else at the club.'

As for the added pressure of McPherson re-signing for the Light Blues, Reid said, 'Davie's signing means I have to work even harder to get into the side. It's just another challenge I have to face, but I'm taking the season game by game, and if I get my chance I aim to take it.

'My confidence has also been helped by those few games I managed towards the end of the season. I sometimes worried if I would be able to make a comeback at all, but I played through those games quite well and that has given me a boost.'

The former Scotland under-21 man also spoke about winning the tough mental fight associated with such a long lay-off, and said, 'I don't think I'll worry about tackling as I said to myself when I was out for a year that I was going to shut it from my mind because if I thought about it my performances would be affected. And the signs are good as I haven't thought about the injury during training games.

'Rangers have a big squad, but last season we used all our recognised central defenders, so I'm hoping to get my chance and take things from there.'

Prior to the opening league match of the season against St Johnstone, Rangers hosted French champions Marseille in a challenge match which drew in excess of 40,000 fans to Ibrox. The fixture had been organised as part of Trevor Steven's £2.4m switch to Rangers a week before the start of the season.

The 28-year-old midfielder had moved from Rangers to the southern French port less than a year previous for a stunning £5.5m – although his dream of playing abroad soon turned sour. Steven said, 'I had problems as my contract wasn't being honoured and that cast a shadow. Those problems didn't make it easy for me to settle and at times I simply had to grit my teeth and get on with producing the performances on the pitch.

'But it was always an ambition of mine to go and play abroad and see what life was like and I thoroughly enjoyed that aspect of my move to France. It was an experience which broadened my horizons, and that's now the way I'm looking at my time on the continent.'

During his short spell in France, there was almost constant speculation that Steven's contractual problems would lead to his departure, and a host of English clubs were reportedly ready to battle it out for his signature. But Rangers got there in the nick of time to help end his French farce.

Steven added, 'A move to Leeds United in particular was being discussed, but even then I was always hopeful Rangers would maintain their interest. I always dreamed I would end up back at Ibrox and thankfully that has happened.'

However, Steven was forced to limp off after 70 minutes of the game against Marseille with a hamstring injury – and that ruled him out of the league opener against Saints. Two goals in two minutes – the first from Rudi Voller and a wonder-goal by Didier Deschamps – gave Marseille a 2-1 win. Mark Hateley hit a late consolation from the penalty spot. Marseille, one of the favourites to win the inaugural Champions League, included stars such as Marcel Desailly, Basile Boli, Franck Sauzee and Abedi Pele.

DAVE McPherson would have been at Ibrox most weeks even if he hadn't been fortunate enough to sign for the team he supported as a kid: that was never in doubt, but perhaps he has former team-mate Billy Davies to thank for saving him the admission money each week.

The duo turned out for youth side Pollok United – where politician Tommy Sheridan was also a team-mate – and when a Rangers scout came along to watch Davies in action, he quite liked the look of big 'Slim' and the rest, as they say, is history.

McPherson said, 'I was a Rangers fan as a boy and was born and brought up in Pollok, which wasn't too far from Ibrox. I signed a schoolboy form at 14, and was fortunate enough to join the club two years later, 1980, on a professional contract. I made my debut during the 1982/83 season while still a teenager and consider myself very lucky to have done so at such a young age.

'Rangers didn't have a boys' club at the time, and it was pre-academy. Basically you got picked up from school or while playing youth football. Billy and I played for Pollok United, and also played for the same school team. When he got picked up by Rangers, the scout must also have noticed me and he invited me along to Ibrox. So from those early days I was always connected to Rangers.'

However, despite the interest from Rangers, McPherson revealed how the move was almost derailed at the 11th hour. He explained, 'Around that time, I was contacted by a few clubs from England who wanted me to go down for trials, but being a Rangers supporter I decided to stick with what I had. In those days, you would have headed down south during the school holidays for trials, but with

Rangers on my doorstep I could train on a Tuesday and Thursday night at Ibrox. Rangers had decided long before the summer holidays they wanted me, and that was when they offered a schoolboy contract, which I was delighted to sign.'

He added, 'John Greig was the manager at the time but I didn't have too much contact with him. Willie Thornton was responsible for overseeing the youth side of the club. I looked upon Willie Thornton and Willie Waddell as the two key figures at Rangers – and you certainly wouldn't mess with them. They seldom smiled, always stern, but they were always immaculately dressed. I had real respect for both gentlemen and they just oozed Rangers; the class and dignity you expected from men like that.

'Willie Thornton would come on the trips to France with the youth team but would remain in the background and not say much, just offering little bits of advice here and there. I wouldn't say he was a big influence on my career, but I did have a lot of respect for him.'

The Rangers youth side were invited to participate in the prestigious Croix youth football festival every year, and scouts from the top European club sides used the event to spy on the continent's top talent.

McPherson said, 'Rangers had a great record at Croix, although I'll never forget being there and being scouted by Ajax, and one of their representatives actually asking Willie Thornton if they could sign me when I was 16!

'I suppose I was one of the early football-playing centre-backs, which was probably why Ajax recognised me and picked me out. I wasn't just lumping the ball up the park, I loved to play football.

'I remember breaking into the Rangers first team and the first-choice centre-backs were Tom Forsyth and Colin Jackson, who were great players, but older-style defenders, and any time I tried to pass the ball out from the back I would get a row! They would say, "What do you think you're doing?" But that was just how I played, and I had been heavily influenced by the Dutch side, and players like Ruud Krol, and even the German captain Franz Beckenbauer. They both played football from the back and that was the way I wanted to play. It was kind of unknown in Scotland at that time, and I suppose it wasn't until Alan Hansen moved to Liverpool that he developed into more of that kind of player, as well as Gary Gillespie to a certain extent.'

McPherson managed to score on his Rangers debut, in a Scottish Cup tie against Albion Rovers, and said, 'I don't remember too much about that day, but I scored a penalty. I think we were winning quite easily and when we got the spot kick, the players decided the "young boy" should take it! I was a bit nervous but was definitely glad to get the goal.'

McPherson enjoyed seven good years at Rangers, and played for a season under new boss Graeme Souness, but was shocked when his phone rang just after arriving back from holiday. He takes up the story, 'I played for a season under Souness and we won the league. In fact, he played me in every game apart from when I was suspended, and I chipped in with quite a few goals, but Graeme was adamant he wanted to build his own team and it didn't really matter who he had inherited because he had his own ideas.

'But I was still shocked when he called me during the close season to say Hearts had put an offer in for me – and that he thought I should go! I had just been on holiday with Chris Woods and Terry Butcher in Spain and the call came completely out of the blue. My first thought was, "My God, what's this all about?"

'I went over to Ibrox to try and find out a wee bit more and I met Walter Smith. I said to him, "What's going on here Walter, we've just won the league and I scored all these goals?" He didn't say much at all, certainly nothing that convinced me I was wanted, so I decided there was nothing else for it but to pick my boots up and just go.

'It was one of the most difficult moments of my career. I had returned from holiday on a high, I was looking forward to the new season knowing we'd just won the league for the first time in a few years and that I had been a big part of that, but there I was, walking out the front door of the club I loved, into the street and gone. Just like that. The fact it had come from nowhere left me shell-shocked, but I had a decision to make; a very important one, and the last thing I could afford to do was mope around. Luckily for me, Alex McDonald and Sandy Jardine were in charge at Hearts and that made the decision a bit easier.

'Hearts are a big club but moving there initially felt in complete contrast to Rangers. There weren't the same expectations in terms of what was expected of the players at Ibrox, although I have to say that changed over the years.

'When I signed for Hearts, they had been unlucky not to win the league just a couple of years beforehand, so I think Alex was trying to rebuild and bring players in with that wee bit of experience of winning a title, and that was why he had targeted me. I signed at the same time as Shuggie Burns, and the fee paid to Rangers was £440,000, and I used to kid Shuggie on that Hearts had paid £435,000 for me – and even then I think I overvalued him!

'I found it really difficult to settle at Hearts, and the first six weeks or so weren't great. The training was different – not that it was bad – but the facilities weren't as good. The standard wasn't the same as it had been at Ibrox, although Alex and Sandy were working very hard to improve it, and they eventually improved it massively, although naturally it took time.

'As for the football itself, I had just moved for a big transfer fee so I felt quite a bit of responsibility on my shoulders, and not long afterwards, Alex made me captain, which was even more responsibility. I'm not sure a player pays too much attention to the fee; I don't believe he thinks, "I better step up to the plate here." Nowadays it's different. We're talking about players moving for 80 and £90m, but when I moved to Hearts, I didn't look at the fee. With me, it was more that I was a supposed big player coming from Rangers, therefore the pressure was on me to perform. It was the days before Bosman, so more or less everyone moved for a fee, whereas clubs can now pick up brilliant players for nothing towards the end of their contract.

'The Hearts fans were great to me. Initially, I didn't play well, so there were the usual murmurs of discontent; the usual, "He's a waste of money," but once the first month or so was out the way I settled down and they were right behind me. It's a smaller stadium so you tend to hear more, but the atmosphere is fantastic and it's a great place to play your football.'

There is usually a touch of irony involved in any unwanted player move, and McPherson's 'karma moment' arrived at the tail-end of his first season in maroon, when Hearts faced Rangers. He recalled, 'It was at Ibrox and I scored in a 2-1 win. It meant we finished above them in the league, so you can imagine how pleased Graeme Souness was. Graeme had sold me, a centre-back, and the big-name player he brought in, Terry Butcher, broke his leg, so no wonder he was mad.'

While at Tynecastle, McPherson was also an integral part of the national team, and played in all three of Scotland's games at the 1990 World Cup finals in Italy, with the match against Brazil an obvious highlight. He said, 'I remember talking to a few of the players before the match against Brazil, and it was the game everyone wanted to play in, because to say you'd played against Brazil in the World Cup finals was something special.

'We were up against guys like Romario, Careca and Muller; special players, but what a great experience. It was a real challenge but one you wanted to try and enjoy. We felt confident about getting a result against Brazil that night, but the surface was really greasy and when Jim Leighton palmed the ball out, Muller – like all good strikers – was waiting to pounce. It was a great shame, because we felt we could have qualified from the section, so to lose 1-0 to Brazil was very frustrating, especially as a draw would have taken us through. In fact, we nearly qualified through default. We were waiting on the Uruguay result, although it didn't go our way in the end. I suppose it was the typical Scotland story of so near yet so far.

'After the match against Brazil, I was asked to do a press conference with Andy Roxburgh. I met Pele, and he said, "You had a very good game," and I replied, "Thanks very much, you weren't such a bad player yourself!" It was the time when FIFA had started doing all the stats and someone passed me a sheet with all these figures, and my passing success rate was something like 87 per cent, which was great. I always thought I was quite a good passer of the ball but when you see it down on paper it's pleasing.'

After five years in the capital, and more than 200 games, there were rumours that McPherson would soon be on the move. As Hearts' most saleable asset, and the club reportedly ready to cash in on the player, an orderly queue began to form.

McPherson said, 'I was very settled at Hearts and loved it there. I had broken into the Scotland side and things were going well, but I had a fair idea I would be moving when my contract was up. I remember getting calls from the likes of Borussia Dortmund and Seville, and they were interested in signing me. Both clubs said if I joined them they would give me £1m over three years. This was in the days before agents and I'm sitting in my front room open-mouthed, mumbling, 'Yeah, uhu, I'll take that, good!' But I couldn't accept their offers as it was pre-Bosman. I eventually met up with representatives from the clubs but my hands were tied. I think had I gone to Germany, the style of football would have suited me but it just never happened.

'A couple of months before the end of the season, I'd heard Rangers were interested. One day my mobile phone went and it was a journalist asking a few questions. We were getting changed for training at Tynecastle so I went into an empty room to take the call. I was sitting next to the fax machine, chatting away about the game the previous Saturday, when the machine started making a noise.

A fax was coming through and it was on Southampton FC headed notepaper, so being a nosey parker I waited to have a look – but I couldn't believe my eyes. It read, "Southampton FC offer £1 million for the services of Dave McPherson!"

'I kid you not. I immediately stopped concentrating on the phone call, told the guy I had to go and thought, "I need to get out of here. I shouldn't have seen this." And guess what, Hearts didn't tell me about it. At the time, Southampton were a big club; a club I had always admired, to be honest, but I couldn't say anything about it because I wasn't supposed to know about the offer. To be fair, Hearts should have told me that somebody had put an offer in, but they didn't. It made me wonder if anyone else had been interested in signing me. I suppose players get to know more these days because of agents and middle men.'

McPherson was in Norway for a Scotland friendly in 1992 when he met up with Rangers manager Walter Smith. He said, 'Walter asked me if I was happy to come back to Rangers, and if I was he would put an offer in. I said I was and he put the wheels in motion with a £1.3m bid. I wasn't really surprised. I knew I was doing well and through reading the papers it was clear there were clubs interested in me outwith the ones I knew about, but I hadn't really given Rangers too much thought as I believed I would be going elsewhere, so when Walter spoke to me I thought, "Well, I'm still a Rangers supporter." I had been really disappointed to leave Rangers the first time, but perhaps this meant I had proved in some way that Rangers were wrong to let me go.

'I was delighted to be unveiled as a Rangers player for a second time but I just wanted to get going as soon as possible. When you move somewhere, it's the waiting until you play, and getting to know all your team-mates, but it was easier for me because I'd been at Rangers previously. A lot of the staff were still there and they seemed happy to see me back, which helped. And then there was Durranty and McCoist – and you know what sort of wind-up welcome awaited!

'So it was easy to settle back in, although the expectation levels had risen a couple of notches because they had invested heavily in players. There was also added pressure because they had won four titles in a row and even then people were talking about getting to nine, so you felt that as well. Rangers are a massive club and you definitely feel the expectation from supporters, every member of staff does, not just the players. We all demanded success from one another.'

When McPherson first joined Rangers, the club had their own dedicated training ground at the Albion, but when he re-joined, that had gone – and hadn't been replaced.

He said, 'The facilities we were using were good, but we had to travel to them every day. Once you got there, though, it was good, and they were private. It was what we were used to, but I think at that time everybody just thought Rangers would have their own facilities because we were such a big club. Fortunately, things have changed and the club now has Murray Park, which is a fantastic place.

'But as soon as I returned to Rangers, we were off to Italy for training, at Il Ciocco, which was just what we needed at that stage as it allowed us all to get back to full fitness after the close season. It was secluded. We were on top of a mountain, in 80 degree heat, but I can assure you it sounds better than it actually was – but it was necessary. What it also did was allow me to get to know guys I hadn't played with before, like Mark Hateley, so it was great for bonding.'

McPherson added, 'I think the priority at Ibrox at the start of any season is to win the league, and anything else is a bonus, so I think any talk of a treble simply wouldn't have been on anyone's radar. As it was, we became only the fifth ever Rangers side to win the treble, but that fact alone didn't sink in right away, probably because I grew up a Rangers supporter and remembered us winning the treble in the 1970s and thinking then what a magnificent achievement it had been.

'It was only after I left Rangers, and took the time to look at the three medals that it fully sank in. I realised I was a treble winner. It's not something which should be taken lightly as not too many players will achieve it in their career.'

McPherson reckons Walter Smith swapped star individuals for an all-round talented squad that season – and he reckons it paid dividends. 'I don't think there was any one individual star in the squad,' he said. 'We were all very good players, and Walter did a great job putting it all together and playing players in certain positions. I played right-back in the majority of games even though he had signed me as a centre-back. It's a case of when you're playing for Rangers you just get on with it and do what's best for the team. I think that was the feeling regarding every player. Everybody in that squad gave everything they had in every game; we had a tremendous never-say-die spirit, so we knew very early on that for a team to beat us, they would have to be either very lucky or absolutely brilliant. We were certainly not going to lose games easily.

'Gary Stevens was our regular right-back, but he'd picked up an ankle injury and it was giving him a lot of trouble, so Walter called me in to his office one day and said, "I know I signed you as a centre-back, but I need to play you at right-back because Gary is still injured. I know you're comfortable playing in a number of positions, so what do you think?" I told him as a Rangers player I would play anywhere for the club. Bomber Brown then filled in at centre-back and I played most of the season at full-back. We had a great balance to the team that year, which was another important ingredient.

'I played 53 games that season, and something like that can work both ways. Naturally I was happy to be a regular in the team, but that amount of games can also have a detrimental effect on your body. It takes its toll. Even the seasons I played at Hearts, I played just about every game, maybe 70 games a season at times, when you include domestic cup, European games and internationals. It all adds up to a pretty hectic season. If you are playing in a World Cup or European Championships during the summer, you're not getting a break, but it's worth it as it means you're successful.'

And like every other player that term, McPherson was incredibly proud of what Rangers achieved on the European front. He said, 'On reflection, I think we might even have been able to win the Champions League. Of course, I'm very proud that we reached the group stages but then to go through that unbeaten leaves you wondering what might have been.

'Sometimes all it takes is a wee break here or there. I was disappointed we didn't win our last game, against CSKA Moscow, but to be fair, they were a very good side and perhaps tiredness was a factor by that point, because we didn't have a massive squad. At that time we hardly trained because we were playing so many games, but there is still a certain amount of training you have to do to keep your fitness levels up.

'The build-up to both games against Leeds United was amazing. We were all looking forward to playing in the Battle of Britain, as the tie had been billed, but then Gary McAllister sticks one in the top corner in the first minute of the first leg at Ibrox and we're thinking, "Where did that come from?" It was probably the best thing that could have happened as it spurred us on even more and we managed to win the game.

'Leeds had a great team. When we went down to their place, there was a ban on away supporters, but I remember thinking there were some dodgy Leeds fans in attendance, and when we scored they started to cheer – which just confirmed my suspicions! We went down there thinking we could get a positive result, maybe not win the match, but I was convinced we wouldn't lose. They fired everything at us but we were well set up, got the early goal and held out for a famous win. I think the English press thought Leeds would beat us no bother, so they were sick when we won.'

McPherson added, 'We were playing virtually every midweek, and it's sometimes hard to get motivated for every single game, but I think adrenaline keeps you going. I'm not decrying our league but you're going from an elite European level to a lower level. You might be playing one of the lesser lights in the SPL, and they want to beat you every bit as much as Leeds United do, but you do tend to back off a wee bit because you're tired – and have just come down from a massive European high – but one thing Walter always emphasised was the next game was all about getting a result, and we often managed to battle through games without playing well, and get a positive result.'

Speak to Rangers fans about 1992/93 and each will have their own special memories. The most popular might just be the Hateley/McCoist partnership, which proved more potent than the F-22 fighter jet, but McPherson is keen to talk up the case for the defence, and said, 'We had the best defensive record in the league, so every part of that team was doing its job. The team spirit was also great and everyone worked together really well and that's what makes a great team, rather than two or three outstanding individuals.

'I see a lot of players coming through at different clubs these days and the emphasis seems to be more on individuality than team ethos. They are brought up through the academy system and it's all about how the manager wants them to play, but they don't really know the game. Going back to '92/93, each player at Rangers knew how their team-mates played. It was more important for us all to know each other's strengths and weaknesses, and that's how you covered each other.

'I knew exactly when Andy Goram was going to come off his line and punch the ball away, so I knew when to get out of the way. It might sound like a small thing, but add them all up and it's good team play. It's a sort of in-built intuition that I think was far more prevalent when I played than it is now.

'I would say that winning the treble and the run we put together in Europe means '92/93 is my most successful ever season in the game, and the fact I'd just come back from the European Championships meant it was a massive season. I'm not so sure we managed to fully enjoy it at the time, given the number of games we played, but we had some great nights out! Mind you, they were few and far between because of the number of games, but when we got one, we enjoyed it!'

Was McPherson surprised that Aberdeen were Rangers' main challengers in 1992/93? He answered, 'I know a few Aberdeen supporters and they hate me when I bring that season up in conversation. I suppose most people think Rangers and Celtic will challenge each other every season for the honours, but back then Aberdeen had a really good side and we had to be at our best to beat them. The games against the Dons were really tough – and close – but we had the Indian sign over them.

'We believed we were the better side and that attitude helped us. I think we got inside their heads and over a long and hard season that definitely worked in our favour. It doesn't matter if it takes a last-minute goal to win the game, but you have the belief that you will do it at some stage.'

But McPherson wasn't finished yo-yoing between Glasgow and Edinburgh, and in 1994 he was heading back to Tynecastle. He explained, 'Rangers were looking to bring some fresh players in and Alan McLaren was doing well at Hearts. Rangers put an offer in and I believe the Hearts manager Tommy McLean said that if Rangers wanted Alan they would have to offer a player in return, and we would like Davie McPherson if he's available! We had a chat about it and I decided to go for it. It was a lot smoother and easier to make the decision than it had been the previous time I'd moved from Glasgow to Edinburgh.

'I enjoyed my second spell at Hearts, although probably not as much as the first. I think there was a wee bit of turmoil at the club and Tommy and Eamonn [Bannon] struggled somewhat. Jim Jefferies then came in and Hearts won the Scottish Cup in 1998, which was a tremendous feat, given the number of years it had been since Hearts had won a major trophy. In my first spell at Tynecastle, we had come so close to winning silverware so it was nice to finally get over the line. It was a massive relief for everyone at the club – and to win it against Rangers at Celtic Park!'

He added, 'I had nine years at Ibrox and ten at Tynecastle. When I look back at my career I'm very proud of what I achieved, and to get into the Rangers Hall of Fame was a real privilege. Being a Rangers supporter, that was a huge honour for me, especially when you look at some of the names that are there. I also like to see Scottish players getting recognised in this way because nowadays it is more about foreign players, but to be brought up a Rangers supporter and be inaugurated into the club's Hall of Fame is something truly special. When you take into consideration the number of players who have represented the club, there is only a very small percentage in that exclusive club, so it's something I will never take lightly.

'I've had a great career overall, although it's almost like two careers. I think a modern footballer would be lucky to do what I did at Rangers, but I did just as much at Hearts.'

McPherson left Tynecastle in 1999, and at the age of 34, decided he needed a new challenge. He was soon on a flight to the other side of the world.

He said, 'I needed a fresh challenge. I had played all my career in Scotland and as you're getting a bit older, the thought of playing another winter here filled me with dread. I had a chance to go and play for Carlton SC in Melbourne, Australia, get a bit of sunshine and play in the summer, and I thought I would give it a go. I loved it but financially it wasn't as good out there as it is now; it was a bit unsettled, but the actual standard of football was good.

'There were some very good players in Australia, but I think being older and playing in the heat made it a bit easier for me. The pace was slower and I could read the game quite well. It was quite often around 40 degrees, so there weren't that many people running about, which made it more comfortable for me. A lot of games took place on Friday nights, but it was really humid, and that took its toll on you as well, although I thoroughly enjoyed the experience.

'Sadly though, the club was struggling. It was a franchise and the owner wasn't putting any money in. I then had a chance to go to a club in Sydney but it wasn't a 100 per cent secure contract so I made the decision to come back to Scotland.'

And that was to Greenock, to take up a role as player-coach at Cappielow. McPherson recalled, 'I'm sure I won't be remembered for my time at Morton but I'm glad I gave it a go. I went there as player-coach, and then player/manager. Let's be honest, when you get the chance to become a manager it's hard to say no but with the benefit of hindsight I shouldn't have taken it, because when you're sacked from your job as a manager, it's difficult to get back into it.

'It was a bit frustrating because the team was doing well but I just didn't get on with the chairman. He was trying to be too influential. When you get someone with my background in football, you bring them in as a manager to manage the team. Have an opinion, don't get me wrong, because you own the club, but don't try and pick the team. He used to come into the dressing room before the game, at half-time and again at the end, but I eventually locked him out and he wasn't best pleased. You can imagine how frustrating it was for me.'

McPherson still follows the fortunes of Rangers very closely, and said, 'In recent years, Rangers did overspend massively, which was completely wrong, and a lot of mistakes were made, including some of the people who were brought in to run the club. I bumped into Paul Murray and he has always come across really well and I was chatting to him about the future of our club, but I'm just looking ahead and thinking, what has happened in the past has happened, and you can't make it disappear, but let's look forward and get on with the job of rebuilding the club.'

3

League Flag Flies Proudly on Opening Day

THE first day of August brought the opening game of the season but the excitement of a new campaign soon morphed into a nervy afternoon as the Light Blues limped over the finishing line by a single goal at home to St Johnstone.

And while the occasion had started with chairman David Murray unfurling a fourth successive league flag, it was left to arguably Rangers' greatest ever goalscorer to ensure both league points would remain on Edmiston Drive. With 34 league goals to his credit the season previous, Ally McCoist ensured he was off the mark on day one this time around although 80 minutes had elapsed before one of the Scottish game's greatest ever predators pounced to clinch both points.

Just ten minutes prior to grabbing the only goal of the game, McCoist had squandered a glorious opportunity when he fired wide after good build-up play by Ian Durrant. But there were no mistakes later on when Stuart McCall chipped the ball into the box and Richard Gough climbed highest to knock it down to McCoist, who squeezed it over the line.

The relief among the 38,000 crowd was palpable, and fans were celebrating moments later when Paul Rideout powered home a header only for the Englishman's effort to be ruled offside. Saints posed little threat but when they did, Andy Goram was equal to anything they threw at him.

Afterwards, a pragmatic Walter Smith said, 'It was the type of game I expected it to be and I think it's the kind of match we will get at Ibrox for the majority of the season.'

Ever the joker, McCoist reckoned he was on course to smash every record going, and laughed, 'I had two chances and scored one – that's a 50 per cent success rate and if I can keep that up, I'll end up with 450 goals this season!'

Once Super Ally had calmed down, he gave a more serious view of the season ahead, 'Last year we had a phenomenal record when we averaged well over two goals a game. It will be very difficult to match that this time, or even get anywhere near it, but I don't care if we only score 50 goals this season, as long as we win the league.'

But if the first team were sweating over the final result, the reserves had no such problems in Perth. They thumped St Johnstone 10-0 and could apparently have notched another EIGHT as the scoring ended on 70 minutes! John Spencer led the way with four goals. Also on target was Gary McSwegan, with a double, along with Lee Robertson, Sandy Robertson, Steven Pressley and David Hagen.

Meanwhile, Rangers' midfield dynamo Ian Ferguson was ready to consider a move away from Ibrox in a bid to get first-team football. The forgotten star was fit and ready to answer the call from Smith – and warned that if it didn't come within a month, he would move on.

Ferguson, who was 25 at the time, admitted, 'I want to stay with Rangers, but I don't want to play reserve team football every week. The next month is crucial. I will work hard in training and matches and hope reports filter back to the gaffer. But if I'm not involved in the first team set-up within a month then, unfortunately, I will have to see where my future lies.'

Injury and illness had dogged Fergie almost constantly since his £800,000 move from St Mirren in February 1988, but even though he had put these worries behind him and was back to full fitness he had started just six first team games since the beginning of 1992.

That prompted speculation that he was about to move on from Ibrox, with a transfer to one of the top London clubs most heavily touted. Ferguson added, 'The speculation hasn't affected me this time as I seem to have been in a similar situation throughout the last two years and nothing has come of it. But last season I let the whole thing get to me. It annoyed me that I wasn't involved much and my head went down, but I'm determined it won't happen this time.

'For a start, the gaffer had a talk with everyone at the start of the season and told us straight there was no room for huffs in the dressing room because it would only cast a cloud of gloom over the place. It's going to be hard to get back into the first team. I really think there will need to be injuries before I get a chance, but I'll continue to work hard to prove to the gaffer that I'm worth a place.'

Fergie was part of a strong Rangers side that headed for Inverness to play in a testimonial match for Billy Urquhart, the former Ibrox striker. The likes of Ally Maxwell and Oleg Kuznetsov helped form a guard of honour for the man who had cost Gers £15,000 – and then showed no mercy by hammering five past Caley, with no reply. Ferguson staked his claim for a top-team return with a couple of goals.

Urquhart said, 'I have many highlights of my time at Ibrox, such as winning the League Cup against Aberdeen, and obviously playing in Europe. I literally came from the Highland League and within six weeks I was on the bench against Juventus in the European Cup.

'I was very disappointed to leave Rangers, but at the time I felt it was the right move. There was a lot of competition for places and I couldn't see myself getting first team football with guys like Derek Johnstone, Derek Parlane and Gordon Smith up front and Gordon Dalziel just breaking through.'

Urquhart, who ran a successful builders' merchant, was due to hang up his boots at the end of the season and insisted that would give him more time to get down to Ibrox to see the Rangers!

One guy desperate to get back to his old ways was England international Dale Gordon. The talented winger had toiled with injuries in the second part of the 1991/92 campaign but was hoping that a close-season shoulder op would help him recapture the form he had shown when initially landing the big-money move to Ibrox. And apart from trying to help Rangers clinch a fifth successive league title, Gordon was also keen to earn a call-up to the England squad for the forthcoming World Cup qualifiers.

During the previous campaign, his shoulder had required constant strapping for training and matches as the result of a re-occurrence of an injury he had picked up for Norwich against Manchester United. He then suffered ankle ligament damage against Hibs in March which sidelined him for most of the month and left him fighting for fitness for the rest of the season. Doctors ordered Gordon to rest his shoulder for 12 weeks after the operation, even though he turned in a starring role against Forres in pre-season when he scored a hat-trick.

He said, 'My shoulder has reacted brilliantly to the operation and my knee is giving me no problems, so I like to think I can start the season afresh, which would be a major boost to my confidence. I haven't done myself justice at Ibrox yet. My form did slide a little towards the end of the season, but even though I had problems with my shoulder and knee I can't use them as an excuse. But now that I'm over my injuries and have my first pre-season with the club under my belt I'm looking forward to the new season.'

Gordon's upper-body injury was the best-kept secret at Ibrox. His shoulder joint needed tightening after wear and tear of the original op three years previous started to take its toll. He said, 'The re-occurrence of the injury was a gradual thing which started about mid-February. It just didn't feel strong at all. I played with a shoulder harness towards the end of the season to hold it in place and I had to be careful not to overstretch it in case it came out. Luckily it didn't during games, but I felt it jar in training a couple of times and when that happens it's hard to get the strength back in such a short space of time.

'It wasn't a muscular problem which could be built up with weights, it was the actual joint which was giving me problems and that made it harder to recover between matches.'

Gordon also revealed how he had been set to win a call-up to the England squad for the friendly against the CIS (a combined Soviet Union team in 1992) in Moscow at the end of April. He said, 'Both Mark Hateley and I were in line for inclusion, but unfortunately injury ruled us out. Graham Taylor was in contact with the manager then, so I've got to produce the goods this season so that he is in contact again.'

The winger added, 'There is always going to be speculation on who's arriving or leaving when you're at a club the size of Rangers. The club is the biggest in Britain and so tends to breed that kind of press. When you play for Rangers you have to be prepared for such media coverage, but I just put the papers down and refuse to worry too much.

'I look back on my first season with Rangers and I've won two medals which I will treasure and, ultimately, I've played 28 games and only been on the losing side once.'

Gordon was hoping to be involved in the next league game, against Hibs at Easter Road, but the thorny matter of reconstruction was dominating Scottish football, and Rangers chairman David Murray was at the forefront of the proposed Scottish Super League.

Murray vowed, 'Nothing and nobody will stop it going ahead.' He also accused the Scottish Football League of mismanagement, and revealed there was no room for compromise with the SFL, while insisting a super league was the best option for Rangers, its players and the supporters.

His hard-hitting comments came just days after 12 clubs outside the proposed super league line-up put forward a motion to introduce four leagues of ten in Scotland. They also recognised the need for reform within the set-up, but Murray blasted, 'It's too little, too late. I find their proposals rather amusing, especially when the Scottish Football League didn't even want to meet us for discussions. Now their own members are split and divided about what course to take.'

Murray also hit out at the personal comments made against him and Hearts chairman Wallace Mercer, who was also chairman of the Scottish Super League. He said, 'Most of the criticism hasn't come from supporters but members of the Scottish League, most of whom are old men hanging on to their positions as they have much to lose under the current set-up.'

Murray was hoping to have the new league up and running in time for the 1994/95 season and insisted it would be the most radical ever shake-up of Scottish football. He said, 'These changes have been forced upon us by the mismanagement of the Scottish Football League. There can be absolutely no compromises now.'

The latest meeting of the Super League committee proved far more entertaining than the Light Blues' cross-country trip to face Hibs. Easter Road boss Alex Miller had decided most of his players would go into hibernation for 90 minutes and remain within the confines of their own box. A five-man defence put the shutters up on Ally McCoist and co. as Trevor Steven and Stuart McCall worked tirelessly to produce an opening.

Dale Gordon missed Rangers' best chance of the day, five minutes after the break. David Robertson, a constant threat on the left, crossed low for McCoist, who instinctively squared to Gordon, but with the goal gaping he side-footed the ball past the post from eight yards.

With just five minutes remaining, Hibs almost grabbed both points. Pat McGinlay launched a piledriver from the edge of the box and Andy Goram pulled off a world-class save when he dived high to his left to palm the ball over the bar. Had that gone in, it would have given the hosts an undeserved victory as Rangers had dominated the majority of the match.

Despite the capital stalemate, there were celebrations of a kind for one Ranger as Richard Gough racked up his 200th competitive appearance. The 30-year-old centre-half, who joined Rangers from Spurs in October 1987 for £1.1m, had raced to the impressive milestone in less than five seasons.

Gough said, 'I didn't realise I was approaching the 200 mark. The only record I can remember reaching is the 50 league game mark with Spurs. Now, though, I've set myself a target of at least another 200 games for Rangers. I still have four years left on my contract, so if I steer clear of injuries I should make it. And I would hope to score more than 14 goals in my next 200 games!'

Only two of Gough's team-mates at that time had played more games than him: Ally McCoist (395) and Dave McPherson (225).

Meanwhile, manager Smith reckoned that being made a director wouldn't save his job if his team suddenly stopped getting results. Smith became only the third Rangers manager in history to be given a place on the board, following in the footsteps of Bill Struth and Graeme Souness.

He accepted the post without hesitation following an offer from David Murray over dinner in Edinburgh, and said, 'As a boy who supports the club, your first wish is to play for Rangers. That didn't happen to me, but as I moved into coaching I began to think what an honour it would be if I was ever to become manager. However, if you can't be any of those two I think anyone who is a supporter would love to become a board member. I'm lucky to have achieved two out of the three.

'Coming into Ibrox every day is a big thrill for me, but there's no doubt the game in general is facing exciting times. Almost every club is improving facilities for fans and they will be keen to make sure we project the best image for Scottish football. To be involved in the football side gives me a big enough buzz, but there is now an added dimension of being involved in the decision-making process at the club.'

Rangers' lowest home league crowd in more than a year – 34,613 – turned up at Ibrox for the midweek visit of Airdrie, and if truth be told those absent didn't miss much. The highlight was a mesmerising move made in Russia involving Oleg Kuznetsov and

Alexei Mikhailichenko, who traded passes before setting up Dale Gordon to fire home. Mark Hateley scored the other goal in a 2-0 win.

Second-string player Neil Murray was on the fringes of the first team and would play a significant role in bringing the Scottish Cup to Ibrox later in the season but when it came to brains, Murray was smarter than your average Bear! The youngster had just emerged from three years of studying at Glasgow University with a degree in accountancy – and was now the only Ibrox player with letters after his name!

The 19-year-old – the regular right-back in the reserves for the previous 18 months – had been on a part-time contract with Rangers while studying but was now concentrating on making the breakthrough into the top team. He said, 'I'm pleased that I can now call myself a full-time footballer. It's been hard being part-time for the last three years.

'I feel I have been improving since I joined Rangers, but now that I can concentrate on the football, hopefully I can improve a lot more. I'm proud that I completed the degree. It wasn't something I really thought about until I was just about to leave school. I left when I was just 16 and felt I should do something in case the football didn't work out.

'Rangers have been brilliant. They let me take as much time off as I needed to study. The hardest time wasn't last year, but my second year at university. That was the toughest part of the course and there were quite a few occasions when I left a lecture at five o'clock, came straight to Ibrox and got on a bus to go to a game that night. It was hard to prepare myself mentally for the football after concentrating on my studies. But that's all behind me now and I can concentrate fully on my future at Rangers.'

And staying with the reserves, young gun John Spencer staked a claim for a first-team squad place when he bagged his second hat-trick in eight days during the 4-1 home win over Hibs.

But there were mixed fortunes for the first team as they crashed to their first league defeat of the season (4-3 at Dundee), and swept aside Dumbarton in a Skol Cup tie at Hampden.

Those with a liking for fast and furious football would have enjoyed their visit to Dens Park, although Rangers supporters would no doubt have described it as a defensive horror show. Despite a double from Ally McCoist and one from Ian Ferguson, it was the four they lost – including two by Billy Dodds – that would have driven Walter Smith mad. Three times Rangers went behind, and three times they equalised, but when Dodds struck from the spot seven minutes from time, there was to be no fairy-tale fourth equaliser for Gers. Sadly, the Iron Curtain defence proved to be more of a net curtain!

Rangers had been expected to thump Dumbarton four days before their Dens Park horror show, and they did just that thanks to goals from Durrant, Gordon, Hateley, McCoist and Mikhailichenko. Sounds easy, but Rangers had squandered 11 chances before Durrant opened the scoring five minutes before the break.

That match served as the final game of Paul Rideout's seven-month-long Ibrox career and he departed the south side of Glasgow for Everton on his 28th birthday. He said, 'I really am sad to leave Ibrox because I have thoroughly enjoyed my time with the club. I was never unhappy and was kept constantly involved with the team.

'The fans were tremendous to me and the lads at the club are terrific. I really enjoyed the laugh and the crack. The move north has done wonders for my career. I have nothing bad to say – and that's unusual for any player who leaves a club!'

Once again though, it was the curse of McCoist and Hateley which was responsible for Rideout's decision to leave Rangers AND the departure of another club favourite, when John Spencer made the tough decision to join Chelsea as a result of seeing better first-team prospects at Stamford Bridge than at Ibrox.

Spencer was just 21 when he upped sticks and left, but it wasn't a decision the young goal-getter took lightly. He said, 'I've grown up with Rangers. I've been associated with the club since I was 12, so leaving and saying cheerio to the boys and the staff was really tough – like a hammer blow to the head.

'No doubt I'll be back up the road at some point, standing on the terraces or sitting in the stands, watching the games. I'm naturally disappointed I didn't play more for the first team, but my ambition was to play for Rangers and I achieved that. I played in an Old Firm game as well, which we lost unfortunately, but I achieved what I set out to do – I played for Rangers!

'I love Rangers and they will always have a place in my heart, but I've got to wipe the slate clean and now I'm looking forward to playing in the English Premier League. It gives me a great boost that [Chelsea chairman] Ken Bates has put his money where his mouth is, because the club has spent a lot of money on me when you consider that I'm really unproven and haven't played as many first team games as I would have liked.' But Spencer joked that the hefty price tag wouldn't bother him, 'I would say I was a snip at £500,000!'

Before walking out of Ibrox for the final time, Spencer left a positive message for the Ibrox coaching staff, saying, 'I'd like to thank John McGregor and Billy Kirkwood, as well as the gaffer, Archie and Doddsie – but especially John, who gave me a kick up the backside when I needed it and did a lot for my game.

'Even though I played for the first team, my favourite memory is winning the Reserve League last season. Just seeing John and Kirkie's faces at the end of the game made me feel really, really good, as if we had really achieved something.'

With the squad lighter by two, it was a busy August for the Light Blues and they played their sixth of nine competitive matches that month at Stranraer in the third round of the Skol Cup. Rangers cruised to a second successive 5-0 victory in the competition with McCoist scoring three times and Hateley twice.

Youngster Neil Murray also made his first-team debut, although the teenager would remember the occasion for clattering into a photographer – and almost picking up a bad injury! He said, 'Coisty touched the ball back to me and I managed to get it across goal, but momentum carried me into a photographer. There was nothing I could do about it and thankfully neither of us were hurt, but the poor guy was left taking pictures of the sky!'

Despite that little hiccup, Murray acquitted himself very well on a night he would never forget. 'The game itself was enjoyable. Early on, I had a lot of scope to attack because they only played with three in midfield at the start and there was room down the flanks. But later in the game, perhaps in the last ten minutes, I was getting a bit tired so I didn't get forward as much.'

He admitted that the first-team call had come as something of a shock, saying, 'I was surprised to get a chance so early on. I had played quite well in the three reserve games beforehand, and I just tried to maintain that level of consistency.'

It was honours even after the first Old Firm match of the season, with Ian Durrant leaping from the Ibrox bench to equalise in the 70th minute following a goal by Celts striker Gerry Creaney.

But Rangers were left fuming by a decision to disallow a Trevor Steven goal in the fifth minute. Pieter Huistra found David Robertson, who clipped the ball forward to Mark Hateley. The big man played the ball into the path of Steven, who shot past Gordon Marshall.

Huistra admitted he was furious when the linesman raised his flag, and said, 'It was a terrible decision. The full-back at my side played Trevor onside and I can only guess the linesman didn't see him when the ball was put through, and he put his flag up too early.'

Had that goal been allowed to stand it would have given Gers an early psychological boost, but instead both teams were left to scrap out the remainder of the first period.

After Creaney's goal, Smith replaced Steven with Durrant, and less than ten minutes had elapsed when the Kinning Park lad repaid his gaffer – and some. A Huistra cross was knocked into Durrant's path by McCoist, and the talented midfielder shot high into the net.

Smith said, 'It was an excellent finish. Perhaps people expected too much from Ian when he made his return from injury last season, but he showed in patches that he was capable of regaining his form. He is as physically fit now as he'll ever be, and I hope his sharpness is back too.'

After five league matches, Rangers occupied fourth spot, just a point behind joint leaders Aberdeen, Dundee United and Celtic.

To illustrate just how big a club Rangers were in the early 1990s, one only has to look at replica shirt sales. Between 1 May – the week before the Scottish Cup Final – and the middle of August, the club sold more than 100,000 jerseys, and the Stranraer firm charged with making the shirts were pumping out an incredible 6,000 home and away tops and 1,500 pairs of shorts every week. Pasolds Sunchild had been working flat out since the end of January 1992 to meet the demand for strips, and the trend was showing no sign of receding.

Adidas manager Brent de Boeck revealed how the strip was well on its way to becoming the biggest seller in Europe. He said, 'Only Liverpool sell as many jerseys in Europe, but Rangers are pushing them very close and their sales will probably move ahead very shortly.'

As a result of huge kit sales, Pasolds Sunchild had increased staff numbers from 135 to 168 and at one point had NINE production lines working round the clock to keep up with demand. It took a metre of fabric to produce one Rangers jersey and enough had been sold to stretch from Glasgow to Edinburgh – and back! Rangers' five-year deal with adidas was the most lucrative in European football.

As usual, the last week in the month brought two matches and both were successfully negotiated. First up was Dundee United at Tannadice in the quarter-finals of the League Cup, and Rangers progressed to the last four after extra time. In a ding-dong battle, goals by McCoist and Gough in normal time and Huistra four minutes into the additional 30 sent the Rangers supporters in the 15,716 crowd home happy. It was a fantastic victory and just the tonic for a battle against league leaders Aberdeen four days later – even though the Light Blues would be without four internationals; Trevor Steven, Stuart McCall, Mark Hateley and Gary Stevens.

Roy Aitken put Aberdeen ahead on the half hour and it remained that way until the break, and until Ian Durrant took hold of the game by the scruff of the neck. Durrant was outstanding. First, he fired home an equaliser before setting up McCoist for the second. Alexei Mikhailichenko finished off a great afternoon's work by volleying home a killer third, and the win put Rangers just a point behind new leaders Dundee United.

Ian Durrant was rewarded for a string of impressive performances with a call-up to the Scotland squad for the opening World Cup qualifying match against Switzerland in Berne. In-form Durrant joined team-mates Dave McPherson, Richard Gough, Stuart McCall, Ally McCoist and Andy Goram, while Neil Murray and David Hagen were included in Scotland's under-21 squad.

One youngster who continued to impress the reserve team coaches at Ibrox was 16-year-old Charlie Miller. Described as a 'midfielder-come-centre-forward', the teenage Glaswegian had already played five times for the reserves, and made his full debut against Aberdeen reserves in a 0-0 stalemate at Pittodrie, where he was in direct opposition to Alex McLeish.

The youngster said, 'I was pretty nervous when I found out I'd be playing against someone like Alex. Even though he's just back from injury, and probably wasn't match fit, he's still got the football brain to take him through a game. But I didn't do too badly against him. It wasn't a bad debut although I should have scored in the first half and that would have made it an even better one.'

Miller had been at Ibrox since signing an S form in 1989 and had continually impressed at youth level with Rangers and the Supporters' Association Boys' Club.

He said, 'I'm glad I signed for Rangers as it means I can now concentrate full-time on making a career in football. Even after only a couple of months full-time, I notice a big difference in my play. I feel a lot quicker and sharper and I've learned a lot about the game.'

ALLY Maxwell would have been damned if he did, and damned if he didn't!

As a young lad making his way in the game he decided he would prefer to be at the sharp end of the team, up front and scoring goals, and he did not a bad job too.

Ultimately, though, he swapped the number nine jersey for number one, and found his sanctuary between the sticks.

He explained, 'True, I was a centre-forward when I was a kid and I managed to score a lot of goals at that age, but we still seemed to lose most games. One day, I said to the manager, "Forget this, put me in goals." He did and we won the game. The rest, as they say, is history.'

Which brings me to my opening line. Instead of trying to depose Andy Goram in the Rangers side, he could have been in direct competition with Ally McCoist. Out of the frying pan and into the fire, unless Maxwell could have contributed in excess of 50 goals a season!

So the talented keeper decided to remain between the sticks and was just 17 when he made his debut for Motherwell against Aberdeen – with the game indelibly etched in his mind due to an unforgettable Archie MacPherson quote.

Maxwell said, 'It was incredibly nerve-wracking. I was up against guys like Gordon Strachan and Alex McLeish, who were top class players at that time, and I was no more than a kid. Within five minutes of the start, I was still shaking like a leaf when a shot came in and I thought "here we go" but it bounced straight in front of me and ended up in my arms.

'To this day I still have no idea how I managed to catch it, but I do remember legendary commentator Archie MacPherson's immortal line, something along the lines of, "This team is so young the manager doesn't know if he should be taking them to Pittodrie or Aberdeen Beach to build sand castles," which is exactly what it was like.'

Mind you, one could have been forgiven for thinking Maxwell was still playing centre-forward the day he hit the bar in a match against Celtic. He remembers it like it was yesterday, and said, 'It was typical Motherwell weather the night we played Celtic. The wind and rain were coming at us sideways – you know, a real fine Scottish day, and we had endured wave after wave of Celtic attacks in the first half when they had the wind at their backs. In the second half, we obviously had the elements working for us. The manager wanted us to pile on as much pressure as possible and we were soon causing them all sorts of grief.

'I remember getting the ball in my hands and punted it down the field. It was just a bit too far and Pat Bonner had to rush from his goal to collect it. The next time I got the ball, the Motherwell fans were screaming for me to SHOOT! I thought "what the hell", so I punted it as high as I could and let the wind carry it. And it did. It bounced almost in the exact spot as before and Paddy started to come out, but didn't realise how high it bounced – and it sailed right over his head and hit the bar!

'The fans went crazy and loved it. However, our manager Tommy McLean wasn't sharing the love and I could tell by his expression that he wasn't impressed. Because it was so windy, he wanted our strikers to have a chance to reach the ball and he told Tom Boyd to tell Craig Patterson to tell Chris McCart to tell me that I was an idiot!'

Maxwell admits he has many special memories of his time at Fir Park, although the obvious highlight is the Scottish Cup win over Dundee United – despite the fact it is tainted by such an awful injury.

He recalled, 'Winning the Scottish Cup is obviously a career highlight, as it was my first major trophy as a professional football player. Winning the Premier League and the League Cup with Rangers was also fantastic and gave me the complete set, so they are all highlights.'

But there was a dark side to that Scottish Cup win of 1991 as Maxwell played a large chunk of the game – most of the second half plus extra time – with broken ribs, a ruptured spleen and double vision after a dreadful collision with Dundee United defender John Clark. Despite suffering such horrendous injuries, Maxwell still somehow managed to pull off a world-class save from Maurice Malpas in the dying moments of added time to ensure Motherwell hung on for a famous 4-3 win.

Most folk who recall the game wonder how Maxwell managed to get through it all – including the man himself. He said, 'I ask myself that same question every day. Not a lot of people know this but when Motherwell asked me to participate in a DVD for the 25th anniversary of the cup win, it was the first time since the actual day itself that I had seen footage of the match. I was sitting at ASU [Arizona State University] being interviewed and it brought all these memories flooding back – and let's just say they aren't all good.

'For years, I asked my family not to talk about it and if someone ever brought it up I would leave the room. Until this year, I couldn't watch it at all, but for the DVD interview they wanted me to go through it play by play and it was very tough. There were parts of the game they replayed, and I remember looking at my wife and saying, "I don't remember that." When you watch the DVD you can tell from my face that it still isn't a pleasant experience for me – even 25 years on!'

The moment the cup final was over, Maxwell – and his team-mates – had etched their names into the history of Motherwell FC. What they achieved would never be erased, from the history books or the memories of the thousands of Well fans that attended the match.

But he said, 'If I'm being honest, at that point I thought I'd be spending the rest of my career at Fir Park – I had zero intention of leaving Motherwell, so when it did happen it was very sad. I didn't want to leave and I never played a competitive game for them after that Scottish Cup Final.

'One of the big regrets is that I never received a testimonial. I signed my first competitive contract on 1 November 1981 and left "officially" in June of 1992, which is 11 years, and that isn't including the five years I spent in the youth system at Fir Park. Yes, it was definitely a tough one to take.'

But every cloud has a silver lining, or so they say, and Maxwell's salvation came in the shape of an official approach by Rangers – in Liverpool manager Graeme Souness's office at Anfield!

'Yes, that's true,' said Maxwell. 'I was on loan at Liverpool when Graeme Souness was in charge and one day I was asked to go and see him in his office. When I walked in, Graeme was on the speaker phone with Walter Smith. I sat in the office listening while they were talking, and Graeme suggested Walter should make a bid for me. I was astounded to hear Walter's answer.

'He told Graeme he had already made an offer for me AFTER the cup final, and that Motherwell had turned it down. They certainly didn't tell me. I had no idea! I later confronted Tommy McLean about this and he insisted Motherwell had received no such offer. Obviously, I was now on the radar of Rangers and Walter decided to monitor my situation from that point on.'

Maxwell eventually moved to Rangers for £300,000 – and that's when his big challenge began: how to depose Andy Goram as number one, although he said, 'It was never my intention to take the jersey, honestly. I knew my place. I was at Ibrox to learn and who better to learn from?

'So here is how this story plays out. Just before joining Rangers, I was offered two jobs. The first was the first-team goalkeeper's jersey at St Johnstone, which was a huge honour, but I was also offered the back-up spot to Andy with Rangers. All I could think of was that you only get one chance to play for Rangers and that it would probably never happen again. I was already friendly with Andy through the international squad and loved working with him personally, and as part of the Scotland set-up. I grabbed the opportunity with both hands and held on for what was sure to be a bumpy ride!

'As I said, I already knew Andy well through working with Scotland, but I loved working with him on a daily basis. He was a mentor to me in many ways. He was and will always be "The Goalie" to me. I loved Andy to bits.

'I was friends with most of the guys at Rangers, but other than Andy, the guys I got on best with were probably Davie Robertson, Pieter Huistra, Gary Stevens and John Brown. I had a great relationship with these guys during my time at Ibrox.'

One of the biggest differences between playing for Rangers or Motherwell is the size of the attendances. In 1992/93 the Light Blues were averaging just over 42,000 for league games at Ibrox, a huge difference from the few thousand who were turning up at Fir Park on a regular basis.

Maxwell said, 'It's a massive difference for a player. For a start, the bigger the club, the bigger the scrutiny. Normally, one end is giving you 45 minutes of abuse, while the other is, depending on the day, not as abusive. I can remember one game where the Rangers fans were in full voice (there wasn't much action at my end of the pitch) and I could feel the crowd singing underneath my feet; they were actually making the ground vibrate! There is massive pressure on you but you realise the unbelievable strength of the fans behind you and it can be a big help.'

The Hamilton-born keeper made a dozen appearances for the first team during the treble-winning campaign, and insisted it was a bittersweet experience. He explained, 'Naturally it was a big thrill for me every time I wore the Rangers jersey, but if that appearance had come because Andy Goram was injured then it was tinged with a bit of sadness, so I suppose it was something of a double-edged sword.'

After signing on the dotted line, Maxwell was quoted as saying Rangers were the biggest club in Britain, but did he really say that, or was he misquoted? He reflected, 'Having just been at Liverpool, which was one of the biggest clubs in Europe, and who just happened to make a habit of winning, and seeing both stadiums and both sets of fans, it was easy to see why Rangers were one of the top clubs in Britain. At that time, I saw some of the biggest clubs at their peak and Rangers were right up there.'

When exactly, if at all, did he realise the 1992/93 squad was a bit special? 'Just really with the way the day to day things went. We trained hard and played hard, that was generally how we did it. It wasn't talked about. It was the way it was, and that's special.

'Walter and Archie had a great way of bringing new players to the club that would be cohesive to the players already there. That is a very special talent in itself – retain your core and make additions that complement those core players. That's why we were special. McCoist and Durrant were such huge personalities, and bringing in a new player that didn't get on with those guys could potentially have been a disaster. But it wasn't. It was a great time to be at Rangers.'

During the following season, Maxwell was playing in goal for Rangers against Celtic at Parkhead when he was the subject of an unprovoked attack by a pitch-invading Celtic supporter. I was wondering if there was more pressure on Old Firm players, or was it just business as usual? He said, 'Being a goalkeeper, no matter what club you play for, brings enough pressure to last a lifetime, but playing for Rangers at such a young age definitely added to it! Mind you, if you are attacked on a football field and you have someone like John Brown looking after you, well, it certainly makes it a little easier to handle.'

Maxwell played in ten of the last 18 games of 1992/93, which was no doubt a case of Walter Smith utilising his squad to the max. The player agreed, and said, 'I think so. He was rotating the squad to ensure we had fresh, fit players in most games. The good thing was that everyone had to compete for their starting jersey, which meant competition for places was healthy.'

One of the highlights of a great season was definitely the run in Europe, which saw Rangers go undefeated in ten European Cup/ Champions League matches. But was there a belief among the players that they could actually win the competition?

Maxwell answered, 'There was a belief about the place that we could win any game we played, but we weren't allowed to look too far ahead. Everything we did was geared up to focussing on the task in hand, then we would look no further than the next game.

'Our European run that season was incredible, and once again there were mixed feelings about how it all ended. We knew we had just been on the most incredible ride, but going so close and missing out meant there would always be that disappointment there.'

While Maxwell was at Motherwell, he worked under legendary Rangers boss Jock Wallace and cited the great man as a big influence on his career. He added, 'Jock was a legend, there is no doubt about that, and the players had a lot of respect for him. He was just old school; he was strong and everything with him was black or white. As a young guy, that was what I needed. You did as you were told, you respected your coach and he led by example.

'The best story I have for you gives an insight into how Jock was in the dressing room – and it goes like this. We were getting a half-time team talk and our goalkeeper had just lost a soft goal. The ball had trickled through his legs, and he apologised to big Jock, saying, "Sorry boss, I should have kept my legs closed!" To which Jock replied, "Naw, son, maybe yer mother should have kept HER legs closed!" It's a true story.'

When Maxwell signed for Rangers, he admitted it was a relief to finally have Ally McCoist on his side. He said, 'It definitely gave me a bit of respite because I have never had a player from the opposition team make me laugh so much as him.

'I remember we were beating Rangers 3-0 at Fir Park in the season before I moved to Ibrox. During the game, Rangers were awarded a corner and Motherwell were up 3-0 at this point and he comes up to me and says, immediately before the corner is taken, "Maxie, I can't believe we're losing, I'm playing really well!" Then I come to Rangers and think, "Thank god he is usually up the other end of the field." He is just one of these guys that makes you laugh. Coisty is hilarious.'

Maxwell added, 'I would sum up my time at Ibrox by saying it was such an honour and privilege to play for Rangers. I was given a chance to work with some of the best coaches, players and staff around. Not to mention the fans, who were absolutely magnificent with me.

'Nowadays, I am the director of goalkeeping for SC del Sol in Phoenix, Arizona, which is a youth development programme. I am also a coach for the Women's Arizona State University Soccer Programme and a regional advisor for the United States Women's National Soccer Team.'

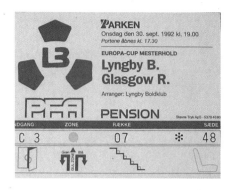

5

Lyngby are 'Dane For' in Euro Qualifier

THERE was good news of sorts for Gary Stevens when his surgeon, Mr Browett, advised him to walk down to his local shop for a pint of milk! A mundane task at best for most of us, but for the England full-back it was the first step on the road to recovery.

It was the beginning of the second stage of his recuperation after twin ankle operations in the close season. Stevens had travelled to Harley Street in London for examinations by the same surgeon who had treated Lazio midfielder Paul Gascoigne, and the medic was satisfied with the progress being made by the 29-year-old, who had ditched the hi-tech ankle support boot he had been wearing since his op in June.

Stevens said, 'The surgeon is satisfied with my progress, particularly as he had to perform two operations – on a stress fracture and chipped bone – at the same time. He has given me exercises in what is termed functional walking – around the house or down to the shops. And then after a week I can progress to walking round the pitch. It doesn't sound a lot to look forward to, but it has been drummed into me that it is for my benefit in the long run and if I don't treat the injury properly I could lose the whole season, and that would be a total disaster.'

Stevens was on target to make a comeback at Christmas, and had been on a strictly controlled diet to make sure he didn't pile on the pounds. He was also on a self-imposed ban from hanging out with his team-mates.

He explained, 'Watching the lads at first was difficult, but the last three games have just flown by. I've been concentrating on my own work and steering clear of the lads in the dressing room which I definitely think has been to my advantage.

'Initially, I was sitting around the dressing room chatting with them, and then they would head out to training. But seeing them go off made me feel down and I ended up leaving for home shortly afterwards feeling worse than when I arrived. Now I only see them fleetingly and I concentrate solely on working hard. I've got to be philosophical. If I can keep progressing and don't threaten the healing process too much then I can be reasonably fit by the time it actually comes to kicking a ball again. And hopefully my return won't be too long after that.'

But while Stevens was desperate to get back into a Rangers jersey again, another player was eyeing a move back down south. Nigel Spackman was believed to be in talks with Chelsea, with the £500,000 signing from Liverpool keen to get back playing regularly again.

Meanwhile, as part of a new sponsorship deal, several Rangers players – including Ally McCoist – were presented with brand new Ebel watches. The timepieces, valued at £1,300 each, were made of 18-carat gold, and while there was a rumour doing the rounds that the deal had been struck to help McCoist with his timekeeping, the players felt it was just a ruse to allow him to trot out his favourite line, 'This is the earliest I've been late all week!'

But the jester's hat was put into cold storage when he bagged his second hat-trick of the season. Rangers mauled Motherwell 4-1 under the floodlights at Fir Park to return to the top of the league, albeit on goal difference from Hearts and Celtic. Bomber Brown was also on target but it was McCoist's treble which had everyone talking. He latched on to a chip from Brown to fire home his first, before being in the right place at the right time to seal the points, with the third goal his 12th in just ten games.

A couple of days later, Scotland's biggest crowd of the day – an incredible 8,200 – turned up at Ibrox to watch Rangers and

Motherwell RESERVES in a league match. Sadly the Ibrox second string, who were top of the league, lost 1-0.

One week in mid-September was shaping up as a pivotal moment of the season with games against Lyngby, in the first round of the European Cup, challengers Hearts in a league match, and St Johnstone in the League Cup semi-final. It meant three fixtures in eight days which would tell Walter Smith an awful lot about his players – and his chances of success in the coming season.

Twelve months previous, a similar situation had arisen with Sparta Prague (European Cup), Hibs (Skol Cup semis), and Aberdeen in the league. All three games were lost and Rangers exited two competitions as a result. Smith was adamant there would be no repeat, and said, 'The players who were involved last season should remember what it felt like to go out of the Skol Cup and Europe, and to lose an important league game against Aberdeen. If they need any incentive to do well this time around, that setback should provide it.'

He added, 'We must look to improve our prestige. We've won the domestic championship four years in a row, but we have to gain more credibility in Europe to ensure our name is spread over the continent more than it has been in recent seasons. And financially, it is important we reach the group stages after the commitment we made in building the extension to the Main Stand.'

Rangers went into the match against Danish champions Lyngby on the back of a second successive 4-1 league win on the road – this time against Partick Thistle. And the Firhill run-out proved just the tonic as goals by Hateley and Huistra eased the Gers to a comfortable 2-0 win over the Danes.

Apart from short spells at the beginning of both halves, when Lyngby sprung from the traps with gusto, Rangers were dominant, although the victory still had to be earned. Bomber Brown said, 'They were a useful side and I think those who expected us to hammer them were wrong as they proved they can play some good football. But we saw enough at Ibrox to suggest we can score over there and if we do I feel it will be enough to put us through to the next round.'

Next up in a trio of important games was a league match against Hearts at Ibrox. Prior to kick-off, the sides were joint top of the table with Rangers in front by just a solitary goal, but the first half soon descended into a midfield slog, with both teams battling for supremacy and no quarter asked, or given. But things settled down after the break and the Light Blues' superior blend of football saw them grab both points thanks to goals by McCoist and McCall. Mind you, at the other end, Andy Goram was in stunning form and pulled off two world-class saves.

The final game – against St Johnstone – saw Rangers book their place at Hampden thanks to McCoist's third hat-trick of the season. There were chances for both sides before McCoist edged the Light Blues ahead midway through the first period from just four yards. Europe's Golden Boot winner scored a second a few minutes before half-time and finished in style on 69 minutes by clipping the ball over Andy Rhodes. Paul Wright netted a consolation for Saints from the penalty spot after John Brown had mistimed a challenge on Steve Maskrey.

Meanwhile, Rangers completed the final piece of the Chris Vinnicombe transfer jigsaw by taking a team down to his former club Exeter for a challenge match – and then the talented young left-back spoke of his need to get away from Ibrox!

The former England under-21 skipper had signed for the Light Blues in November 1989 but had struggled to cement a first team place, playing second fiddle to Stuart Munro, John Brown and David Robertson. UEFA's controversial 'three foreigner' rule was also against him.

Middlesbrough were apparently keen to sign Vinnicombe, who said, 'I must look to the future and get back to playing first-team football. It would be sad to leave Rangers but I can't play reserve football for ever. I spoke to the gaffer at the start of the season and he told me that if the right offer came in he would consider letting me go.

'I have learned so much from the coaches at Ibrox and I'm definitely a better player than when I arrived. Coming here was the best move for me, but my worry now is that I might get a little stale if I sit in the reserves too long.'

But as Vinnicombe shaped up to ship out, Rangers were ready to come out fighting in their bid to get the ruling overturned. Vice-chairman Donald Findlay wrote to the SFA asking them to back Rangers – and most of Scotland's leading clubs. Findlay also said Rangers had the support of several top English and continental clubs – including influential Italian outfits.

Findlay insisted he would take his fight all the way to the European Court of Human Rights if necessary. He added, 'We are asking the SFA to support an approach to UEFA, not to ask for an increase in the number of non-nationals allowed, but to ask for no limit to be set at all.

'It is contrary to principle to impose any kind of limit and we take the view that anybody, regardless of colour, creed or nationality, should be able to ply their trade wherever they wish. But if at any stage we stick on this, or we are not successful with the SFA, we are determined to go to whatever lengths it takes to have this ruling changed.'

The success Rangers were achieving on the field was being replicated on the terraces – or should I say, stands! With the season less than seven weeks old, more than 320,000 had taken in Rangers' 13 matches. Six of those had been played at Ibrox, and attracted an incredible 239,440 fans through the turnstiles – an average of 39,906 per game, which was the highest in Britain.

Chairman David Murray said, 'The supporters know my views on the number of games we are asked to play and watch each season. It's ridiculous and is putting a strain on both players and supporters. But our fans' reaction to the team this season has been unbelievable and I would like to say a huge thank you to them all.

'All over Britain average gates are falling, with the exception of ourselves and Blackburn Rovers, and we like to think we are showing our appreciation to our fans by pegging costs and offering matches such as the Marseille friendly as part of the season ticket package.'

Murray's comments were echoed by assistant gaffer Archie Knox, who vowed Rangers' Euro ambitions would NOT be thwarted by a demanding domestic programme. Knox, one of the most respected coaches in the country, hit out at the number of games the top players in Scotland were being forced to play.

He insisted it was starting to take its toll on his players just two months into the season, with both Richard Gough and Dave McPherson forced to give in to niggling injuries and pull out of a trip to Tannadice. He also revealed how just two players – McCoist and Hateley – were fresh enough to report for training the morning after the Skol Cup semi-final victory over St Johnstone.

Less than a quarter into a lengthy campaign, Rangers had already played 15 matches, and Knox said, 'None of our squad are playing with the spark or freedom of a couple of weeks ago and it's all down to the number of games they're asked to play.'

And, on the eve of the European Cup return match with Lyngby, Knox warned, 'We must make sure our European ambitions aren't compromised. We might have to consider resting players in different games and giving some of our squad a break in some matches, but that is why we have a big pool of good quality players.

'However, it isn't always easy to do that, particularly when you are on a winning streak. Not only do we not want to change the line-up, but players don't want to sit out any matches either. As far as that goes, we will need to rely on our judgement at the time.'

Despite being without international defenders Gough and McPherson, and Alexei Mikhailichenko, Dundee United were no match for rampant Rangers and the Light Blues racked up four goals for a third successive away match. It was United's heaviest home defeat since 1971 – when Rangers had stuck five past them.

This time, stand-in skipper Ally McCoist was on target along with Trevor Steven and Pieter Huistra, who scored twice. Ian Ferguson was back to his old self and bossed the game from the middle of the park. After the game, Fergie said, 'I had picked up a thigh knock the previous week and during the game the pain became sharper. It meant I had to be substituted, but to go off to a standing ovation like that felt very nice. If the truth be told, I had a lump in my throat. It makes such a difference hearing encouragement rather than having the fans shout at you.'

The win put Rangers four points clear of the chasing pack.

Rangers held their AGM at a packed Royal Concert Hall and after formalities such as the annual accounts had been scrutinised and accepted by shareholders, and directors Jack Gillespie, Walter Smith and Ian Skelly were re-elected on to the board, shareholders asked some tough questions.

These included the 'harsh' treatment of former director Hugh Adam; a rumour that Rangers had only bought Dave McPherson to help Hearts out of a cash crisis; a question asking why the Russians weren't playing more regularly; did Walter Smith have full control over signings, or did the purchase of Trevor Steven come from 'a-high'; criticism about Scotland games taking a toll on the Ibrox pitch; damage caused to the Broomloan Road stand by Celtic fans, and one gentleman who asked if Rangers could seriously expect to compete pound-for-pound with the likes of Barcelona!

In answering the final question, Murray said, 'Barcelona don't have a support like Glasgow Rangers in terms of loyalty. I've been to Barcelona in my basketball days and I've seen what a massive club they are. But I would think the improvement we've seen at Rangers over the past six years would show something. I'm not here wasting my time. I only have one ambition and that's to see Rangers win a

European tournament and we will do it together. I have no doubts about that.'

Next up for the Light Blues was a trip across to Denmark to face Lyngby, and the opportunity to qualify for the second round of the European Cup. McCoist was adamant his side was just 'one quick goal' away from the second round of Europe's premier competition.

He said, 'If we can get a goal over there, especially a quick one, it would make it very difficult for them. In fact, the tie could be over if we score first, and that's our aim. However, they will want exactly the same thing, so we have to play with a degree of caution. The last thing we want to do is concede a goal which would put the tie right back in the balance. Lyngby are no mugs.'

More than 3,000 Rangers fans were present in the Parken Stadium and they looked on as Ian Durrant fired home the only goal of the game to send the Light Blues through to a meeting with either Stuttgart or Leeds United.

It might not have been the early goal Coisty craved, but with 85 minutes on the clock Durrant started and finished the move in terrific style. He laid the ball off to the in-form Ian Ferguson, who supplied a perfectly-timed return ball. Durrant outpaced the Lyngby defence and coolly took the ball around goalkeeper Kim Brodersen before slotting it home.

Earlier on, it had taken two great saves from Goram to keep the scores level and had Lyngby managed to score there's no telling what could have happened. Durrant said, 'People keep saying that goal and our victory must be the icing on the cake, but it just keeps getting better and better. The games can't come quick enough and I feel great. I was delighted to score against Lyngby, especially in front of so many of our supporters. They were different class.'

Not long after dumping the Danes out of Europe, Walter Smith waded into the debate on the number of games the top sides were being asked to play – and he backed plans for a Super League in Scotland. He also said he would prefer just one national cup competition, with the League Cup being laid to rest. And by following the examples which had already been set in many European countries of playing only one match a week, Smith felt, 'Coaches would be given more time to work with their players; the playing standards of Scottish football would improve; there would be a drop in stress-related injuries, with players being fresher, and that fans and players would look forward to their football more than they were under the current "two games a week" system.'

The Gers boss added, 'It's not just because I'm the manager of Rangers that makes me say these things. If I was involved with another club my thoughts would be exactly the same. Everyone keeps telling us European sides are better than Scottish clubs and that their players are more prepared and technically gifted. But European clubs would never consider playing the amount of games we're forced to play in Scotland. Surely it is only common sense that we follow them and cut down on the number of matches.

'The League Cup, for example, is a tournament we could well do without at the start of a season. Players normally play in four competitions at that stage of the season and it can only affect their performances at one time or another. There is no professional player, regardless of his standard of fitness, who can play that many matches and maintain both his enthusiasm and fitness.

'If we took away the League Cup and left the important European matches and internationals as the only games to play in midweek at that stage of the season it would be far more beneficial. We would still have the Scottish Cup to play for after the New Year, but with the amount of fixtures we have we could do without the League Cup.

'The reason we play so many games is because some people thought more matches would increase revenue, but the days are long gone when people would turn up the moment you open the gates.'

But one player who was glad to be back playing games was Ferguson, one of the main reasons the Light Blues were enjoying a 12-match unbeaten run – which included just the one draw.

But Fergie, while pleased with his form, felt there was one aspect of his game still letting him down. He explained, 'A lack of goals is all that's missing for me at the moment. It seems that every time I try a shot, a defender gets in front of it or the keeper pulls off a fantastic save. But I'm not going to let it get me down. I'm quite happy to leave the scoring to Ally McCoist and Mark Hateley, and if the goals start to come for me I'll be delighted.

'Just as long as I'm playing well and the team is getting the results, I'll be happy, but that doesn't mean I'm going to stop going for goal.'

He also admitted he was delighted to be back in Andy Roxburgh's Scotland squad, and said, 'It was completely unexpected, so it was a pleasant call to receive. What international experience I have, I've enjoyed very much, but I'm not getting my hopes up about getting a game against Portugal.'

Ferguson was one of six Rangers players named in the squad for the friendly at Ibrox. The others were Andy Goram, Dave

McPherson, Stuart McCall, Ian Durrant and Ally McCoist, while David Hagen and Neil Murray retained their places in Scotland's under-21 squad.

Meanwhile, staff at the Ibrox ticket office were bracing themselves for an avalanche of applications for two of the biggest matches of the season. Workers were expecting more than 60,000 letters to arrive from supporters looking for briefs for the Skol Cup Final and the European Cup second round tie against either Leeds or Stuttgart.

Ticket office manager Matt Cook pleaded with fans to be patient and said, 'Please don't panic if you don't receive your tickets right away. In relation to the timescale involved, we would obviously and ideally aim to look after the applications for the European match first, then turn to the Skol Cup. These are two prime fixtures and the clerical and administrative effort involved is enormous.'

B OMBER Brown is the epitome of the young supporter who went on to play for the club he loved – and boy how he enjoyed every moment of it. And it's not just the 17 major honours he won while at Ibrox, but the matches he played in, the friends he made and the fact he wore the club crest so close to his heart on more than 300 occasions.

But as with every other professional player, his career had its ups and downs, with arguably one of the biggest negatives coming near the start of the 1991/92 season, when Rangers lost three vital games in a week. But that setback would provide the motivation for success the following season.

Brown recalled, 'I think expectation at Rangers is always high, and season '91/92 was no different. The result against Sparta Prague in the European Cup first round was a huge disappointment and, if I remember correctly, their player drilled one home from about 30 yards with the last kick of the ball to put us out – and that was a classic case of the fine margins we talk about.

'But we went on to build a bit of momentum ahead of the 1992/93 season. Archie Knox came in after Graeme Souness had left and Walter [Smith] had taken over. The gaffer had words with us regarding the Scottish Cup, and told us we had to do better in the competition, and that season we won it. We then had about an 18-month spell where we won every domestic competition going, from the double in 1991/92 to the treble the following season.

'There was also a real buzz surrounding the advent of the first ever Champions League and I think that lifted the boys. Mind you, we had a really good side, perhaps without any world-class players, but a squad packed full of real good pros, and Walter and Archie put together a side that we all thought was good enough to qualify for the group stages of the Champions League. That was the first aim, and then putting on a good display once we got there was number two.'

That season's European competition began with a tie against the relatively unknown Copenhagen side Lyngby, with the first leg at Ibrox, and it was up to Bomber Brown and co. to ensure there would be no fairytale win for the side who inhabited the land of Hans Christian Andersen.

Brown said, 'We had played many pre-season games in Scandinavia and always found their sides were big physical units and well disciplined, so we knew we wouldn't have it easy, and that's the way it panned out. We won 2-0 at Ibrox and 1-0 in the national stadium in Copenhagen, thanks to Ian Durrant. It was a hard game in Denmark but we had a good solid unit at that time and everybody worked their socks off for one another. We worked hard to win the ball when we didn't have it, and had players like McCoist and Hateley that were lethal. You would have hated playing against them week in, week out. I had to do it in training and it was torture, but thankfully we managed to get over the Danish hurdle and were left to await the outcome of the Leeds–Stuttgart tie.'

Bomber didn't realise it at the time but 1992/93 was shaping up to be the best season of his career – and he played in a few! He said, 'I played at a good level for around 18 seasons but that one was quickly becoming one of the best, and being a supporter made it all the sweeter. We did the treble, went on a 44-game unbeaten run and had an amazing run in Europe, so it must be up there with the club's best ever achievements.

'By winning the European Cup Winners' Cup in 1972, that side will never be forgotten. It remains the most famous game in our history, but in 1992/93 we were on the brink of doing something very special – on many fronts. To be so close to winning the first ever Champions League was in itself an incredible feat.

'It's not until many years later that you realise just how special that squad actually was. We had just beat Aberdeen at Parkhead to win the Scottish Cup and afterwards in the dressing room, Walter said, "It will be a number of years before you realise just how special this season has been." Once everything had settled down, it soon started to sink in.

'I always look at Hateley and McCoist, and the fact they never played together against Marseille in either game, and I think that was a defining factor, because I reckon we would have won at least one of the ties, and that would have been enough to get us through, especially with the way the games went.'

The Class of '93 would become just the fifth Rangers side in history to win the treble, an achievement which provided instant entry to the Ibrox record books – and then to play ten games in Europe that season and not lose a single tie is surely filed in the 'fantasy football' category! Brown said, 'Playing ten games in Europe, remaining unbeaten and then hearing what had allegedly gone on with Marseille was hard to take.

'During my Ibrox career, which spanned eight years, we won the league every time, so we played in either the European Cup or the Champions League, and never once dropped down to a Cup Winners' Cup or a UEFA Cup, so we didn't have that safety net. I think out of the nine times Rangers were in the top European competition, five of the nine teams who went on to win it had knocked us out along the way.

'But season 1992/92 will always be very special for everyone connected with the club and something that to this day I'm very proud of. Some amazing memories were made that season.'

When Graeme Souness arrived at Rangers in 1986, rebuilding the defence was a priority. Walter Smith was no different. Brown said, 'I struck up a good partnership with Richard Gough, but we had some smashing defenders round about us, and the likes of Ian Ferguson, Stuart McCall and Ian Durrant working very hard in midfield. Even Hateley and McCoist worked tirelessly to close down opposing full-backs, so it genuinely was a great team effort. One of our best qualities was a simple one: you lose the ball, you work hard to win it back, and that was something Graeme had drilled into us.

'Our defence was top drawer. Goughie and I played well together, and we had David Robertson and Davie McPherson round about us too. We developed a good understanding of how to play the back four and work the offside, stepping up or dropping off, and if Goughie was attacking the ball I would drop off and Slim [McPherson] would tuck in, so we all knew what one another was doing and, of course, we had a right good goalie behind us, which meant we could squeeze up to go one-on-one with strikers.

'Andy Goram was second to none and that confidence flowed throughout the team and allowed us to press forward and push on. We had a good unit but it was pretty basic stuff really. Walter and Archie put the jigsaw together and let the boys get on with it.

I remember both of them saying that for around 18 months they didn't need to coach, they just had to manage because of the squad they had assembled. You would receive simple instructions before a game and you just went out there and got on with it. That period of about two years, from 1991–93, was exceptional.'

Brown isn't one to single out team-mates for special praise but decided to make an exception in the case of Ian Durrant. He said, 'Ian had a knack of scoring in the big games. The bigger the better for the wee man. But when you consider how long he had been out injured, to come back and perform at the level he did was incredible. That season's Champions League was the true essence of the competition, with all the league winners from their respective countries involved, so that was the level Durranty was playing at. He was sensational.'

Once Rangers got past Lyngby, they were looking at a second round tie against either Leeds United or Stuttgart, as a replay had been ordered by UEFA. Rangers didn't have a great record against German sides so the players craved a second round match-up with Leeds.

Bomber said, 'We knew they had a fantastic side, and had beaten Manchester United to the league the previous season, but we all felt we had a good chance of progressing in the competition if a Battle of Britain became reality.

'We had boys that were born in England, but played for Scotland, like Goram and McCall, and we had the likes of Mark Hateley coming up here and wanting to get back into the England squad. There were also guys like Dale Gordon who were pumped up for a match against Leeds.

'The fact the Elland Road side had Scottish guys like McAllister and Strachan made us want the tie even more. It's the type of match you dream of playing in as a wee boy, and it certainly didn't come much bigger than Rangers v Leeds that season.

'We might have lost an early goal in the first leg, but I felt we won the tie in the tunnel – before a ball was even kicked. It was something Graeme Souness had told us a few years previous. He said, "Clock your opponent in the tunnel and stare them out and if they can't stare back at you, you're one up." I'll never forget standing there, waiting to go out, and the roar we could hear from inside the ground was absolutely deafening and when I looked at some of the Leeds players, they were staring ahead like rabbits caught in the headlights.

'And even though Gary McAllister scored early on, I always felt we were going to win the game, because we knew that when Hateley and McCoist were playing together we would get goals. It ended up a great night and our supporters created a brilliant atmosphere.

'The build-up to the second leg was also incredible. Even with a slender 2-1 lead, we were being written off, and getting a pounding in the English media. But Alex Ferguson was sending Archie Knox all the cuttings from the papers down south prior to the second leg – and Fergie made sure we didn't miss any. Walter and Archie had both previously worked with Fergie, but there was also the added ingredient of Manchester United hating Leeds, so the cuttings were coming up regularly and Archie was gathering them all up.

'Mind you, we weren't allowed to see them straight away. We had a couple of league fixtures to get out the way first, but once we were free of distractions, Archie pinned up the cuttings in the dressing room and we had a good look at what Leeds would do to us, and how the game was just a formality. It was music to our ears because we certainly couldn't have been described as a frightened or timid bunch of players. We were desperate to get down to Elland Road and get in among them, and prove to the English media that Leeds weren't as good as through to the group stages!'

It wasn't just the newspapers south of the border that were crammed full of stories about the upcoming second leg at Elland Road; the Scottish media were also clamouring for any little titbit they could find on the match. It was shaping up to be the biggest cross-border clash in decades.

Bomber said, 'We flew down the night before and stayed in Manchester, the Holiday Inn at the airport. The bus picked us up at the hotel prior to the match and we were pumped up and desperate to get going. When we were only moments from Elland Road – well aware that it was strictly home supporters only – the volume of supporters grew and the tension was building. I recall one of the lads saying, "I can't believe the number of Leeds fans giving us the thumbs up and waving to us. They're really friendly!" Walter Smith turned round and said, "It's Rangers fans with Leeds tops and scarves on ya stupid bugger!"

'We all started laughing and it helped ease the tension. Then we started picking out people we knew. Someone would say, "Look, there's Willie with a Leeds top on, and there's Shug with a yellow scarf!" Not everyone was "1people spotting" though. A few of the guys were playing cards to take their mind off the game. But it definitely helped knowing there was a good number of Rangers supporters in the ground that night, and the "welcoming party" was a nice touch. My brother took my car down with a few of his mates, while big Andy Smillie had a corporate hospitality box, so there were plenty of our fans inside Elland Road.

'I roomed with Ian Ferguson and my brother stayed in our hotel room that night and drove my car up the road the next day. It was great that my family were able to share in such a top experience.'

Bomber insists the memories of being knocked out so early the previous season helped drive the team on that night, and added, 'We were very aware that the 1992/93 campaign could be a special season for us and we were determined to knock Leeds out and get to the group stages. And we had some great momentum at that time.

'Elland Road can be an intimidating place, and Leeds United are a big club down south, but they aren't massive in comparison to Rangers. Our club is an institution, so the whole build-up to the game didn't intimidate us at all. I remember standing in the tunnel and their PA system was blasting out "Eye of the Tiger", the *Rocky* tune. I was delighted because I love that song, and I looked round and there was Ian Durrant shadow boxing their big centre-half, Chris Fairclough, and the Leeds player was just staring nervously ahead.

'And it was against Fairclough that Durrant won the header for our first goal, so the wee man had got right inside his head. It's amazing how such a small thing can have a huge effect on a match. Durrant won the ball and flicked it on to Mark Hateley, the ball bounced twice and the big man knocked it home. All these wee things contributed to a great victory. We had a great dressing room and the players who could easily lighten a tense situation.'

Hateley's early goal settled Rangers down, and while Leeds created a number of good chances they found Andy Goram in exceptional form. However, Bomber and his team-mates knew a second goal would all but kill off the tie, and the flame-haired defender had a hand in the game's defining moment.

He recalled, 'I won the ball from Eric Cantona, played it to Durrant and he played a great ball out wide to Hateley. The big man looked up and sent a cracking cross into McCoist, who stooped to head past Lukic. Coisty very rarely scored with his head, but it was a cracker. They got one back, but we had a bit of a cushion and were reasonably comfortable.'

Rangers had done it. They had beaten the champions of England home and away and could look forward to the Champions League group stages, but for the victorious players the night was just beginning. Brown said, 'When the final whistle sounded, the first thing I noticed was McAllister and Strachan sprinting straight off the pitch, and right down the tunnel. After a couple of minutes I heard this applause getting louder and louder and it was the Leeds fans applauding us off the park. It meant the world to us, that they had just watched a team that was well deserving of victory on the night – and over the two legs – and they recognised that and showed their appreciation.

'We were walking down the Elland Road tunnel, proud as punch at becoming the first British club to qualify for the Champions League group stages and who was there to meet us but Sir Alex Ferguson. He shook each and every one of us warmly by the hand. You would have thought he was the Rangers manager that night.

'He then came into our dressing room and Walter congratulated us on a famous victory and said, "Boys, go out and have a few drinks, you've earned it. Enjoy yourselves, but be on that bus for the airport at 7.30am." I think Walter perhaps felt relieved and maybe some of the pressure was off him because millions of pounds were up for grabs for the teams that qualified.

'As soon as we were changed, and out of the dressing room, the first thing I wanted to do was phone my dad back home in Blantyre, but there weren't any mobile phones in those days, so I asked a club steward where the players' lounge was. When I walked in, there was only one table occupied, so the Leeds players had obviously decided to give it a body swerve.

'Anyway, I went up to the bar and the barman gave me the phone – the old one with a cord and the round dialling circle. I had a good chat with my dad, who was absolutely delighted, and he told me to enjoy my night. I hung up and turned round and there was Eric Cantona and David Rocastle, and Rocastle's mate, Dennis Waterman, the actor from *The Sweeney* and *Minder*, sitting in the corner.

'I had swapped jerseys with Cantona after the game, and when I was walking away from the bar in the players' lounge, he once again congratulated me on the win. Some of our lads came in and we had a beer, but we never saw Strachan or McAllister. Perhaps it was the embarrassment of them being Scottish, and losing to a Scottish team, I don't know, but we were certainly no slouches and in Andy Goram, I would say we had the best goalkeeper in the world at that time.'

Bomber added, 'I remember we all headed for this Rastafarian nightclub, with Stuart McCall – can of lager in hand – leading the way. We walked in, in boisterous mood, and about 30 big Rastas walked straight out! We took over the club that night and sat with a few of the Manchester United boys – including Ryan Giggs, Gary Neville, Nicky Butt, Lee Sharpe and David Beckham. We had a great night, enjoyed a fair few pints and laughed and joked until we got back to the hotel in the wee small hours. We had a bus to catch in the morning.'

The big games were coming thick and fast and next up for the victorious Bears was a mouth-watering clash with Celtic just a few days later. Brown recalled, 'We didn't kick a ball between the final whistle at Elland Road and the pre-match warm-up at Parkhead on the Saturday. We came up the road, recovered from Leeds, slept a bit, came in on the Friday morning and Archie and Walter took us for a walk round Bellahouston Park and then over to the Place Cafe on Paisley Road West for pie and beans, coffees and ice cream sodas. It was time to refuel.

'We then went to the hotel in the afternoon, caught up with a bit more sleep, and the adrenaline just kept us going. That season was primarily about rest and recovery because we were mostly playing Saturday–Wednesday–Saturday, and it was all about Walter and Archie managing people and bodies. I think I played almost 60 games, while those involved with their respective international teams had another ten or so games on top of that.

'But we went to Parkhead on the Saturday and beat Celtic 1-0, with an Ian Durrant goal, and our fans were once again in great voice. They were also waving their European flags, which was just fantastic. It was a great sight.'

When Rangers were drawn against Marseille, Bruges and CSKA Moscow in the group stages, Brown picked out the ties against the French champions as the ones which could prove significant. He was proved right, and enjoyed playing in both the home and away legs.

He said, 'We got battered in the match at Ibrox – they were a very good side. Hateley was up front, but we were without McCoist, and they had Alen Boksic and Rudi Voller playing up top. It was the old Ibrox playing surface and it was really heavy, and cutting up badly. We were 1-0 down at half-time and Goughie had to go off injured.

Young Steven Pressley came on and we then found ourselves two down.

'For the first hour that night, Marseille were unbelievable. They were one of the best teams I ever played against, and that includes the Juventus side of '96, when they had Del Piero, Vialli, Ravanelli, Deschamps, Desailly etc, but Marseille were right up there.

'We showed real spirit and determination to come back that night and draw 2-2. We never knew when we were beaten – which was one of our great strengths. Maybe at 2-0 they thought it was a case of job done, but we kicked on, got a goal back and it lifted the roof off the stadium. We then got a second and I reckon another five minutes and we would have won the game. I think Marseille got a shock that night, but at the end of the 90 minutes they knew they had been in a game.

'We came off the park feeling we had secured a moral victory; we knew we had played a quality side and afterwards we started to feel it could be between ourselves and Marseille to win the group. It also gave us the belief that we could go to Marseille and win.'

Next up, though, was a match against Russian champions CSKA Moscow – in Germany, and Bomber recalled, 'It was the second week in December, and it was cold in Germany, so you can imagine what it was like in Moscow! It was a wee bit surreal, being an away game for us, and there was this wee group of Russians in the stand, and they all had the big Cossack hats on, complete with red stars, but it was a great goal from Ian Ferguson which won us the game. Any victory in the Champions League, whether home or away, was always welcome, but to get the victory against CSKA gave us that bit of momentum going into the double header with Bruges.

'The match over in Belgium was played in a tight, old-fashioned stadium, but we had a great support cheering us on. Whenever we played abroad, it wasn't about sight-seeing, we were there to do a job, and Pieter Huistra got our goal that night – the equaliser – and even though we had chances to win the game, it was still a good point to collect away from home. It also meant we remained unbeaten in the group, which was important. Our aim was to get something from all the away games and win our remaining home games, and we knew if we did that we had a right good chance.'

Rangers won the return game, with the contest living long in the memory because of a certain player scoring a certain goal. Brown laughed, 'We beat Bruges 2-1, and as much as we were overjoyed at getting the two points, I'll never for the life of me work out how Scott

Nisbet's cross into the box managed to bounce over the goalkeeper and into the net. The pitch was sodden so I can only imagine big Nissy located the only firm part of the playing surface and there was a good bit of topspin on the ball.

'Mind you, it was an eventful first half as Ian Durrant had scored for us and then Mark Hateley was red-carded a minute before the break, so we did well to get the goal in the second period and go on to win the game. Later on, big Mark was adamant that a bit of jiggery pokery had played a part in his sending-off. He would claim that Marseille had made a few phone calls to ensure he was out of the next group game, which just happened to be against the French side. So while the victory was massive that night, we didn't realise just how big a loss he would be until we got to France three weeks later.'

That was the crunch game in the group. Marseille v Rangers in the Stade Velodrome. Rangers were now dining at the top table in Europe.

Bomber said, 'Given Marseille had a far better goal difference than us – thanks to their 6-0 win against CSKA – the game in France was crucial. We knew their fans would crank up the pressure on us but we were looking forward to it because we had loads of big-time players in the squad. And let's face it, if you had played for Rangers at Parkhead, especially in front of the old Jungle, then Marseille were never going to intimidate us.

'As it turned out, their fans – and ours – created a cracking atmosphere and the big drums were banging long before the players took to the field. It was their old stadium, with the fans all housed behind wire fences. We were there a couple of days before the match and had a walk round about the harbour area. We had been well warned about which areas to avoid, and where was safe to visit etc.

'Going into the game, we knew that whoever won would progress to the final. The last round of games wouldn't matter and AC Milan, who had won all their games, would provide the opposition in that game.

'In their last game at home, Marseille had destroyed CSKA 6-0, but we had already played CSKA and knew they weren't a "6-0 team"; they were a solid unit, so there was talk that something had happened to influence the course of the game, but we still went into the penultimate tie full of confidence and with nothing to fear.

'It was a big game for us and we had our wives and partners – who had travelled over on a second plane – there to cheer us on. It was a tough game, but we were always in it, even when Franck Sauzee bagged the opener. Ian Durrant scored a cracking equaliser and we had chances in the second half, but there is one incident in particular I will never forget. Walter Smith had pushed me forward and when Gary McSwegan cut in from the right, I was screaming for him to square the ball, as I had a tap-in, but he shot from quite a tight angle and the opportunity was lost.

'There are defining moments in football matches and that was perhaps it in that game. If we get the goal we're going to the first ever Champions League Final, but we didn't and we left that night with a point, but I suppose it shows just where we were at that time that we were disappointed coming away from Marseille with just a point. When we arrived back in Glasgow we were reminded that it was still everything to play for in the last group matches, but deep down we were thinking, 'have we missed our chance?'

Rangers had to win their final group match, against CSKA, and hope Marseille slipped up in Belgium. There would have been long odds on offer at the bookmakers of such a scenario taking place, but where there's hope...

'We absolutely pummelled CSKA at Ibrox,' said Brown, 'but we just couldn't put the ball in the back of the net, and then we found out Marseille had beaten Bruges 1-0, so that's how tight it was. The majority of games in the group were settled by a draw or a one-goal margin of victory. So it was frustrating and disappointing that the campaign ended in the manner it did.

'Afterwards, people were calling for Rangers to appeal, to try and get the Marseille v AC Milan final halted, and I suppose when you look at what's happened in the Olympic Games, with Jessica Ennis-Hill being awarded a third gold medal because of dodgy dealings in Rio, then perhaps there was a case to say that Marseille had robbed Rangers of a place in the final.

'It's not something I dwell on massively, but I feel that had Hateley and McCoist played together in the games against Marseille, it would have made such a difference. I think we would have won in France, as Marseille were terrified of Hateley, the threat he posed in the air and just his all-round presence. Basile Boli wouldn't have fancied meeting him even on his own patch, because in his day, Hateley was a beast, and the way McCoist fed off him was different class. They were a fantastic partnership.

'If you look at the history of our club; to win every domestic trophy, and go through the Champions League – qualifiers and group matches – undefeated, and miss out on the final only through possible skulduggery, I would have to say the '92/93 season is arguably the best in the club's history. Through speaking to members of the Barcelona Bears side, I know they had targeted the European Cup Winners' Cup that season, but we targeted the lot – and almost did it. It has to be one of our best.

'I think any of the players involved in the nine-in-a-row seasons would also say that 1992/93 was their favourite. I know it's definitely the case for me. I played professionally for just under 20 years and the 1992/93 campaign is an absolute standout.'

Brown concluded by revealing how his brief shot at international glory came to a grinding halt during the season in question – and it still rankles with this proud Scot.

He said, 'I had been in one Scotland squad that season, for a World Cup qualifying tie against Portugal at Ibrox, but hadn't made the team. The manager Andy Roxburgh then lined up a friendly against Germany in the March – the month before we played CSKA – and I was hoping for some game time, and to win my first cap. There was no prouder Scot than me, so I was gutted when I didn't even make the squad, and more so when I found out the reason. Roxburgh said he didn't want to put 30-somethings into a squad for a friendly international!

'So, the night we drew with CSKA at Ibrox, Archie Knox came into the dressing room and said, "Bomber, Andy Roxburgh is in with Walter and wants to add you to the squad for the World Cup qualifier in Portugal next Wednesday." I said to Archie, "Tell him to fuck off! I was too old to play against Germany last month, and it was headline news, so I'm too old to be in his squad for Portugal."

'Walter then came in and spoke to me about it, and I said, "We've just missed out on a Champions League Final, we have a chance at the Scottish Cup to win us a treble at Parkhead. That's my priority. Tell Andy Roxburgh to stick his call-up." I would love to have represented my country, but I wasn't allowing anyone to mess me about and treat me like a pensioner. I was 31 years old at the time, hardly ready to be put out to stud.'

7

Goals Galore for Super Ally

OCTOBER started much the same way as September had ended – with Rangers winning games and Ally McCoist taking centre stage. In the first match of the month, a newspaper headline read 'McCoist 4 Falkirk 0', and who could argue? Of course, the other ten players – and substitute Ian Durrant – played their part, but it was goal machine McCoist who earned his 'Super' tag by netting a couple in each half to take his hat-trick tally for the season to four.

Could life get any better for the hot-shot striker, best-selling author, occasional team captain and goalscorer supreme? Stuart McCall had the answer, and after the win, which was achieved in cruise control, he said, 'After the trip to Denmark, and the number of games we've had recently, there were a lot of tired legs among us. Thankfully, Coisty's legs were fine, but he made it worse for the rest of us by making us chase him each time he scored!

'I think he is on a high, and although some people might say he is a lucky so-and-so, he makes some tremendous runs to get into the right place at the right time and get on the end of things. Mind you, we all felt a bit sorry for big Mark Hateley. To see Coisty score four and have two goals chopped off himself must have been tough.'

The win over the Bairns signalled the end of the first quarter of the league season and Rangers' record read played 11, won eight, drawn two and lost one. But the most important statistic was the four-point lead over second-placed Celtic.

Just four days later, Walter Smith's side travelled up to Perth for a potentially difficult league match, but St Johnstone proved no match for rampant Rangers who smashed five past their hapless opponents. This time, Hateley's luck was in and the big Englishman scored twice. Mind you, McCoist was also on target twice, with Ian Ferguson's goal drought ending in some style when he let fly from 25 yards to notch the fifth and final goal.

For Hateley, though, it was goals number seven and eight of the campaign, although his celebrations were cut short when he found himself in plaster the following morning. He had been troubled by an Achilles injury, but a course of treatment and a ten-day break due to the international recess meant he probably wouldn't miss too many games.

Smith said, 'Ally McCoist is scoring a lot of goals for us at the moment, but it's good for his partner to get a couple too. Mark's game is essentially about setting up chances, so he has no qualms about doing that for Ally.'

But Hateley contradicted his gaffer when he joked, 'I'm fed up making all these chances for Ally. Mind you, it was nice to get a couple against St Johnstone, especially after having two chopped off against Falkirk. But to come away from home and win is the important thing. To score is a bonus.'

Hateley added, 'I think we're applying ourselves much better this season. We are more professional in our approach and buzzing from the start of games, whereas last season we were a bit apprehensive in our approach – but winning week in, week out definitely helps.'

The only thing which had blighted Hateley's season to date had been a series of niggling injuries which had sidelined him for four of the 17 matches. He said, 'I can do without these persistent injuries. But I'm pleased we have a break at the moment and after that hopefully things will settle down.'

As for McCoist, 23 goals by the middle of October was real *Roy of the Rovers* stuff. And as the 30-year-old was preparing for the Scotland v Portugal match, he revealed how he had once 'played' for Benfica. He explained, 'I was on holiday with my wife Allison in Albufeira, in the Algarve, in 1983, shortly after I'd joined

Rangers. I was standing at the hotel bar one day and got chatting to a Portuguese guy who told me his name was Umberto Coelo.

'He asked me if I was interested in football and I told him I was, but didn't tell him I played for Rangers. He then asked if I fancied a wee game the following afternoon, and I thought, "Why not?" Next day he picked Allison and me up at the hotel and drove to a big indoor sports arena.'

McCoist told of how lengthy queues had formed outside the building, but little did he know he would be one of the star attractions for the crowd – and he was in for the shock of his life when his new pal Umberto took him into the dressing room.

McCoist explained, 'I was introduced to the rest of the team as Ally from Scotland, and then someone threw me a Benfica strip! We ran out on to the pitch and there were 5,000 people there to see the Benfica first team play the local side Emortal, who turn out in the Portuguese Third Division.

'Apparently it was a challenge game which was played every summer. It turned out Umberto has played over 80 times for the national side. Only the great Eusebio has more caps for Portugal. I was playing alongside other Portuguese internationalists such as Frederico Rosa and Carlos Manuel, who both played for Benfica at the time.

'I thought it was just a bounce game among a few local lads, but we ended up winning 7-3 and I scored a goal, so it wasn't too bad! After the match both teams were invited to an outdoor banquet and we had a meal and a few beers together. It was a fantastic day.'

Long-serving Ibrox ace Scott Nisbet was used to playing in front of 40,000 supporters at Ibrox, but admitted the thought of speaking in front of 2,000 folk terrified him. The 24-year-old was guest of honour at the prestigious Rangers Supporters' Association Rally, which was due to take place at the Royal Concert Hall in Glasgow for the first time.

Nisbet had been a full-time professional at the club for seven years, and it was this service that led to him receiving one of the biggest honours to be bestowed upon a Rangers player by the club's supporters. The Edinburgh-born defender was set to follow in the footsteps of legends such as Jock 'Tiger' Shaw, Derek Johnstone, Tommy McLean, Ally McCoist and Ian Durrant by delivering the keynote speech to fans at the 43rd Rangers Rally, which was expected to be a 2,000 sell-out.

Nisbet said, 'I was approached after the match against Falkirk and was shocked at first, but it's a great honour. I don't know what makes me more nervous, playing in front of a packed house at Ibrox or speaking in front of 2,000!'

Well-known Bluenose comedian Clem Dane was the compere for the evening.

Meanwhile, the man they called 'The Judge' handed out another stiff sentence to Premier League opposition when he came off the bench to score the only goal of the game against Hibs. McCoist, supposedly resting after picking up a knock the previous week while on Scotland duty, was the hammerer of the Edinburgh side ... just when it looked as though they would leave Ibrox with a point and a clean sheet. McCoist scored with just nine minutes remaining, and while his latest goal was scored from just a yard out, it was a vital extra point for Walter Smith's battle-hardened troops.

McCoist had picked up the 'Judge' nickname after spending most of the 1990/91 season on the bench but had since gone on to set plenty of goalscoring records and his strike against the Easter Road men was his 16th of the season.

Just a few days before the match, staff and players at Ibrox were mourning the death of club legend, Willie Waddell. The former Light Blues player and manager, who was 71, died after suffering a heart attack in a Glasgow hospital. His funeral was held at Linn Crematorium, and around 1,000 people gathered to pay their final respects. Rangers' stars past and present were in attendance. The entire first team was joined by Walter Smith, the board of directors and members of staff who worked alongside Mr Waddell at the club.

Great Rangers from the past, including Bob McPhail, John Greig, Jim Baxter and Graeme Souness were present as were other well-known figures from the Scottish game including Billy McNeill and Andy Roxburgh.

Greig, who under Mr Waddell had captained the side to its greatest achievement in winning the European Cup Winners' Cup in Barcelona in 1972, led the tributes. He said, 'Willie lived for Rangers. I was absolutely shattered at the news of his death. He was like a father to me and always impressed upon us the fine traditions of the club. It was bigger than any one individual.'

Smith added, 'His advice over the last six years has been invaluable. When Graeme Souness and I first arrived at the club, he helped us enormously. He was held in high esteem by everyone connected with the game.'

Chairman David Murray also praised Mr Waddell's contribution to Rangers, and said, 'The club owes him a tremendous debt for his forward planning and progressive thinking.' That vision was captured in the magnificent Ibrox Stadium, which stands as a monument to Mr Waddell and also the 66 fans who lost their lives in the 1971 Ibrox disaster.

After the saddest chapter in Rangers' history, Mr Waddell, the manager at the time, took control and set about ensuring such a tragedy could never happen again. He visited the top stadia in Europe, and Ibrox was remodelled along the lines of the Westfalenstadion in Dortmund.

Willie Waddell served Rangers for over 44 years as a player, manager, general manager, vice-chairman and honorary director. He first joined the club in 1936 as a 15-year-old and made his first-team debut in August 1938. It was a debut to remember as he rushed to Ibrox straight from school and scored the only goal of the game against English champions Arsenal.

Nicknamed 'Deedle', he was a stunning right-winger who built up an almost telepathic understanding with centre-forward Willie Thornton, who headed home many goals from the pinpoint crosses of his good friend. Mr Waddell was revered by the Rangers fans, who even composed a song in his honour, titled 'How Can You Buy Willie Waddell?'

In a playing career spanning 20 years he played 558 times for Rangers and scored 143 goals. He won four league championship medals, two Scottish Cup badges and 17 Scotland caps. After leaving Rangers, he became manager of Kilmarnock and led them to the Scottish First Division title in 1965, the first provincial club to do so since the 1930s. He later became a journalist before returning to his first love, Rangers, in 1969.

With the Skol Cup Final on the horizon, full-back David Robertson had three good reasons for hoping Rangers could beat his former club Aberdeen at Hampden. Not only would victory mean he had completed the full domestic set of medals since his move from Pittodrie to Ibrox 15 months previously, and not just because it would mean all three trophies would sit proudly in the Ibrox trophy room at the same time, but it would allow Robertson to go back to his native city with his head held high.

He explained, 'When we were already in the final and it was Celtic v Aberdeen in the other semi, I was hoping Aberdeen would win because they are my old team. That said, I would obviously get a lot of satisfaction if we beat them, but if we lose it would be a long time before I could go back up to Aberdeen.

'Since I came to Rangers, I've been quite lucky against them. We have lost just once, drew once and won the rest of the games, but the Dons haven't won a trophy for a good while and will be tough opponents. Willie Miller won't be thinking about going to Hampden to be second best. We will need to be on our guard, but hopefully we can play well and win.

'To complete the domestic set of medals just over a year into my Rangers career would also be incredible.'

And Robbo played his part as Rangers did just that. True blue grit and determination were just as important as skill, as more than 45,000 supporters saw Stuart McCall's 14th-minute opener cancelled out by the prolific Duncan Shearer on the hour mark. But 24 minutes of extra time had elapsed when Robertson sent a tantalising ball across goal looking for Mark Hateley, only for the unfortunate Gary Smith to knock it past Theo Snelders.

It was the seventh time in ten years that Rangers had won the League Cup, and just four days after the energy-sapping Battle of Britain the Light Blues had somehow found the strength to overrun their opponents. It was a thrilling encounter which saw both teams create a number of chances. In the 13th minute, Ian Ferguson picked up a pass from McCall and rifled in a 25-yard shot which came back off Snelders's post. Rangers were in front 60 seconds later. David Winnie played the ball back to Snelders, but the keeper allowed the ball to cannon off his chest and McCall nicked in to poke it into the corner of the net.

Shearer took advantage of some good play by Eoin Jess and David Winnie on 62 minutes to lash home with Andy Goram well beaten, before Rangers lost both Richard Gough and Trevor Steven to injury. In extra time, Snelders saved well from Durrant, while Ferguson, Mikhailichenko, McCoist and Robertson all squandered good chances before the late own goal ensured it was Rangers who lifted the trophy.

Goram played a huge part in bringing the cup back to Ibrox, and then insisted Rangers' mean streak was responsible for their success. He said, 'It's a big blow for the game in Scotland that we won the cup. Had Aberdeen won, every other team would have been given a boost. That was their best chance of the season so far to win a trophy, but they didn't manage it, so they will be wondering what they have to do to win.

'But no one will get any sympathy from us because the only thing our boys care about is Glasgow Rangers. We don't care about the rest. As long as we win the league and cups available to us, then we're happy. The greatest thing we have going for us as a squad is that none of the lads like losing – and we deserved to beat Aberdeen because we were the dominant side.'

The League Cup medal completed a domestic set of badges won by Goram at Ibrox since he signed from Hibs in June 1991 for £1m. He was Walter Smith's first big-money signing, but scoffed at suggestions that Rangers only had to wield the cheque book to guarantee success in Scotland.

He said, 'Rangers don't just buy good players – there's a lot more to it than that. You've got to be a good professional and a winner, because if you're not, then there's no point in being at Ibrox.

'It probably took Rangers a while to sign players such as David Robertson, myself and a few others, but they were the players the club wanted. There are a lot of players here with a right good attitude – they are winners and they want success. That's what gets us through. An average team can get away with being average as long as they fight for each other. But if you put the same amount of fight into a team such as ours, which is a good one, then it's a difficult formula to beat.'

Walter Smith hailed the efforts of his players, but cautioned, 'Coming off the back of a domestic cup final and a big European match there is a worry that the players might put the league to the back of their minds. But if that happens it could undo all our good work. We must guard against it.'

One player who had to wait to get a good look at his medal was Alexei Mikhailichenko. The former Dynamo Kiev and Sampdoria star had fought his way back into Walter Smith's side in the weeks leading up to the Skol Cup Final – and then played a starring role at Hampden.

But Miko was unable to enjoy the post-match celebrations as he had a flight to catch and had to leave Hampden straight after the final whistle. Once outside the stadium, he simply hailed a passing Rangers fan in his car, told the bemused driver 'Bothwell' and was driven straight home!

He explained, 'I had to catch a flight from Glasgow to London and then to Kiev as I had to meet up with the Ukrainian national squad, and had just enough time to go home and get changed. I actually received my medal in the dressing room but I was disappointed I couldn't hold the cup in my hand and celebrate with the team and the fans.'

It was challenge matches only for both Miko and his team-mate Oleg Kuznetsov, as they had chosen to remain loyal to their native Ukraine. After the break-up of the Soviet Union, several Ukrainian-born stars such as Sergei Yuran, Igor Dobrovolski and Victor Onopko had opted to play for the Russian national team, but Miko and Kuznetsov decided to stay put.

Miko said, 'In some situations I can understand Ukrainian-born players turning out for Russia. My good friend Dobrovolski, for example, although born in the Ukraine, was brought up in Moldavia and played his football for a long time in Moscow.

'Perhaps in other cases morale and national feelings have changed for the sake of material interests, although the situation is very complex. When the break-up of the Soviet Union began, both Oleg and I made it clear we would play for Ukraine and no one else. And our appearance in Kiev last week played a political role more than anything else.

'We will do our best to help our national team in the process of its creation. However, by the time we play organised football again we will both be over 30 and won't have much time to be successful with our country, but the important thing is we do our best to help the Ukraine.'

The midfield maestro then spoke of his admiration for Ally McCoist – who had scored 28 times in just 22 games, and it was still October! Miko raved, 'Sometimes I feel the ball is tied to his feet because he gets into the most incredible positions to score an impossible amount of goals. In fact, I get the feeling if Ally were to stand in the centre circle and close his eyes, the ball would hit off his head and still end up in the back of the net!

'But there is no luck attached to his skill. Any striker who gets into these positions must have an incredible sense for goals and Ally has shown he has great speed of mind and thought. He has the ability to cause problems for any defence.'

Mikhailichenko, 29, felt McCoist could cut it in the Italian league, and said, 'It is difficult to make a comparison, but he is on a similar level to forwards I have played against because he has great technique. But to fully compare, Ally would have to go to Italy and play.'

Miko's comments were timely as Super Ally notched up his fifth treble of the season in a 4-2 demolition of Motherwell at Ibrox.

The talented front man had picked up a bottle of champagne for an earlier hat-trick just before the game, but showed he had a real liking for bubbly with another three-goal blitz.

It was Halloween and Super Ally had the Steelmen running scared – after Ian Angus's opener had given the 38,719 supporters inside Ibrox a bit of a fright. But three from Coisty and a Bomber Brown strike had Gers on Easy Street before Tommy McLean's visitors struck a late consolation. The win maintained Rangers' four-point cushion at the top of the Premier League.

October ended with Scott Nisbet playing a starring role at the Rangers Rally – and McCoist and Ian Durrant 'allegedly' rendering the big man unable to speak!

Rangers supporters packed out Glasgow's Royal Concert Hall for the annual fans' bash and they were joined by directors, management and the full first team and reserve squads, as everyone enjoyed an evening of cabaret, expertly compered by Clem Dane. But the highlight was the speech by Nissy, which had everyone in hoots of laughter, especially the big man himself. The popular defender had spent all week working on his notes, but crumbled shortly after taking centre stage and found it difficult to continue.

His team 'mates' stood behind him as he attempted to deliver his speech, but the word from behind the scenes at Ibrox was that Nissy was being 'out-pattered' by two well-known jokers in the Rangers camp. They were throwing some friendly banter in his direction and every time he tried to continue they would crease him up with another one-liner. Suffice to say the pair are just as sharp on the park, and they forced big Nissy into a major own goal when he couldn't continue his speech due to the tears of laughter running down his face – but the supporters loved it!

8

Battle of Britain

RANGERS were desperate to exorcise the ghosts of the previous season's (relatively) shock European Cup exit to Sparta Prague – when they suffered extra-time heartache following a Scott Nisbet own goal. So, with the first hurdle against Lyngby successfully negotiated, Walter Smith and co. patiently awaited the outcome of the Leeds–Stuttgart tie.

While Rangers were beating the Danes home and away, Leeds had lost the first leg 3-0 in Germany, a result that looked likely to see Stuttgart through. However, spurred on by the magnificent Gordon Strachan, United turned it on in the return game at Elland Road and, roared on by a partisan crowd in excess of 31,000, goals by Gary Speed, Gary McAllister, Eric Cantona and Lee Chapman gave the home side a handsome 4-1 victory.

The counter by Andreas Buck levelled the aggregate score at 4-4 and took the Germans through on the away goals rule – or so they believed.

Just hours after the match, a member of the victorious Stuttgart party noticed his side had exceeded the permitted number of non-Germans in their squad. At the time, UEFA allowed clubs to use a maximum of three foreign-born and two 'assimilated' players (those who had played for five years in the country their club was based in, including three at under-19 level), and it transpired Stuttgart had breached the tournament rules by using four foreign players.

The big question for UEFA was what to do about it. They held a meeting, which lasted for five hours, and while the main point was to decide how to punish Stuttgart, the meeting soon became a debating ground to discuss the hated rule. The general consensus was that if a team could win its national championship using players from 'X' amount of countries, then why couldn't those same players represent their club in the European Cup?

But while Leeds were grateful to Stuttgart for noticing, and admitting to, their mistake, they felt the only avenue open to the game's governing body was to expel the Germans from the competition. UEFA didn't agree. It was pointed out that the German FA had been one of the main driving forces behind the three-foreigner rule being implemented, but UEFA felt expulsion was too harsh a punishment.

Midway through the meeting, Leeds's representatives in Zurich became incensed when Stuttgart attempted to discredit them by suggesting Gary Speed had also been ineligible to play in the match. Leeds immediately pointed out that although Speed played for Wales, he was fully qualified to play for them under UEFA rules. UEFA agreed that Stuttgart's accusation was spurious and fined the club 10,000 Swiss francs.

In summing up, a UEFA official announced that the organisation was awarding the Elland Road side a 3-0 victory as Stuttgart had fielded an ineligible player. This left the clubs level on aggregate at 3-3 and UEFA decreed a play-off game should take place at the Nou Camp in Barcelona. The decision was seen as a cop-out, not for the first time, by European football's bigwigs.

In the meantime the victims of the delay and controversy were Rangers, who were forced to play a waiting game, although it was suggested in certain quarters that they might just want to avoid Stuttgart as teams from Germany had knocked them out of European competition four times in the previous ten years.

And so to the Nou Camp, and a second opportunity for the Germans. The official crowd was given as just 7,400 (in a stadium with a capacity of 120,000) but the prize at stake was priceless. The game was played in an eerie atmosphere with the travelling Leeds support situated in a small section of the upper tier of one stand. But the Yorkshire supporters were cheering loudest as goals by Strachan and Carl Shutt handed them a 2-1 win – and an opportunity to book their place in the group stages of the inaugural Champions League. But first they had to get past Rangers!

One of the first decisions made by both clubs, after talks with their respective associations and the police, was that away fans would be banned from both ties. Rangers were also ordered by UEFA to cut their standing capacity by 40 per cent, which meant that only 42,000 tickets would be available for the Ibrox leg. The game was also stamped with a 'High Risk' classification by UEFA.

Still, that didn't prevent queues forming outside the Ibrox ticket office as season ticket holders clamoured to exchange vouchers for match briefs. Ticket office manager Matt Cook insisted his staff were 'almost under siege'.

Rangers secretary and director Campbell Ogilvie said, 'In my time at the club, this is the busiest I've ever seen the ticket office. This is the match everyone wants to see.'

He added, 'Banning Rangers fans from the second leg at Elland Road is a decision we regret having to take as we have a good travelling support and many of our fans will be disappointed. However, this is not a decision we have taken lightly. We considered every option, but in the end we were in agreement with Leeds United, the police and both national associations on the matter.

'Had we taken between 1,500 and 2,000 tickets for Elland Road we would have had to reciprocate and that would have meant even less space for our fans at Ibrox. Given our support, we could easily have taken between 15,000 and 20,000 supporters to Leeds.

'For the sake of Rangers Football Club, I would ask our supporters not to travel to Elland Road.'

The Battle of Britain was on!

Archie Knox insisted he was looking forward to the tie, and revealed how he and Walter Smith had been in Barcelona to run the rule over their second-round opponents. He said, 'There is no doubt Leeds deserved to beat Stuttgart. I think they were the more positive and better team on the night. In fact, they were probably the better team over all three legs.

'That said, they didn't have to do anything particularly special to beat the Germans. They will play a lot better against us than they did in Barcelona. I hope they don't, but they will, simply because we will give them a tougher game.

'The English First Division, or Premier League as it is now, is a hard one to win and achieving that last season will have given their players bags of confidence. I've seen them quoted as saying they think they can win the European Cup, so that is the level they think they're at.'

Meanwhile, Smith reckoned the decline of the age-old Scotland v England international was in part responsible for the over-hyping of the encounter. He said, 'There has been a lot said and written about this match, but it doesn't surprise me as the annual Scotland–England match has fallen by the wayside in recent seasons.

'The English press have stated Leeds will win, but I didn't expect anything else because the Scottish press are giving the advantage to us. Certainly, I don't feel we have anything to prove to the English. And what is written will have no real effect on the team.

'Our players know they will have to perform particularly well if they are to progress in Europe and that is something we are keen to achieve if we are to enhance our reputation on the continent.'

Mark Hateley and Alexei Mikhailichenko missed training in the build-up to the big game but both were expected to make the squad. Smith had already decided on the three foreigners he would play, but was keeping his side under wraps until the last minute.

He said, 'Leeds play to win and score goals, and I would hope that anyone who watches Rangers think we approach games in a similar way. I don't think there will be any particular attention placed on trying to stop the opposition playing. The emphasis will be more on each team trying to influence the game by playing their own type of football and trying to score.'

One man in particular had a vested interest in the match-up. Stuart McCall insisted he used to be a bag of nerves before games against his first love, Leeds United. Of course, he would love to have played for his boyhood idols but had established himself at Bradford City – who played just nine miles along the A647.

He said, 'When I was younger I used to suffer badly from nerves before matches, and when it came to playing against Leeds things just never came off for me on the pitch. My problem was I tried too hard and I was just too wound up.'

Those early-career jitters vanished as McCall gained more experience with Everton, Scotland and then Rangers, and he said, 'As the years wore on the matches I was playing in got bigger and bigger and that experience helped me overcome my nerves.

'It's an understatement to say this match is just a case of Rangers against Leeds United. It's much more than that. Everyone has been buzzing so much that it has become Scotland versus England, and the Battle of Britain. The game has overshadowed everything else and has been hyped so much I can't wait for it to start. It is without doubt the perfect chance to show the rest of Britain just how good a team Rangers are. The view down south is that we are a reasonable side in a poor league. We know that's not the case. Anyway, no one is actually dominating the game down there just now, with teams like Norwich and Coventry at the top of the league.

'A victory over Leeds would show we are a good outfit and shut the English up!'

Naturally, comparisons were made with the last time these two great clubs did battle on the European stage – in the 1968 Inter-Cities Fairs Cup. It was a quarter-final tie, and the first leg was played at Ibrox. At the time, both teams were top of their respective championships and boasted numerous internationals among their ranks. From being a Second Division outfit four years previously, Leeds had emerged as arguably England's leading team. Manager Don Revie had put together a blend of skill and steel which, combined with his own tactical shrewdness, was beginning to reap the rewards in the shape of silverware.

Just three weeks before the crunch tie with Rangers, a Terry Cooper goal had given Leeds victory over Arsenal in England's League Cup Final. In the crowd at that match was Gers captain John Greig, who reported back to his manager on an impressive Leeds performance.

In the first leg at Ibrox, Leeds showed their less acceptable face as they set out to close the play down and contain the Light Blues. A huge Ibrox crowd of 80,000 looked on in disappointment as both Willie Johnston and Alex Ferguson squandered chances to put the Gers ahead before half-time, and two minutes before the end, Welsh international keeper Gary Sprake denied Orjan Persson to secure the 0-0 result Leeds had obviously sought.

A score draw at Elland Road would have seen Rangers progress but disaster struck in the 25th minute when Ferguson handled in his own box and Johnny Giles scored from the spot. Seven minutes later, Peter Lorimer scored a killer second and try as they might, Rangers failed to silence the 50,000 crowd with a goal and Leeds went on to win the trophy.

To present day, though, and when the teams emerged from the tunnel to do battle the noise inside Ibrox Stadium had reached fever pitch. It was bedlam – and it looked as though it just might be getting inside the heads of some of our visitors. But just 64 seconds after Belgian referee Alphonse Costantin had sounded his whistle, Rangers were behind. Gordon Strachan pinged a corner to the near post, David Robertson headed clear, but Gary McAllister met it perfectly on the volley and smashed a sensational opener past a despairing Andy Goram.

The Ibrox crowd was stunned into silence. Not for long though as Rangers were soon on the offensive and taking the game to their illustrious opponents. The home side created chance after chance, but the Leeds defence stood firm and keeper John Lukic was inspired – but contributed to his side's downfall with 21 minutes on the clock. A Trevor Steven cross was headed behind by Chris Whyte and when Ian Durrant swung the corner into the area, Lukic miscued his punch and sent the ball into his own net.

And eight minutes from the break, Rangers were in front. A corner from the right was met by Davie McPherson and Lukic parried his powerful header, only for ace poacher McCoist to hit the loose ball down into the ground and over the outstretched leg of David Batty.

The home fans were in fine voice and Rangers went for the kill. Durrant, McCall and McPherson all had chances to extend the lead, but a combination of good defending and Lukic conspired to keep the ball out. The visitors were clearly glad to hear the half-time whistle and escape, albeit briefly, the cauldron Ibrox had become. In truth, the second period could never live up to the thrill-a-minute stuff of the first, and despite creating a few decent chances, Rangers would take the narrowest of leads down to Yorkshire for the second leg.

Stuart Munro was among a galaxy of former Rangers stars at Ibrox that night. Others included Nigel Spackman, John Spencer, Ray Wilkins, Trevor Francis, Kevin Drinkell, Terry Butcher and Mo Johnston.

And after watching 90 minutes of pulsating action, Munro tipped Rangers to progress to the group stages. The 30-year-old defender, who was playing with Blackburn Rovers, admitted he had been shocked at the ignorance of media pundits down south in the run-up to the first leg. Munro said the whole of England would now expect Leeds to conquer the Light Blues in the return fixture.

He said, 'In England, they are very naive about Scottish football and Rangers, and that was obvious before the match. I read a few of the newspapers and they were comparing players at different positions and giving them marks out of ten. But they were picking Rangers players at right- and left-back and various other positions who don't even play there. They haven't got a clue!

'The English will expect Leeds to win – and win comfortably in the return – but I know it won't be that way at all. There's no doubt in my mind that Rangers will score at Elland Road and I can't see them being beaten down there either. Rangers can play even better than they did at Ibrox and I'm very confident they will go through.'

Munro reckoned Rangers could make vital gains in both central defence and midfield, although he felt certain his old side would be able to exploit Leeds' vulnerability in the right-back channel.

He said, 'I hear Mel Sterland isn't far away from being fully fit and so he may return for the second leg, but at present they don't have a recognised full-back playing there. They have tried John Newsome and Chris Fairclough in that position and they could struggle again if Sterland isn't ready.

'I also think David Robertson and Pieter Huistra link up really well on the left, so they could have important roles to play in the return.'

But he also sounded a warning when he added, 'Rangers have a problem because they are pulling so far ahead of everyone else in Scotland. They aren't getting the competition they require week in, week out to maintain a high standard of football. I feel they can play at a level in Scotland that is enough to win the league without being seriously pushed.'

When it was known that in the second leg, Leeds and Rangers would emerge from the Elland Road tunnel to the sound of the *Rocky* theme, assistant manager Archie Knox was hoping it was his corner who would be delivering the knockout blow.

Knox had savoured the unique atmosphere at the home of the English champions while assistant at Manchester United, and said, 'The atmosphere there is absolutely tremendous. The music gets everyone wound up, but the Leeds fans are the type who cheer throughout the game anyway, not only when their side is on the attack. There is continual noise, the same as there was in the first leg at our place, so there is no way that will intimidate our players. Anyone would like to play in an atmosphere like that and our players are experienced enough, so it should inspire them.

'You deserve to go out of the competition if you go away from home a goal up and try to sit on that lead. We're going down there to try and win the match, but even if we score first we can't afford to relax. Leeds are the kind of team who, if they go three goals down, will still play with the same style in the hope of getting back into the game.'

Dave McPherson revealed how he was going into the game looking for a fourth career win over the Yorkshiremen. Big Mac had played in the first leg win, while he was also a member of the young Ibrox side which triumphed over Leeds at the prestigious Croix tournament in France in 1981, and he was even part of the Light Blues side which cuffed Leeds – at pillow fighting!

He explained, 'I went to Croix three times with the Rangers under-18 side and we won the tournament twice. In 1981, Leeds also entered and we shared a school gymnasium with them, which was used as our sleeping quarters.

'We beat them 2-0 on the way to winning the final that year against Dynamo Kiev and the following morning we decided to surprise Leeds with a pillow attack. They could afford a lie-in because they were flying home from France, but our lads faced a three-day camel trip by bus, train and boat to get back to Glasgow, so we had to be up earlier. To compensate, we sorted them out with the pillows, but it was all in good fun as there was a great camaraderie between the sides.

'Willie Thornton was in charge of our team, which included players such as Billy Davies, Hugh Burns, Kenny Black and even Gordon Marshall who eventually signed for Celtic. It was a great achievement to win at Croix because it was one of the top youth tournaments in Europe at the time.'

But when Rangers travelled down to Yorkshire for the second leg of the European Cup, second round, it was the real deal: and apart from national pride, there was also millions of pounds at stake for the victor. The 11 players entrusted with holding on to the narrowest of advantages were Goram, McCall, Robertson, Gough, McPherson, Brown, Gordon, Ferguson, McCoist, Hateley and Durrant.

Elland Road was a cauldron. Home fans only, they said, but a small sprinkling of diehard Rangers supporters – sporting the light blue under Leeds scarves and hats – were there every step of the way with their heroes, determined to make sure Goram and co. were never alone.

Back home, millions watched on television through cracks in their fingers as Goram and Brown combined early on to deny the enigmatic Eric Cantona. It would be the first in a long line of unforgettable Goram saves that would ultimately break Yorkshire hearts. And while the left boot of Hateley and head of McCoist would silence the Leeds faithful with stunning goals, every single Rangers player – sub Alexei Mikhailichenko included – played their part as the Light Blues pulled off a sublime 2-1 victory to progress to the group stages.

There had been great performances during 1992 such as the New Year win at Parkhead, the Scottish Cup semi-final against Celtic and the Skol Cup Final victory against Aberdeen to name just three, but the skill, effort and determination the players demonstrated in Leeds put them all in the shade. And for those of a Rangers, or even Scottish persuasion, it was quite something to see the English media men in the press box sitting in stunned silence as the team they had written off as no-hopers proved them wrong in magnificent style.

McCoist's diving header was arguably one of the most important goals he had ever scored as it put Rangers 4-1 ahead on aggregate, and sparked the post-match celebrations which lasted long into the night. He said, 'Without doubt, that is the most important goal, in terms of financial contribution to the club, I have ever scored. It was a terrific build-up and cross from big Mark [Hateley] to set the goal up, and when the ball hit the back of the net, the celebrations were sparked by a sense of relief because we knew there was no way back for Leeds. The after-match party lasted well into Thursday morning and I only hope in the future we have cause to spend a few more early Thursday mornings like that.'

Hateley also helped silence the most partisan crowd in England, and immediately laughed off suggestions that his third-minute volley would have ended up in the seats behind John Lukic's goal 99 times out of 100. He said, 'It's just one of those things. Sometimes you can hit them and they end up in the stand, and other times – like this one – they fly into the back of the net. The thing is, unless you try them now and again, you will never find out. I just remember the ball bouncing in front of me, running on to it and thinking, "Go on, hit it." I did, and we all know where it ended up!

'I think all goals are important, and even though it was a good one, if it had bobbled over the line I would have been just as excited, because it was an important lift for the boys. We grew in confidence from there, we defended well and attacked in strength. And when it came to putting our chances away, we did that as well.

'I think we all showed so much character after being written off by a lot of folk down south. A lot of people focussed on Andy Goram's performance, but he has been playing well all season. Even at international level he has been doing what he does best – shot-stopping. But everybody from the keeper to the front line did very well. We all help each other because we know Andy is going to save shots and I think he knows the rest of the team do their bit.'

Hateley added, 'I never thought of it as an England v Scotland game. It was just another match for me and I think that's the way a lot of the lads approached it. Football is football, it doesn't matter who you play against. I like to win against English teams, Italian teams, Scottish teams, or whoever.

'It was a very rewarding win for the club, for the fans and for the players. It means more games for us, but I don't think you can ever have too many games in the European Cup.

'We regard ourselves one of the biggest, if not THE biggest club in Britain, and one of the biggest in Europe. I would rank us among the top five clubs in Europe, so hopefully we can reproduce on the field what we already have in our stadium – the best!'

Hateley looked on as the draw for the group stages pitted Rangers against Marseille, Bruges and CSKA Moscow, and he was delighted that the Light Blues had missed out on home and away ties with his old club AC Milan. He said, 'I think we have to be happy with the draw. We are not up against Milan and there are also two other former winners of the European Cup in the other group, while no one from our group has won it previously.'

As a postscript to the win in Leeds, West Yorkshire Police reported that between 150 and 200 Rangers fans had been in the crowd for a match which had been billed as for 'home fans only'. But Chief Superintendent John Ellis, in charge of matchday operations, had nothing but praise for the 25,000 strong crowd, and said, 'I was markedly pleased with the crowd behaviour on the night and the fans must take full credit, not only for their support, but also for remaining behind at the end of the game to cheer both teams off the field. It was widely recognised that the decision to make both games for home fans only was an unusual step but, on reflection, there is no doubt it was the correct one.'

9

Old Firm Joy for Gers

RANGERS stretched their unbeaten run to 17 with perhaps their most pleasing victory of a magnificent sequence. The Light Blues went into the Old Firm game at Parkhead on the back of an energy-sapping European Cup tie against Leeds United, but still had too much in the tank for their cross-city rivals.

And once again Andy Goram was an inspiration between the sticks. Outstanding saves from Dariusz Wdowczyk, Stuart Slater and Gary Gillespie earned him the man of the match award, although it was a Kinning Park lad, steeped in the traditions of Rangers, who scored the only goal of the game.

On the half-hour, a slip by Mike Galloway allowed Dale Gordon space on the right-hand side of the box. His chip to the far post was headed back across goal by Ally McCoist for the onrushing Ian Durrant, and he made no mistake in firing past Pat Bonner.

The win kept Rangers four points clear at the top of the table, but saw Celtic move from second to fourth, with Hearts regaining their place as main challengers. However, gaffer Walter Smith blasted claims that Rangers had already disappeared over the horizon with the league championship trophy. He said, 'I don't listen to that kind of talk and no one at Rangers will listen to it either. If you don't have respect for your opponents you will lose games. We have the greatest of respect for every side we face.'

Durrant's Old Firm winner – his second of the season against Celtic – rounded off arguably his most successful period in a Rangers jersey. The 25-year-old was at the heart of the Skol Cup Final win over Aberdeen, as well as back-to-back wins over Leeds United, while the Old Firm win was the icing on the cake. And his influential role was officially recognised when he was named Scottish Brewers Player of the Month for October.

Durrant said, 'The only word to describe the last four weeks is frantic. It has definitely been the most intense and most successful period of football I've ever been involved in, and I'm sure the rest of the players feel the same way too. I just wish it was always like that.

'The spirit among our squad has never been a problem, but we're doing well just now and everyone is very perky, but I just hope we can go through the rest of the season feeling the same way. There is a bit of tiredness among the boys just now and a few are playing with knocks, but every match we play is a big one and that is enough to carry us through. And at this stage of the season we're beginning to feel the benefit of a good pre-season programme.

'Scoring the winner against Celtic was a bonus. It's especially pleasing to come away from Parkhead on top after a very hard week. Old Firm games are always the same, but we were full of confidence going into this one and we all worked very hard. Losing Goughie and Bomber through injury meant we had to put Stuart McCall at right-back and big Mark Hateley in the middle and they did a great job.'

Meanwhile, Rangers' victory over Leeds put the club back among the elite of European football, and the prestige value they were set to receive from Champions League involvement was just as important as the cash boost which would come from the glamour games against Marseille, CSKA Moscow and Bruges.

That was the view of Campbell Ogilvie, who was speaking enthusiastically about the new league set-up on his return from the Euro draw in Geneva. He said, 'I've been at many European draws and meetings and this is the first time we have been viewed alongside the elite on the continent. For us to have reached this stage is a major target achieved.'

It was Rangers who first proposed to UEFA that a league system be introduced for the last eight in the competition in mid-1989, and following the success of the 1991/92 competition, UEFA attracted a record sponsorship cash haul of £35m for the 1992/93 group stages. The eight qualifiers were set to receive a share of 54 per cent of the cash, with Rangers' involvement set to earn them at least £4m. The remainder of the cash would be invested in improving the game from the bottom up.

From 1992/93, UEFA was taking complete control of the league to form its own unique and individual identity. No longer would participating clubs be allowed to wear shirt advertising when they played in the Champions League. Only manufacturers' logos would be permitted and the Champions League logo would be displayed on the shirt sleeve, while all trackside advertising would be under the control of UEFA.

Matchday programmes would be completely redesigned to reflect the identity of the Champions League, and UEFA also held control over television rights, which it had sold to 23 companies, including ITV, in almost every country on the continent. The governing body had even commissioned a Champions League anthem to be recorded by the Royal Philharmonic Orchestra and played before every game. However, clubs would still keep their own catering and ticket revenues.

Ogilvie added, 'The whole concept has been very professionally organised. UEFA have invested a lot of money in getting the promotion of the league right and the public will clearly see this.' He also insisted there would be no rift with Rangers' sponsors Scottish and Newcastle Breweries as the tournament banned the use of the McEwan's Lager logo on the club jersey. He added, 'We talked about this with our sponsors 18 months ago and they have been kept fully aware of developments. They understand our position.'

Every Rangers game would be shown live on TV throughout Scotland, and perhaps even Britain. But with so much off-the-field activity, Ogilvie was quick to point out that the football itself would remain the most important factor. He said, 'First and foremost we are a football club serving a football public. And there is no better way to serve our supporters than the matches we have to look forward to. Our aim is to be the best, so we want to play against the best and the Champions League will allow us to do just that.'

On the pitch, European Cup hero Dale Gordon praised his team-mates in the aftermath of the win over Leeds – and took it a step further by insisting Rangers were good enough to win the English Premier League. The £1.2m signing from Norwich made his prediction after helping steer Rangers past the English champions. He stressed that victory in both legs would send his fellow countrymen home to think again on the standard of his team and Scottish football.

He added, 'People are blinkered down south because they don't see the Scottish game on a weekly basis. With us winning four in a row and taking control in the league, all they see is Rangers, Rangers, Rangers, but they don't see how big and how good a club we actually are.

'I'm sure a lot of the English who came up for the first tie were given the shock of their lives, not just in terms of the football we play, but also to see what our facilities are like. They are without doubt the best in Britain. And I believe that if we were in the English Premier League we would be good enough to win it!

'From what I've seen on satellite television and from what I know of my own personal experiences down south, there aren't any teams that would challenge us. There isn't anything better than Rangers. After the Leeds games, the English can only have the greatest respect for us and I'm sure when we go on in the competition the only team to watch, from their point of view, will be ours.'

Next up for Rangers, domestically, was Dundee at home, and it was a game that presented Walter Smith's men with an opportunity to gain revenge for their only defeat in the first half of the campaign. Rangers had lost 4-3 to the Dark Blues up at Dens Park in August, a loss which prompted a 19-match unbeaten run.

Smith said, 'Although we've had a successful run recently, it has to end sometime, but I hope it won't be a home match we lose – and certainly not this one against Dundee. Over the years we have been beaten by other teams during the course of the league season, but we aren't often beaten twice in the campaign by the same team. I hope that won't be the case now and we can show a continuation of our form and carry on our unbeaten run.'

In the meantime, one player who had been left out in the cold during the fantastic run was planning his comeback – and the victory over Leeds had hastened his thinking. Gary Stevens had missed the first six months of the campaign with an ankle injury but was desperate to force himself back into the manager's thoughts for the forthcoming Champions League fixtures. That provided the motivation for him to pull on a jersey in a reserve team match against Celtic, which ended in a 3-0 loss.

Stevens said, 'My first game was going to be the home match against Dundee, but I didn't realise how quickly the Champions League matches were starting. I was surprised when I found out it was only three weeks until we played Marseille – and that changed my outlook in training.

'I want to be in the manager's thoughts for the Marseille game at Ibrox but if I had waited until the Dundee game, that wouldn't have left me enough time. Two weeks still isn't a lot of time, and I know they will fly past, but I would never forgive myself if I didn't give it a go, without being stupid.

'Personally, the game against Celtic reserves went well for me because I got what I wanted from it, which is probably a bit selfish as it was a bad result for the team. They're all disappointed, but the fact I got 90 minutes was more than I expected, so I was delighted with that, but it also proved to me there is still a lot of work to do.

'I've been playing professional football for 11 years and the longest I've been out before this was two months. It's hard work to get back, because you're doing it by yourself and not in the best of conditions, as you can appreciate in November and December. The problem I have is the first team are involved in so many games that they're not doing as much training as I need. For instance, I went down to Leeds which meant me missing two days of ball work. I have a lot to catch up on, but I'm determined if nothing else.'

Stevens did indeed make his top-team return in the midweek match against Dundee – but once again it was that man McCoist who took centre stage with another two goals in a 3-1 victory. Super Ally struck in the 31st and 48th minutes to ensure Rangers stretched their unbeaten run to 20 games, while Mark Hateley was also on target in the dying moments.

Stevens played the entire 90 minutes, and said, 'I had my own views about how my comeback should progress, but circumstances meant it turned out a bit different, and when the gaffer asked me the morning before the game if I fancied turning out, my answer was a massive YES.

'I was surprised to be considered so early, but in retrospect it was a good game to come back in. I thought Dundee might try to push a man on me to put me under pressure but I didn't really have anyone in direct opposition. It was more full-back against full-back. It wasn't the best of games for the fans to watch but I think that was to be expected given all the games the lads have been asked to play recently.'

It wouldn't be completely accurate to say 'the lights were out and no one was home' with regards to the Dundee match. A crowd of 33,497 attended but sadly a brand new power generator failed and Rangers lost an estimated £12,000 in catering revenue, while thousands of fans went hungry. Rangers' aptly-titled maintenance manager, Tom Onions, said, 'After the transformer went down, we were left with a choice – restore the catering facilities or turn off the floodlights. The problem was fixed before the match was finished, but thousands of pies, burgers and sausages had to be destroyed!'

Just after the match against Dundee, a high-powered UEFA delegation visited Ibrox to run the rule over the stadium ahead of the Champions League ties. Marcus Studer, the Swiss number two to UEFA general secretary Gerhard Aigner, led the group, which also included representatives from the major sponsors and television companies. They were involved in two days of talks with club officials to discuss every aspect of Rangers' involvement in the competition.

Campbell Ogilvie said, 'The representatives are having discussions with all eight clubs involved in this stage of the competition. They wanted to see if the stadium measures up to the requirements of the television companies and major sponsors and that matchday operations were suitable.

'They seemed very happy with the arrangements which have been made. We have struck up a very good relationship with the people involved and that can only be good for the club.'

The forthcoming home tie against Marseille was set to be beamed live to ten countries in Europe including Scotland, France and Germany. And armchair fans were in for a treat, and a completely new angle of events on the field as 18 television cameras and a TV crew totalling 150, far more than ever before, were to be used to cover the action from the Main Stand, behind the goals and on the 18-yard lines. There would even be a special camera positioned in the goal nets!

While many first-team players relished the ten-day break due to the impending Scotland–Italy international, Rangers' stars of the future got the surprise of their young lives when the Italian national team coach stopped outside Ibrox, the venue for the following night's World Cup qualifier. The under-12s were being put through their paces on the pitch opposite the main door on Edmiston Drive by youth coaches Alistair Stevenson and John Chalmers.

Mind you, few of the young players batted an eyelid as the group of tanned men in expensive suits stepped off the luxury coach for a look inside Ibrox, and while many glanced over at the bounce game taking place at the Ibrox Community Centre, two players in particular stopped to watch for quite a while, before making their way round to the entrance and on to the pitch. As they got closer, it became clear they were no ordinary Italians; it was Roberto Baggio and Gianluigi Lentini, who, at that time, played for Juventus and AC Milan respectively. The multi-million pound duo decided to hang around and pass on a few tips to the aspiring young footballers.

Stevenson said, 'The Italians came off their team bus and a few stood at the fence surrounding the artificial pitch and watched the boys play a game. But Baggio and Lentini decided to take a closer look and actually came on to the park and juggled a ball around with a couple of the boys. They took an interest and asked the lads what age they were and about the work they did. They couldn't believe they only came in one night a week. Apparently in Italy the youngsters train together four or five times a week.'

The match between Scotland and Italy finished goalless and when Rangers were next in action, against Hearts at Tynecastle, Ally McCoist joined an exclusive club. With 24 minutes on the clock, Trevor Steven swapped passes in midfield before setting Dale Gordon loose down the inside-right channel. His first-time cross caught out Craig Levein, but McCoist showed his razor-sharp reactions to glance a header wide of Henry Smith and into the corner of the net from ten yards. It was league goal number 200 for the ace marksman – and he also became the fastest scorer of 30 domestic goals since the inception of the Premier League almost 20 years previous.

McCoist also 'scored' a cheeky second when he took a quick free kick from 22 yards and side-footed the ball past a bemused Smith, but the set piece should have been taken five yards back and referee David Syme booked the striker, rather harshly, for his piece of opportunism.

Hearts began to take more of a grip on the game in the second half, with Derek Ferguson causing problems for his old side, and it was his corner on the hour which was flicked on by Levein for Ian Baird to nod the equaliser past Andy Goram from close range. A share of the points meant Rangers remained five clear of second-placed Hearts.

With the match against Hearts out the way, Rangers switched attention to their Champions League tie against Marseille – one of the pre-tournament favourites. On the eve of the match, Trevor Steven revealed how he had spent 11 miserable months in the southern French port, before insisting he would willingly have stayed for another season! The midfield ace, who had ended his French exile by returning to Rangers in a cut-price £2.3m deal, spoke of his time trying to adjust to the erratic leadership of Marseille president Bernard Tapie.

Broken financial promises littered the player's stay at the Stade Velodrome and he never fully settled, despite his ambition to prove himself on the continent – the only thing that would have led to him staying on in France. But Steven, 29, revealed how he jumped at the chance of a return to Rangers when he finally realised that extending his stay at Marseille would have led to an unhappy ending.

He said, 'I went to Marseille for two reasons. I wanted to play continental football and there was also the financial security it would offer. However, my contract was never honoured from day one. I spent the whole time in France with my financial situation unclear and that cast a big shadow over me.

'That was disappointing, because to have done well I needed to be happy in my mind. After all, I wasn't just going to another team, but with my family to another country too. The financial problems made my job more difficult than it should have been. Naturally the situation affected my performances on the park and I don't think they got the best out of me because of that.

'However, I was still disappointed not to have another season there because I think I would have been a lot better, but the situation was out of my control as they wanted to change their foreign players.

'The whole episode was disappointing. It was a great opportunity, but it was clouded due to the financial difficulties.'

Steven's financial dispute with Marseille was finally resolved when the French side came to Glasgow to play a friendly match to mark his transfer back to Rangers at the start of the season. Despite reports linking him with Leeds, he was delighted to return to the Light Blues, a club he considered to be more professional than the French champions.

He added, 'Rangers are better run, and run like a business, but at Marseille I got the feeling that everything depended on how successful you were on the field. At Rangers, everything is budgeted for the club being knocked out in the first round of each competition – with everything else a bonus.

'Our chairman, David Murray, obviously follows the team, but he has no input into playing affairs, whereas it was very difficult at first to get used to the influence Bernard Tapie had in playing matters. In my first week there I couldn't believe it was happening, but by the second I accepted it as the norm. I don't think there is another club like Marseille.'

But Steven had enormous respect for his former team-mates, and pointed out that Marseille had already gone further in the competition than they had the year before. However, he also believed Rangers were in their best position since he first joined the club in 1989 to make their mark among the continent's elite.

He said, 'I think we're a stage ahead of the other Rangers teams I've played with before in Europe. We have improved and are not as naïve as we were a few years ago. In the past we perhaps thought we were ready to take on Europe and got a little ahead of ourselves.

'But now we've a reasonable chance of doing well – although I refuse to say any more than that.'

Meanwhile, Archie Knox turned Euro spy and couldn't quite believe what he saw when Strasbourg took on Marseille. In a stormy 2-2 draw, the French champions – minus German striker1 Rudi Voller – ended the game without a full complement of players, much to Knox's amazement.

Knox said, 'It was a tough game. I was surprised because it's not something I would associate with French football. Marseille got stuck in and played a very aggressive type of game, which surprised me, but Trevor Steven and Mark Hateley said that's the way they play over there. I would have thought it would have been all nice passing, stand back off each other and good skills, but they displayed all their skills under real pressure.

'I think they [Marseille] have been setting their stall out from the word go to do well in the European Cup this year. Since they lost the final two years ago on penalties, they have been desperate to win the trophy. Don't get me wrong, I'm not expecting them to come to Ibrox and try to rough us up or anything like that, but they will certainly be aggressive and competitive, just as we will be ourselves. They had no prima donnas; they all got stuck in and worked hard.'

Mark Hateley insisted he was looking forward to a joust with Marseille's hard-man centre-back Basile Boli, a player he had come up against a few times during his spell with Monaco. He said, 'They don't come much bigger than Boli, and I was flattered to read that he compared us both to a couple of heavyweight champions, and that the Rangers v Marseille match was a title fight. Of course I won't pay too much attention to it. I'll simply get out there and get on with it.

'I've been involved in some big games in my career, and although there is no doubt this is important for Rangers, I'm looking at it as just another game. It's important, of course it is, but I always approach every match in the same way. It's like playing a league match. We've got to be really fired up for all six group matches and hopefully we can get off to a good start.'

McCoist had been doubtful before the start of the match with a calf strain, and the pesky injury ensured he was merely a spectator for Gers' most important match of the season. He was joined in the stand by the suspended Ian Ferguson, and Dale Gordon, Oleg Kuznetsov, Pieter Huistra and Gary Stevens – all victims of UEFA's absurd three-foreigner ruling. So that meant McCoist missed out on an opportunity to become Rangers' top scorer in Europe. He was on 12 goals, alongside club legends Ralph Brand and Alex Scott, but he would have to wait a wee bit longer for the chance to rewrite yet another piece of Rangers history.

And how the Light Blues could have done with Super Ally to partner lone striker Hateley as Marseille went in front with a superbly-taken goal by Alen Boksic on the half-hour. And when Rudi Voller extended their advantage in the 56th minute there looked only one winner, but Rangers refused to surrender to the mega-bucks French side and conjured up a comeback of seismic proportions. Mind you, not before both Richard Gough and Trevor Steven had limped off, leaving young guns Neil Murray, Steven Pressley and Gary McSwegan to top up the already overworked group of battle-hardened pros slogging to get back into the game.

For McSwegan, in particular, the night was about to become unforgettable. There were 22 minutes remaining when the Maryhill-born kid entered the fray. Sensing the game was moving into dangerous territory, more than 40,000 Rangers supporters once again got behind the team, and after a good shout for a penalty was turned down, siege mentality kicked in and the players stepped up a gear.

Ian Durrant picked up the ball in the middle of the park and played a terrific pass down the left wing for Alexei Mikhailichenko. The big Ukrainian looked up and crossed the ball into the box, slightly east of the penalty spot, to where young McSwegan was standing, and Swiggy picked the perfect moment to grab his first ever top-team goal by guiding his header back across goal and into the top corner. Fabian Barthez was left rooted to the spot. There was a brief moment when supporters and players alike awaited the outcome, before McSwegan started off on the run of his life, making straight for the Rangers bench.

And the recovery was complete four minutes later when McSwegan played a brilliant one-two with Durrant, which allowed the talented midfielder to reach the byline, cut the ball back and there was Hateley to guide a diving header past the despairing French international keeper.

Eight minutes remained; Rangers were on the front foot and had Marseille retreating into their trenches, but try as they might they couldn't get the winner. Still, a point and a draw, especially after being two down against a top side, was deemed a moral victory, and who was going to argue?

A couple of days later, McSwegan retained his place for the visit of Partick Thistle and helped secure both league points by heading home the second in a 3-0 victory. The youngster had played his part in Trevor Steven's opener, while McPherson nodded home the third from a Dale Gordon free kick.

After the win over Thistle, McSwegan said, 'My head is still spinning from the match against Marseille, probably because I have waited such a long time for it. I've always dreamed of scoring for Rangers and I've been here more than 11 years, so it's one I'll never forget. And it's not just because it came in the Champions League. It would have been exactly the same had I got my first against Partick Thistle. It was just such a relief to score for the first team.'

The nation's press had descended on Ibrox the morning after the Marseille match, eager to turn the spotlight on Rangers' trio of young Euro heroes. But while McSwegan and Pressley were having their every move captured on film, and every word recorded on tape, Neil Murray was nowhere to be seen. He was, in actual fact, just around the corner, although he might as well have been a million miles away.

Because less than 24 hours after his starring role in front of a TV audience of millions, Murray was pursuing his 'other' career. The 19-year-old was in Broomloan House, in the offices of Martin Associates, with his head buried in a pile of books and figures. Murray, in his first year of full-time training after completing an accountancy degree at Glasgow University, was working towards a professional qualification to add to his university one, and the Irvine teenager said, 'Working in accountancy gives me a break from football and helps me appreciate it more. Perhaps it even helps me keep my feet on the ground, although I'm sure my parents and friends also do that.

'After two years, hopefully I will have a professional qualification to go with the university one and it means I can go back to it anytime – although I definitely see my future in football.'

But now that Murray had savoured the big-time atmosphere at Ibrox he wanted more, and he added, 'It's something I've been working towards since I arrived at the club as a 12-year-old. And to do it in the last eight of the European Cup was quite unbelievable. There is no bigger football stage.

'I found out on the morning of the game that I was playing and I was overjoyed. I could hardly contain myself. I wasn't nervous, it was just real excitement, but I didn't think about the game itself until we arrived at Ibrox 90 minutes before kick-off. I said to Stuart McCall that if we won the toss I would take centre, just to get an early touch, but when I am playing in midfield, I usually do get a good start, get some good tackles in and get an early touch on the ball. I was very happy with the way things turned out.'

It was a fitting end to the month of November, but if the players thought they were in for an easier ride in December, they had another think coming.

IAN Durrant is arguably the most gifted home-grown player of the modern age to pull on the blue jersey of Rangers. But what made Durrant so special wasn't just his phenomenal talent, and eye for the big-occasion goal, but the fact he came back, against all the odds, from a horrendous injury that would have finished off most players.

But that's just the thing: he wasn't like most players. He was blessed with the type of football brain that had he plied his trade in cities such as Liverpool or Manchester, would have seen him revered the world over. The sky was the limit for Durrant, but he chose to give his best years to Rangers, and for that thousands of supporters were grateful.

The Durrant story begins just across the road from Ibrox Stadium, at the Albion training ground, where the 11-year-old would turn up for training twice a week under the watchful eye of former Rangers star Davie Provan.

The Kinning Park kid was just one of 20 hopefuls, so what did it mean to him when he was eventually offered a schoolboy form to sign? 'It meant everything,' he answered. 'I signed an S-form when I was 11 and a half and would come along to the Albion to train on a Tuesday and Thursday under Davie Provan. John Greig was the manager at the time, and I would be there with other young lads on the red ash at the Albion – under three floodlights – and we were all hoping to make the grade. Ultimately, we all hoped we would get the chance to play for Rangers.'

But the Light Blues weren't the only club showing an interest in young Durrant at that time. He explained, 'I was attracting a wee bit of interest from other clubs, such as Dundee United, Morton and St Mirren, while I was told that Celtic were also keeping an eye on me. I played for Glasgow United at the famous Fifty Pitches, and all the local scouts were always up watching games there.

'My family were from Kinning Park, just a half a mile down the road from Ibrox, so when you're born there, the chances are you're going to be a big Rangers fan.'

Durrant's career progressed well until October 1988 when he lined up for Rangers against Aberdeen at Pittodrie. One horror challenge later, and the 21-year-old awoke to find his world in tatters. It was almost four years before he would line up for the Rangers first team again, and even the Scotland international himself admitted he thought he might never play another match.

Durrant said, 'Yes, I thought that many times, especially after failed operations, or when my knee failed to react positively to the new surgical methods at that time. I remember an artificial carbon fibre ligament was introduced to the market but my body just rejected it, so they had to go back in, fiddle about and take it back out again. We then tried the one with the patella tendon and that seemed to work but there was a lot of laxity in my knee [a term given to describe loose ligaments]. I could have played with that, but not at the same level again as it would have kept giving way.'

Durrant was then told that Rangers were packing him off to America, and he recalled, 'The club decided to send me to the States, and the team over there did a good job. They tightened everything up with the so-called "dead man's tendon". Once it was implanted it seemed to give my knee a real solidity. They also did a bit of refurbishment to my medial ligament, totally reconstructed it in fact, and from then on I was fortunate enough to get back. That was at the tail end of 1990 and perhaps for the first time there seemed to be a genuine light at the end of the tunnel.'

The midfield ace 'enjoyed' his first serious pre-season prior to the 1992/93 campaign, but was it really tough or enjoyable? He said, 'It was more enjoyable than anything else. I wasn't allowed to train all the time because of the impact it would have had on my knee, so there were specific days when I would be on the bike in the gym. Mind you, everything was crossed at that time – fingers, toes, everything – just to try and make it through pre-season without breaking down. To be honest, if something negative had happened during pre-season that really would have been it for me, but I sailed through it, which was just such a relief.

'In a way it was like starting all over again, because I had to re-invent myself to a certain extent. I had always been a running midfielder but I had to change things, and go from using my right foot to using my left foot more. It was like a mirror image – what I had done up to then with my right I now had to try and replicate with my left.

'The rehabilitation was incredibly tough, but that was what the long hours in the gym in front of a mirror were for. As well as that I was also doing loads of strengthening exercises. The club doctor taught me that there is a bit in the brain that eventually accepts that you've changed from being predominantly right-footed to predominantly left-footed. Let's just say I learned so much while in that gym!'

Durrant had signed a new contract the season before the all-conquering treble campaign, and he insisted it was a massive relief to get his signature on the document. Looking back now, he said, 'That was a worry for me personally, especially with what had been going on with my knee. It was well documented at the time and the question of whether it would stand up to the rigours of a game were always being asked, so I was fortunate that Walter Smith had the confidence and belief in me to give me a new three-year contract, not just for me, but for the security of my family as well.

'The 1992/93 season was my tenth at Ibrox, and to be honest it was probably my most important. It turned out to be an unbelievable season for the club, and we achieved an awful lot, such as putting together a great unbeaten run – which included ten games undefeated in Europe – the Battle of Britain and so much more. Of course it all culminated in our group of players being one of just seven sides to win the treble with Rangers, and when you take into consideration that the club has been on the go for almost 150 years you realise just how fantastic an achievement it actually was.'

Rangers had a lot of top midfield players at that time with the likes of Trevor Steven, Alexei Mikhailichenko, Stuart McCall and Ian Ferguson all vying for a starting jersey, so how much tougher did that make it for Durrant to get back into the team?

He said, 'You always had to work hard at Rangers, as there was always a whole group of talented players there. What probably helped the likes of myself and Ian Ferguson at that time was the three-foreigner rule.

'Walter Smith was also a stickler for routine so if you were in the team and playing well you tended to stay there, so it was in your own hands to a certain extent and I wanted to make sure I was playing as often as possible. I had missed enough football. But we were all aware that a couple of bad games and you were out the team: it's a constant in your head, and you have to make sure that you take your chance.

'I was fortunate to play in a lot of really big games that season, and having been told I would never play again, to play 46 games that season is testament not just to myself, but to the medical staff who looked after me following my injury. I had a great relationship with Dr Cruickshank, the old Rangers club doctor, who would know exactly when to pull the reins on me and keep me in check.

'I was a wee bit bitter at the time, as I was desperate to get back, but he looked after me so well and definitely prolonged my career. The Doc and the gaffer knew exactly what was best for me. After what I'd gone through, I did get fatigued quicker than the others, but they knew when to get me to slow down and when to step it up a gear.

'But the 1992/93 season is one that will live with me for the rest of my life, not just because of what we achieved, but because we played in some unbelievably big games. Both ties against Leeds are a great example, and then four days later you're playing against Aberdeen at Hampden in the League Cup Final. It was like a roller coaster; big game after big game, but it was all so enjoyable.'

Ally McCoist and Mark Hateley were the 'go-to' guys for goals that term but Durrant still chipped in with his fair share of strikes, and inevitably the dynamite midfielder reserved his best for the big occasion. Of his seven goals in 1992/93, six were scored in massive games.

He said, 'I was always known for scoring in the bigger games, and I thoroughly enjoyed my strikes against the likes of Celtic, Aberdeen and Leeds. I loved playing in these types of games, especially at Ibrox because you're walking down the tunnel towards the pitch and you can hear the noise the supporters are making. It's incredible, and that night against Leeds is up there with the best.

'Perhaps it's surpassed only by one game for atmosphere, and that was in 1987 when we hosted Dynamo Kiev. Ibrox was rocking that night and it still leaves the hairs on the back of my neck standing up each time I think about it.

'Back to the Leeds game, though, and when we were walking down the tunnel that night, you could see your seasoned pros – such as Gordon Strachan, John Lukic, Gary Speed, David Batty, etc – all looking at each other quite nervously because the noise outside was phenomenal.

'You don't often get games like that anymore, but they were special. It was great to be involved in occasions like that: I absolutely loved them.

'When we travelled down to Elland Road for the away match, it was a bit strange knowing that it was supposed to be home fans only in the ground that night, but I was fortunate enough to be able to get my brothers and his mates tickets, and when you're doing the warm-up, you're seeing Rangers fans dotted all over the ground, and they're giving you the thumbs-up.

'When it comes to Rangers fans, where there's a will there's a way, and they will always get tickets. One man in particular springs to mind – big Andy Smillie. He would never miss a game, and he "acquired" a hospitality box at Leeds that night, and when big Mark [Hateley] scored, there were a few things thrown at the box!'

But while Durrant was delighted with the achievements of Rangers that season, there is also a sense of disappointment that they couldn't go all the way in the Champions League. He explained, 'It was frustrating to get so far in the competition, and not to win it, especially with what folk were saying about what was going on with Marseille and their 6-0 win over CSKA.

'But we had chances to win every game and perhaps we were just a little bit unfortunate in the end in that we didn't score enough goals. We got ourselves into some good positions, but we also did things like give Marseille two goals of a start and for half an hour after that we pummelled them. Perhaps if that game had gone on another five minutes we might have beaten them.

'And then there was the game over in Marseille, which was quite similar to our home game against them. We knew that a draw wasn't enough for us so we had to win, and for the last 15 minutes of the game we were well on top. Walter Smith had instilled a great will to win in us but sadly we just came up a bit short over in France.'

But regardless of disappointment and frustration, it was still an incredibly satisfying and successful season, and Durrant thought long and hard when asked what the magic ingredient was. He answered, 'The gaffer was fantastic with us and would always tell us not to panic if we weren't winning games. He made us believe that there was always a way to win and more often than not we found it.

'We could also mix it up with teams and play great football, and knew that if we got the ball wide and then into the box, Mark

Hateley would be there with Coisty always feeding off the scraps. Trevor Steven, Ian Ferguson, Stuart McCall and I also managed to chip in with a few goals. We were also strong from set pieces with Richard Gough and Bomber Brown a real threat in the air.'

Ibrox has witnessed some fantastic double acts over the years such as Miller and Brand, Stein and Johnston, and, to a certain extent, Arveladze and Mols, but the almost telepathic understanding that existed between Durrant and McCoist was a special partnership developed over time, and one that bore some exceptionally sweet-tasting fruit.

Durrant said, 'Super [Ally] and I did have a great understanding on the park. We just clicked in training but I knew if he went right, he would take three steps and then shoot in to his left, and by that time I had already played the pass and before you know it the defender is on the back foot and he is across him.

'But asides from being a great goalscorer, I also thought Coisty was a phenomenal player, and I don't think he ever got the credit he deserved for that. He could certainly play a bit. He actually started off as a midfielder and he was very comfortable playing in the middle of the park. Many a time the gaffer dropped him back into the middle and would bring another forward on, but we were still playing with three forwards as Ally was just playing in a deeper role.'

The 1992/93 season culminated in a treble success for the Light Blues and, being steeped in the traditions of Rangers, Durrant knew exactly what it meant to the legions of fans who follow the club.

He said, 'Winning a treble is something you always strive to achieve at Rangers. That season we thought we could also win the European Cup, but when that fell through we knew we still had the treble to aim for, and that was massive for the lads.

'At that time Celtic were going through a wee transitional period and Aberdeen were our main rivals for the big prizes. Willie Miller was their manager and we had more than a few really tough games against them. We knew the Scottish Cup Final was to be played at Celtic Park so that was an extra incentive for us to beat Aberdeen to clinch the treble. Thankfully we managed to do that and we know that we will forever be part of history and nobody can take that away from us.

'I was very fortunate to be at Rangers for 32 years, including 16 as a player, so to get the chance to play for your childhood team and win what I did was just a dream come true. By signing for Rangers, I fulfilled my dream, but once there I wasn't prepared to believe that it was a case of "mission accomplished". I then wanted to win as much as I could. I was very driven and became greedy for honours.

'The first season I was there I got the Young Player of the Year award under Graeme Souness, and there was talk of me moving away somewhere else, but I had so many great years at Ibrox. Every year I was there was a great year, but there were some really dark times. I had a fight on my hands with the injury and it was a fight I was determined to win, because one of the greatest things in my life was to run out of the tunnel and on to the Ibrox pitch. For a while that pleasure was taken away from me, but I was determined I would experience that feeling again, and I did.'

Durrant added, 'When you're with one particular club for so long, it's difficult to pinpoint your best, or favourite season, but taking away my earlier years, I would say 1992/93 was my best season in a Rangers jersey, in terms of both quality and enjoyment. It was definitely something special.'

11

Fergie Outguns Russians in Bochum

D ECEMBER started off with the club secretary filling in a purchase requisition order for tins of silver polish as the individual awards started to filter into Ibrox.

First up was the Tartan Special Manager of the Month award, which went to Walter Smith for the second time that season. Smith won the gong for the performances of his side throughout November when they beat Leeds to move into the Champions League, and salvaged a 2-2 draw with Marseille in the first match of the group stages.

The Gers also went four games without defeat in the Premier League – with the run including an away win over Celtic – to maintain pole position in the table. It was a worthy award for the gaffer.

A delighted Ally McCoist was then named BBC Sportscene Personality of the Year in a star-studded red-carpet bash in Glasgow. And in typical Coisty style, he said, 'I've been taking some stick from my team-mates since I won the award because when I was giving my acceptance speech, apparently I forgot to thank them for all the help they've given me this year. It wasn't deliberate. I must just have been caught up in the pure excitement of it all!

'But it was a nice way to end a disappointing weekend that started with our game against Dundee United being called off, especially as I was fully fit and raring to go after a fortnight off with a calf injury, which I picked up in training a couple of days before the Marseille game.'

But while Coisty was winning individual silverware, Alexei Mikhailichenko had his eyes fixed on a somewhat bigger prize – the European Cup. Miko was speaking on the eve of Rangers' second Champions League group game against CSKA Moscow, which had been moved to Bochum in Germany because of the cold snap covering Moscow and surrounding areas.

He said, 'The way we finished the match against Marseille showed we have great European potential. This year our players have gained much more experience of playing on the continent, which is so important at this level.

'Last year we weren't as wise. But now, if we can relax more on the field and play with more confidence, I feel we are capable of making the Champions League Final. A comparison between the beginning and the end of the match against Marseille demonstrates my point. We started nervously, but as the match went on we grew in belief and self-confidence. We must show that more often.'

While with Dynamo Kiev and Sampdoria, as well as Rangers, Miko had amassed an impressive haul of domestic medals, but success in Europe at club level had always eluded him. He said, 'At this level of the European Cup, every game inspires special excitement because of the teams involved. I am a football player and I love the game. It is deep in my heart. When I first made the decision to leave Kiev I was inspired to move by the game itself. I knew if I showed my true potential I would be able to play for the best teams and it would be possible for me to have a better career as a footballer.

'If I had only thought about the financial aspects of the game I could have gone to clubs which would have perhaps paid more money, but I don't think I would have been able to play as well. Money is money, but the game itself is the most important thing. I am not disappointed with the career decisions I've made and I hope I can go on and enjoy even more success with Rangers.'

Miko had joined Kiev at the age of ten and made his debut as a 20-year-old in 1983 – ironically against CSKA Moscow in Kiev – when he marked a dream bow by scoring the only goal of the game. However, under the guidance of legendary coach Valery

Lobanovsky, Miko didn't become a first-team regular until 1986, when he was 23.

He said, 'I missed Kiev's Cup Winners' Cup victory over Atletico Madrid in 1985 as I was still playing reserve team football. However, I was not disappointed to miss out because there were things I still needed to learn about the game.'

And Miko showed he still held the Indian sign over CSKA by turning in another sterling performance to help defeat the Russians 1-0 in Bochum. As a result, Rangers were quickly proving they had the ingredients necessary to make a big impact in Europe.

Their display against a top Russian side proved they also had the confidence to compete at the highest level – and that they were strong in every department, a necessary component for success against the big guns. The win elevated them to top spot in Group A alongside Marseille.

Walter Smith immediately homed in on the back-to-back matches against Bruges in the first fortnight of March as the key to Gers' Euro ambitions. He said, 'If we manage the right results against them we will give ourselves a good chance of making the final. Although they lost 3-0 in Marseille, there's no way I would discount Bruges as they have a great home record.'

With victory over CSKA, the Light Blues maintained their 100 per cent record away from home in Europe that season, and it was all thanks to a magnificent team effort, although a number of Rangers players also enhanced their reputations with towering individual performances.

They were: David Robertson, who exploited the lack of pace in the CSKA defence to put in a number of telling crosses; John Brown, who was a rock in defence and twice saved Rangers with last-gasp tackles – his best coming a minute from time when he robbed Oleg Surgueev as he was about to pull the trigger; and Alexei Mikhailichenko, who worked harder than ever before, particularly in defence, while his covering work gave Robertson the confidence to push forward more often.

However, the man of the match was Ian Ferguson, whose powerful forward running constantly troubled the slick Russians. He supported Hateley and McCoist at every turn and capped his finest continental display with the only goal of the game in the 13th minute, which proved unlucky for the Russians.

Only after the game was over did it emerge that Rangers had been forced to prepare for the vital Champions League match on a piece of spare ground behind their hotel. The Light Blues had arranged to do a spot of light training on the morning of the match at the ground of Black and White Essen, a German Third Division side whose stadium was municipally owned. But the players' bus turned up at 10am to find the main gates locked – and the groundsman insisting Rangers could only use the adjacent red ash pitch.

Interpreter George Nuter was furious and phoned Herr Hoffmann, sports director of the city, to register his disapproval, but Herr Hoffmann wouldn't budge, as Black and White had a game on the Saturday and he was afraid the Rangers players would churn up the pitch. Mr Nuter said, 'I told him the players were only there to loosen up, which would take no longer than half an hour, but he wouldn't listen.'

The only option for the Light Blues was to use a piece of parkland behind the Sheraton Hotel, so off went the players for a light jog around the duck pond before putting their jackets down for shooting practice at Andy Goram and Ally Maxwell.

Bemused locals walking their dogs or out with the kids passed just yards away, not quite sure what to make of it all, but thankfully the episode had no effect whatsoever on the players, while the German FA belatedly apologised to Rangers for the problem.

But while everything, well, most things, in the Rangers camp was rosy, Gary Stevens was fuming at a tackle which set his season back six weeks. The England international had only just returned to the side following a lengthy injury but was back on the treatment table after a league match against Airdrie at Broomfield.

The full-back suffered a fracture to his right knee and was put in plaster from hip to toe, and while he refused to name the Airdrie player involved, he said, 'He knows who he is. I am very bitter about the incident and want him to know how I feel. I took a kick on the side of the knee and it was so unnecessary because the ball was two or three yards away. That is the most frustrating thing about this whole episode.

'The tackle came during a ten-minute spell when the player involved was charging about and running into everyone. I knew at the time it was a rash tackle and now I'm out of the game for another six or seven weeks. It's sad, really, if that's what he is being paid to play like. If that was all I had to offer as a player I would give the game up.'

Stevens's frustration was completely understandable as the match at Broomfield was only his fourth game back in the top team. He said, 'Up until the Airdrie game I was growing stronger and stronger and was beginning to conquer the fears I had about coming back after being out for seven months. Now this happens and I'll have to start all over again.'

The match finished one goal apiece, with Bomber Brown putting Rangers ahead in the first half before Airdrie grabbed a last-gasp equaliser. Despite the draw, Rangers remained three points clear at the top of the table, with a game in hand.

Much of the credit for some of the best known players at Ibrox having their shooting boots on went to a 67-year-old woman who worked just a short free kick away from Ibrox Stadium. Ellen Burns, and sidekick Cathie Wells, had the Midas touch when it came to dealing with last-minute boot repairs. Ibrox Cobblers was a one-stop shop for Gers kitman Doddie Soutar, and their customers had a knack of scoring goals once the cobblers had 'breathed new life' into the footie boots!

Mark Hateley's boots needed an urgent repair the day before a match against St Johnstone, and the big man went on to score a hat-trick the following day. Just like Ally McCoist, who found the net three times against Falkirk after his boots had been left in the capable hands of Ellen and Cathie!

And Cathie – the only female cobbler in Glasgow at that time – said, 'We're used to getting jobs which need done yesterday! Doddie once brought in Mark Walters' boots, and they needed a new leather toe as the original was ripping. We didn't have the leather, but because Doddie needed them there and then we were forced to use a big piece of latent leather. Even though I tried to dull the shine, the boots looked daft, but I don't think Mark minded as he scored the following day as well.'

Meanwhile, vice-chairman Donald Findlay revealed how Rangers had joined forces with a host of top English clubs to battle UEFA's controversial three-foreigner rule. Findlay met with lawyers and representatives from Manchester United, Spurs, Arsenal, Leeds and Liverpool at a top London hotel and top of the agenda was finding out the best way to lobby for change to UEFA's unpopular rule.

The legal eagles involved were experts on football and European law and were set to report back to the clubs early in the New Year to advise on the best course of action to take. The clubs, though, were likely to decide on one of two options.

These were: negotiate with UEFA through the European Commission – the governing body in Europe – for change; or take the European Commission to court to declare the three-foreigner ruling unlawful. If it was found to be so, the European Commission would inform all member countries of the EEC that the three-foreigner restriction should not be complied with.

Findlay said, 'We will make our approaches once the lawyers inform us of the best route to take, but we would prefer the first option. We would hope a settlement could be reached between the European Commission and UEFA through negotiation and without taking the matter to court.

'If both parties reach agreement we hope the ruling can be amended in time for the start of next season. However, if we have to take it through the courts it may be another season before changes are made.'

A special SFA sub-committee had also been set up and the members were due to meet with Findlay to hear the case for change. Findlay was also speaking with the backing of the top Scottish clubs, and if the SFA felt its clubs had a case, they would also ask UEFA to abolish the ruling, which many saw as contrary to the spirit of free trade which was sweeping Europe at that time.

Findlay said, 'There is now a widespread dislike of the three-foreigner ruling and we hope UEFA pay attention to this. The English clubs also share our view and we know there are a number of other countries against it, or less committed to it than they were previously.'

After the recent postponement of the Rangers v Dundee United game at Ibrox, work started immediately on tackling the drainage problem and head groundsman David Roxburgh said, 'The main issue with our drains is that they are old. One or more has moved, so the flow of water isn't getting through to the drain as it should be. We are having to take out the undersoil heating pipes so that we can repair the drains that have moved.'

Campbell Ogilvie added, 'A lot of people thought it was caused by damage after the Marseille and Partick Thistle games [when it rained heavily] but that wasn't the case. As soon as we could do something about it we did.'

Rangers' next league match was away from home, at Falkirk's Brockville Park, which allowed the Ibrox track to be excavated and the drainage to be fixed. Meanwhile it was the usual suspects – McCoist and Hateley – who dug the Light Blues out in a tight match with the Bairns, where no quarter was asked nor given. With 18 minutes on the clock, a McCoist effort broke kindly for Hateley and the England international – with his back to goal – controlled the ball superbly, turned on a sixpence, and lashed an unstoppable shot high into the net.

Despite a tough European match on the continent just 72 hours previously, Rangers were on top form and threatened to overrun the home side in the first half-hour but their midweek endeavours soon caught up with them and Falkirk came more into the game after the break. But cometh the hour and a bit and Super Ally curled home a beauty from 20 yards with 75 minutes on the clock for 2-0.

Fraser Wishart's late consolation was more of an annoyance than truly relevant as it robbed Andy Goram of what would have been a fine shut-out.

After the game, the Scotland international keeper spoke of his pride at being given the chance to work with the meanest defence in the league. And while Hateley and McCoist were busy grabbing the lion's share of the headlines, Goram insisted the Rangers defence was worth its weight in gold.

Up until the middle of December the Light Blues had conceded just 23 goals in 30 matches, which had helped make Goram the shut-out king of Scotland with 13 clean sheets from his 28 appearances.

He said, 'When I was at Oldham, our manager Joe Royle always said that the team which concedes the least amount of goals in a season wins the title. Nine times out of ten that's the case. It happened with us last season and before then too. We know we have the players who will always score goals, so it's up to us to keep claiming the clean sheets which will win games.'

But it wasn't always like this as just 12 months previously, Rangers were out of Europe, out of the Skol Cup and trailed Hearts in the league race. Since the turn of the year, however, the back four had tightened up and turned the screw on the hopeful hitmen who faced them every week.

Goram said, 'We've definitely benefitted at the back by playing together for over a year. Last season I was new into the side and so was Davie Robertson, and it was difficult because you don't really know the expectations of the club. Now, however, we all know what it's about and exactly what is required from us, and that has helped.

'There have been a few changes in defence this season, but the players at Ibrox are so good that I never worry about how they will settle into the back four. That goes for the whole team, not just the defence.'

He added, 'Believe it or not, we don't speak a lot to each other on the pitch. It's not quiet, but it could be better. Sometimes, though, it isn't necessary to talk to one another so much because the players in the back four are so good at their jobs, and we all know each other very well.'

And Goram put the shutters up once again when St Johnstone visited Ibrox in Rangers' 21st league match of the campaign. This time, though, it was the Oldham-born keeper's mates at the back who outshone McCoist and Hateley up front, for Richard Gough and David Robertson were on target to secure a 2-0 victory, as the Light Blues maintained their four-point lead over Aberdeen.

Robertson had only ever scored four goals in his career, and two of them had come against Andy Rhodes. He said, 'I scored against him when I was at Aberdeen and he was with Dunfermline. It was a nice early Christmas present for me and maybe if Andy signed for Celtic I would also get the New Year off to the perfect start!'

Pre-match, the spotlight had been on former Gers star John McClelland as he was taking charge of the Perth side for the first time. The Northern Irishman had been a defensive lynchpin of previous boss Alex Totten's team. Totts – assistant to Jock Wallace at Ibrox from 1984 to 1986 – had made McClelland player-coach, but when Totten was mysteriously fired one morning, and he gathered the Saints players in the dressing room to tell them the awful news, and to say his goodbyes, McClelland was the only player missing. It wasn't long before he was given the manager's job, and Totten was left alone at home with just a black bag of possessions and his thoughts for company.

Prior to the game against Saints, one prominent Rangers star was the butt of dressing-room banter – because it was said he was suffering from labour pains! Fans' favourite John Brown was laid low prior to the game with stomach problems, and extensive hospital tests failed to come up with any genuine reasons for the agony. As his wife was about to give birth to the couple's second daughter, the whispering started. In fact, Rangers also received a telephone call (allegedly) from a concerned lady, saying that her late husband had suffered from labour pain while she had been pregnant!

None of that bothered Bomber however, who smiled, 'I've heard all the jokes about me having labour pains, but it can't be too bad if I was actually suffering for my wife.'

But there was good news on the horizon for Rangers secretary and director Campbell Ogilvie as he celebrated Christmas 1992 with an honour from Glasgow District Council. The Light Blues were named Glasgow Professional Team of the Year at the city's annual sporting awards service, held at the City Chambers. And Ogilvie was awarded with a silver plate after winning the Glasgow Services to Sport award for his valuable behind-the-scenes work at Ibrox.

The judging panel, consisting of city councillors, the director of parks and recreation and representatives of the media, awarded the double to Rangers following the club's many successes in 1992.

Ogilvie said, 'I was invited along to receive the award on behalf of the club, not knowing I was also a winner. It came as a great surprise, but both awards reflect well on the achievements of everyone at Ibrox Stadium.'

But while Glaswegians geared up for the festive season, there was no rest for the players, as a Boxing Day fixture against Dundee at Dens Park loomed. Naturally, the match attracted a little extra attention as Rangers had remained unbeaten – in all competitions both home and abroad – since their last visit to the home of the Dark Blues. The team had played 27 matches, winning 23 and drawing the other four. And while defender Dave McPherson was determined to make it 28 unbeaten, he also vowed that Rangers wouldn't lose four goals again that season.

He said, 'The goals we lost that afternoon were bad ones from a defensive point of view. That match is the only time this season that nothing went right for us. After the game we all had a chat and agreed that when we score three goals away from home, we expect to win. We said we didn't expect to lose four goals again this season and I don't think we will. The defeat gave us a kick up the backside and proved that, no matter what anyone thinks, we must work hard, earn each result and take nothing for granted.'

With the match being played on Boxing Day, it meant putting Christmas on hold for the families of the players and management staff. David Robertson admitted it would have been his first real Christmas with wife Kym and daughter Chelsea.

He said, 'Obviously you like to spend Christmas Day with the family, although this year we're training on 25 December but we accept that as part and parcel of the game. You have to take the good with the bad. But it will be my daughter's first Christmas and I'm looking forward to spending time with her in the morning and seeing her reaction when she opens her presents.'

And Robbo received yet another Christmas gift when he helped Rangers beat Dundee 3-1 at Dens Park. Scorers were Mark Hateley, with two, and Ally McCoist with the other, but the afternoon soon descended into a battle of two of the most swashbuckling stars in the Premier League: Hateley versus Simon Stainrod, and it was certainly Rangers' Englishman who came out on top despite Stainrod showing off his complete repertoire of twists, turns and flicks – oh, and a goal to boot.

The points headed back down the road with Walter Smith's men, and there was a couple of days off to enjoy festivities with the family, but a clash with rivals Celtic awaited – and this one would go a long way to deciding whether or not the Parkhead men would remain in the title race, or hand over the baton as main contenders to Aberdeen. The match, to be played at Ibrox, wasn't anything close to a title decider, but perhaps more of a title eliminator.

MENTION the name Gary McSwegan to Rangers supporters of a certain vintage and many will automatically
rewind to his goal against Marseille, which proved pivotal
in the club's extraordinary Champions League run of 1992/93.

But there is much more to the talented centre-forward than 'that'
goal against the French.

Of course, he is the first to admit that he didn't play as many
first-team games for Rangers as he would have liked, but what he
did do was play for the team he loved. And as the first ever British
player to score in the Champions League, he left a legacy that can
never be eclipsed.

But his story starts long before he gained superhero status against
Marseille; in the back courts of Glasgow's Maryhill district, where
'Swiggy' could always be found with a ball at his feet.

He recalled, 'When I was 12, I was playing for my school team
at Woodside Secondary, as well as Possil YMCA, who were a really
good side from north Glasgow. I also played with a team called
Rangers Young Boys, who were based in Scotstoun. One of the top
scouts at that time was George Runciman, who covered the west
end of Glasgow. Woodside played at Blairdardie, which is up near
Drumchapel, and George watched a lot of our games.

'It was the early '80s and I recall him being at the side of the pitch
one day, standing out like a sore thumb with the stereotypical scout's
sheepskin coat and bunnet on.

'I have great memories of these carefree days when I played
alongside all my pals, but looking back, I was naïve and not entirely
sure that I was able to appreciate exactly what was happening to me

then. Nowadays, a lot of the younger kids are wiser in the ways of the world and most have an advisor.

'I was already training up at Dundee, and was there when Dundee United won the league, and beat Rangers 3-1. I had been a guest of theirs that day, but Rangers – through George Runciman – asked me to come in and train with them at the Albion. They didn't have much of a youth set-up back then, and there seemed to be only three or four young boys in training with them, so I ended up playing a full practice match on the red ash, which was full of puddles, alongside players such as John Greig and Tommy McLean. Hugh Burns was also taking part and it seemed to be players of all ages playing in the same match. I scored a hat-trick but it was such a surreal experience.

'My dad, who was a shipyard worker at Yarrows, was with me, and after the game finished I walked over to him to ask how I had done. He had a smile on his face so I knew it had gone well, and then John Greig approached us and said, "I'd like you to sign, son." My immediate answer was, "Yes, okay," and that was that. There was nothing else involved, no long discussions, just a quick "yes"!'

McSwegan, his dad and Greig walked over to Ibrox and climbed the marble stairs to the latter's iconic office, where Greig produced the forms and the youngster added his signature.

McSwegan said, 'That was that. I was an S-form Rangers signing and the wee touch of irony is that I now live close to John Greig and see him most days.

'Truth is, it was an absolute privilege to sign for Rangers, even though my granda had always urged me to support Partick Thistle. My granda was a big Rangers fan but didn't go back to Ibrox after the disaster in 1971. I think it gave him a real fright and he didn't want me getting caught up in things like that, but despite that I always knew he would be proud of me signing for Rangers.

'When I scored my first goal against Marseille I went to see my granny straight away because I knew what it meant to them. To this day I still get emotional thinking about it.'

McSwegan lived in Collina Street, in Maryhill, when he signed for Rangers, and will never forget his first photo shoot. He recalled, 'I was sitting in the house when the doorbell rang. It was a couple of guys from the *Rangers News* who had come up to the house to interview me.

'After answering all sorts of questions, we went outside for some photographs and I was standing on a wall with the high flats in the

*Young guns John Spencer and Gary
McSwegan with coach Davie Dodds*

*Ally Maxwell proved an able deputy for Andy
Goram*

*Alexei Mikhailichenko introduced
Ukrainian fashion to Glasgow!*

*Stuart McCall goes head-to-head with ex-Ranger
Derek Ferguson*

Pieter Huistra has looked out his passport!

David Robertson clears as two Lyngby players close in

Ian Durrant and Ally McCoist show off the Skol Cup

Ally McCoist scores against Leeds at Ibrox

Ian Durrant tangles with Leeds United's Gary McAllister

Mary Hateley has just hit a cracking opener at Elland Road

Andy Goram's goal is under siege in Yorkshire

Goram punches clear at Elland Road

Rangers' Ukrainian duo Oleg Kuznetsov and Alexei Mikhailichenko

Walter Smith in celebratory mood

Trevor Steven and Neil Murray in the thick of the action against Marseille

Gary McSwegan celebrates his goal against the French side

Mark Hateley stoops to head home the equaliser

A selection of Rangers tickets from the 1992/93 season

Scott Nisbet struggles to keep his composure while guest of honour at the Rangers Rally

Bomber Brown goes toe-to-toe with Celtic's Andy Payton

Mark Hateley flies through the air against Celtic

Ian Ferguson leaves the field after a Champions League match

Dutchman Pieter Huistra celebrates

Scott Nisbet is ecstatic!

Archie Knox and Scott Nisbet celebrate the latter's 'fortuitous' goal against Bruges

Bomber Brown gets a shot in against Marseille

And the Rangers star robs Marseille's Rudi Voller

Andy Goram saves against CSKA at Ibrox

Rangers line up before a Champions League match

Richard Gough powers in a header against the Russians

Rangers stars are gutted at the full-time whistle against CSKA at Ibrox

An Alexei Mikhailichenko celebration!

Andy Goram was one of the stars of an unforgettable season

Mark Hateley and Ally McCoist celebrate another goal

Bomber, The Goalie and Slim – three members of the Iron Curtain defence!

Dale Gordon takes on Celtic defender Dariusz Wdowczyk

Gary McSwegan heads home the title-clinching goal at Airdrie

Bomber and Richard Gough celebrate league success

It's five-in-a-row for the Teddy Bears!

Rangers players with the league trophy at Ibrox

Ian Ferguson challenges Scott Booth in the Scottish Cup Final

Dave McPherson and Andy Goram celebrate with Walter Smith after the Scottish Cup Final

background, but the thing I remember most is that I had this really mad haircut!

'At the time I was playing for four teams and had scored something like 120 goals already that season. I was right into statistics and would keep a chart of all the goals I'd scored and for which teams. I always had a target of how many I wanted to get and when I got home from a match I'd fill in the chart with my latest goals.

'They were good days, but I eventually moved further down Maryhill to the Round Toll, and the high flats at St George's Cross. I had left Woodside School at 15 and went straight to being full time at Ibrox. From the group of lads that signed for Rangers at that time, John Spencer and I were the youngest at 15, so we couldn't get paid. We were given expenses and as soon as we reached 16, everything was backdated: it was as though we had won the lottery! Rangers were really good to me and it was a great place to learn my trade as I was constantly learning off the best professionals.'

The talented youngster also played for Glasgow Schools and a Glasgow West representative side, often turning out in a wide role, or in midfield, and said, 'I think when you play in a number of positions, you gain a better appreciation of the game. One week I would be playing left midfield and maybe right mid the next, but I don't ever recall playing up front. I was still scoring goals from midfield, mind you. Back then, nobody paid too much attention to positions, not like now when kids can be over-coached.'

Despite having moved to within a free kick of Partick Thistle's Firhill ground, McSwegan can't recall the Jags ever showing an interest in him. He might have been living virtually on their doorstep, but he said, 'They never made any moves to sign me, but Thistle didn't really have a youth set-up back then. I would play for my school team on a Saturday morning, and if I didn't have another game in the afternoon, I would go over to Firhill and skip in if I couldn't get lifted over, which you could do in those days.

'There was a plank of wood at the back wall which helped kids get over and into the ground. The "hot" plank would move around from game to game, as we didn't want it to be discovered, but it was always there. I remember being about an hour early one Saturday and once in, we had to hide in bushes behind the goal until the crowd came in, so we wouldn't stand out like a sore thumb. That was the days when Alan Rough was in goals and you could run on to the park at half-time and have a kickabout!'

Despite John Greig signing McSwegan initially, it was Graeme Souness who offered the teenager his first professional contract. 'We both signed in 1986,' said McSwegan. 'When he and Walter Smith arrived at Rangers, Peter McCloy was already a coach and was kept on as reserve team manager. Donald MacKay came in as well and you had the likes of Jimmy Nicholl and John McGregor helping out with the kids. It was a good set-up.

'At the time, Souness would occasionally train with the reserves, especially if he had missed a game through one reason or another. He wasn't taking the sessions but on one occasion he absolutely caned me for receiving the ball, flicking it over someone's head and moving off with it. He started screaming, "That's schoolboy stuff, get the ball on the ground and make a pass!"

'From that point onwards I don't think I ever took anyone on again. I got the ball and passed it, just like the gaffer said! At the time I thought he was knocking the natural ability out of us although I soon realised you can't keep playing the way you did at schoolboy level; you just wouldn't get away with it. It was a massive learning curve for me. Let's be honest, if someone like Graeme Souness is telling you to keep the ball on the deck and pass and move, then you listen. I don't know better than him, so you take it on board.

'From time to time he would get some of the first-team squad to train with us and that was how we learned. When I was running at these boys in practice matches it was a hell of a lot different than coming up against someone my own age. Little things like that really helped us improve.'

McSwegan started to make the breakthrough into the first-team squad during 1991/92. He made five appearances for the first team from the bench – so did he see the following campaign as one to carry on the progress? 'I think I would have been daft to set any unrealistic goals. The first team were bang in the middle of nine in a row and we had Hateley and McCoist up front. There wasn't another striker in the league – let alone at Rangers – who would have played ahead of those two, so my mindset was to learn as much as possible from them, and be ready to back them up whenever the need arose.

'To be honest, I wasn't alone. There were others champing at the bit for a top team start. I had a good goalscoring ratio with the reserves and my immediate aim was to keep that going. Plus, a couple of years earlier I had broken my leg and been out for nine months so it was a case of getting going again; that's why I wasn't too disappointed not to be playing for the first team at that time. I was more concerned with re-establishing myself and getting rid of any injuries or psychological barriers as a result of the injury.'

McSwegan suffered a double leg break while playing for Rangers reserves against Celtic. He was clattered by keeper Ian Andrews at the start of the season and ended up missing almost the entire campaign.

He said, 'To this day, I sometimes think about that afternoon. I remember being taken to the Victoria Infirmary and I still had my strip on, and one of the porters asked if he could have my shorts! The first team was playing at Parkhead that day and we got a 1-1 draw, and Graeme Souness and Walter Smith came up to see me straight after the game. Souness seemed really concerned and asked how I was. He could see I was in agony and asked when I was getting taken. When I told him I was in a queue to go into theatre, he walked straight off – and I was taken ten minutes later!

'He had made a few phone calls, talked to a few people and a surgeon from Ross Hall, a private hospital, turned up and I was operated on straight away. I will never forget that. I was so relieved because the ward I was in wasn't the best. It had ripped curtains, cobwebs and the likes, and there were old men just sitting staring out of the window. I was never so happy to get out of there.

'Souness wanted me in at training as soon as possible – so I was back at Ibrox three days after the op! I had something which resembled a big door handle sticking out of my leg with four pins holding it in place. At that time we had a guy in the backroom team who had worked as a rehab specialist at Lilleshall. I reported to him and later that day he had me on a trampoline! I was in regularly for double sessions and it was great.

'Mind you, I was scared stiff to jump on the trampoline but he said, "It's okay, I'll catch you if you fall." To be honest, it was exactly what I needed. Souness told him to be tough on me as he knew I was prone to putting on a wee bit of weight, so he wanted me working hard. I felt quite small, but also knew he was doing it for my benefit. And it's at the back of your mind that had I been at another club, who knows how I would have been looked after, but I was at Rangers and I got the best treatment possible.'

He added, 'I had four or five games in the reserves at the end of the season but got a kick on it again. The boy leathered me from the back and I knew something wasn't right as soon as I put any weight on it. It was like a hairline fracture again, so that was me out until the summer. I was gutted but amazed to discover I had finished top goalscorer that season. The 17 goals I had scored in nine pre-season games definitely helped!

'Everything was sorted in the close season and I was ready to go again when the new campaign started. At the time we played in the Scottish Reserve League and Reserve League West, so I was usually playing two games a week. There were only two substitutes allowed for the top team at the time, and we had a great first-team squad. We also had the three-foreigner rule in Europe, which was good for the young Scottish boys, although not so good for players like Dale Gordon and Alexei Mikhailichenko, who quite often missed out.

'I did a lot of rehab with Ian Durrant, as I broke my leg while he was out injured. He was a brilliant player. I remember his first game back was a reserve match against Hibs and there was 14,000 there, which shows just how much the supporters thought of him.

'At the start of the 1992/93 campaign, I played a few pre-season games which included most of the first team, but when the squad was announced for the training camp at Il Ciocco, I wasn't part of it. It was disappointing but it was mainly the first-team squad that went, with maybe one or two youngsters thrown in. To be honest, I didn't read too much into missing out. One thing I wasn't great at was long distance running. There were guys in the squad who would run all day, but I was more about short, sharp bursts of speed, over say ten or 15 yards.'

But with the season barely a few weeks old, McSwegan was sad to see the boy he had grown up with at Ibrox, John Spencer, decide to move on. He said, 'John and I were good pals, so from that point of view I was sorry to see him leave. But he was far more driven than me, and was desperate to play first-team football, while I was happy to keep learning at Rangers and wait for my chance. Spenny had been over to Hong Kong to play, and been out on loan at Morton, so he was keen to go.

'Looking back, perhaps I was frightened to leave such a big club as any other would have been viewed as a step down, although as the seasons went by, and my first team opportunities and prospects failed to improve, I became really fed up, and would start to resent playing alongside boys just out of school. When I eventually took the plunge and left, I was about 22 but had very little regular first team football behind me.'

Back to 1992/93, and the flip side of Spencer moving on was that McSwegan moved up in the pecking order, although the previous season hadn't quite worked out that way. He explained, 'When you're training hard, doing well in the reserves, and hoping to make the breakthrough, there's nothing worse than hearing the manager has just signed a new striker!

'During the 1991/92 season, one of the first team players was injured and I was training like a demon in anticipation of a call-up – and then the club announced the signing of Paul Rideout, an England under-21 international. I couldn't believe it. Paul was a fantastic guy and we got on very well but personally it was a downer. Mind you, not even Paul, with his pedigree and experience of playing in Italy, was going to displace Hateley and McCoist. That's how tough it was.

'Rangers is the best club in the world, if you're playing regularly, but if you're not it can be a tough place. Perhaps Spenny wasn't more driven than me, but just decided it was time to leave because game time was always going to be limited. When he left, it definitely made me think, but I was at one of the top clubs in the UK, learning from the best, with a great manager, and we were winning everything, so why would I want to move? I was convinced my chance would come.'

McSwegan was a regular scorer in reserve games, and also proved adept at finding the net for the first team when given a chance, but revealed how there was one reserve fixture he was happy to play in, and which offered him the best of both worlds.

'Old Firm reserve games were a sort of middle ground for me. It wasn't first team football, but equally we had to raise our game from run-of-the-mill second-string matches. At the start of the season I played in an Old Firm reserve game at Parkhead and we won 2-0. I scored and it was a cracking game. Once you'd played in a few of these games you got the hang of them quite quickly. We were getting fantastic crowds, sometimes between 15,000 and 20,000, so there was always a great atmosphere. It was quite a step up from your normal reserve game and everyone was pumped up.

'When people asked my favourite away ground, I would say Easter Road or Parkhead – because I used to score all the time! Each time we went there I wondered if I would score two or three. I was always very confident.

'My first-team debut was against Hibs at Ibrox. We drew 1-1 and I came on for Davie Cooper. I was just 17 and was standing at the side of the park waiting to run on and when I saw who was coming off, I thought, "It doesn't get any better than this. I'm replacing Davie Cooper – what's happening here?"

'I made my first start in the League Cup quarter-final at Tannadice against Dundee United. At the time, there wasn't any way of finding out if you were in the team, but you could often gauge it by how training had gone. On this occasion, a squad of 16 was pinned up on the wall, which included three goalkeepers. Then it was a process of elimination. I noticed there were only two forwards and thought I had a chance, and found out for sure when the team was read out in the dressing room.

'It was horses for courses and everyone was different in the way they took the news. Some didn't bother when they found out about their debut, whereas others wouldn't sleep if they knew the day before, so it was all about man management.

'I was then on the bench for our European Cup match against Lyngby in Copenhagen and it felt good to be involved in such a big night, so there was no real frustration at not getting on. Back then, younger players like myself, Steven Pressley, Neil Murray and David Hagen were warmly accepted by the recognised first team players.

'Our dressing room was inclusive, even though we got changed in a separate room. The first team players would pop in and ask if we were coming out to train, etc. Nowadays, it's perhaps a wee bit more of a "them and us" mentality. If anything was happening, the senior players always made sure we were part of it. That season, we perhaps only contributed ten per cent to the games, but when we came on we were always treated as equals.'

When McSwegan looks back on his career, he will always have a special place in his heart for that season's European run; ten games undefeated and a whole heap of great memories made. He said, 'To go through the whole European campaign undefeated was something special, and we all played our part. There were many twists and turns but no one ever let the side down. No stars, no big-time Charlies; everybody was an equal. Back then, the carry on with Joey Barton would never have been allowed to happen. It would have been sorted out on day one. I won't name the names of those who would have sorted it, but I'm sure you can imagine. If truth be told, I was disappointed to see the Barton episode drag on for so long.

'There was a fantastic atmosphere inside Ibrox on the night of the match against Leeds United. Gary McAllister, a good bluenose, scored the opener early on for Leeds and silenced the stadium, but it wasn't too long before it was bouncing again and when you have McCoist and Hateley in your side you always have a chance. In the return leg, they both scored and we got through, and while there were a few times I thought I would never get a game because they were both so good, that night wasn't one of them. We were all caught up in the euphoria of twice beating the English champions, so it wasn't the time to curse my luck.

'I made some fantastic memories in my time at Ibrox, including that goal against Marseille – my first for Rangers. When I was told I was going on that night, my instructions were simple: Archie Knox just said to me, "Go and get us a goal, son." In the days leading up to the match, my finishing had been excellent in training so I felt confident. I had been picking my spot in the goals all week and they had been flying in from all angles, so I thought that if I got on, and got a chance, I was confident I would score. Strikers can be like that.

'Fortunately I got a decent chance and stuck it away, and I genuinely believe that another five minutes and we would have won that game. Just after that, Neil Murray got the ball and I was set up to let fly as soon as it came to me but he didn't lay it off. It was just outside the box and the way I was feeling I was confident I would have scored.

'I was just 22 when we played Marseille but I wasn't in the slightest bit nervous. Every time I played for Rangers it was always about the team; there was no time to worry about yourself. We were all in it together, and that was something I tried to take with me to other clubs when I moved on, but it's not until you leave Rangers you realise other clubs are different.

'The goal against Marseille was, I believe, the first one scored by a British player in the Champions League. And the one slight advantage I had was that even though I wasn't playing for the first team every Saturday, I was still playing regularly at Ibrox as the reserves played their home games there at that time. You always knew exactly where you were on the pitch.

'For that goal, the ball came from the left and the goalkeeper, Fabien Barthez, was moving from left to right so I tried to put it back across him. My first thought was that I'd caught it pretty good. It was a wet night so the ball could easily have gone the opposite way from which I intended. When it came over, I had to check my run, so I got my footing, balance and angles all ready and thankfully it was a good cross. I realised pretty quickly that it was crossbar height and had a good chance of dropping in – and I was delighted when it did.

'We were down to the bare bones that night. Both Neil [Murray] and Steven [Pressley] came on, so the three of us were involved, which might not have been the case had the three-foreigner rule not been in force.

'After the game I swapped tops with Marcel Desailly. What a player he was. In the second game I swapped with full-back Di Meco, but Desailly's was a good top to get as he went to AC Milan and Chelsea after Marseille, and won the World Cup with France.

'As we were walking back to the dressing room, my first thought was for my grandad. He used to come and watch me all the time, from the school team right up to Rangers. I'm sure he used to think, "I hope my boy plays for Rangers one day," although he never actually said it. He loved his football. I went home to my granny's house that night to get changed and my girlfriend Pauline, who is now my wife, and I went back out to the city centre for a few drinks. When I got home, I couldn't get to sleep, which wasn't really a surprise.

'I remember the game against CSKA Moscow over in Bochum. The number of chances they had was ridiculous but we won 1-0. We had some great characters in that team, and the likes of Andy Goram, Richard Gough, Davie McPherson and Ian Ferguson threw themselves in front of everything that night.

'When we played Bruges in the Champions League at Ibrox, I was out warming up when Scott Nisbet scored his famous goal. I always remember thinking their goalkeeper looked tiny, and I thought a taller keeper might have got to it, but it was just a freak of nature. The same night, Marseille beat CSKA 6-0 and there were whispers in the dressing room about what was going on behind closed doors.

'In Marseille there was a great atmosphere in the stadium, but it kicked off a wee bit in the tunnel at half-time. If memory serves me right, I think Bernard Tapie, the Marseille chairman, was trying to get a word with the referee and some of our lads weren't too happy and started giving him a bit of abuse, but overall I thoroughly enjoyed that European campaign.'

The first disappointment of a long and arduous season for McSwegan arrived in the shape of a Skol Cup Final snub – even though the youngster still had a part to play on the day. He said, 'I ended up 14th man. The day before the final, we played Aberdeen in a reserve league game at Ibrox and I scored a really good hat-trick. Walter Smith was at the game. He spoke to me afterwards and told me to get my stuff together as someone had pulled out of the original 14-man squad, and that I was going to the team hotel.

'I was already scheduled to be at Hampden to take part in the Skol Cup Sprint, a sponsors' event to find the fastest player in

Scottish football. I had taken part in the qualifier and made it to the final – and there was a £1,000 prize on offer for the winner, which was a pretty decent incentive.

'But I was now 14th man, which meant if anything went wrong overnight I was in. On the morning of the game, a roll call confirmed the 13 [11 and two subs] were all present and correct so I missed out on the game, but was still able to take part in the sprint. Sadly, I didn't win that either so it wasn't exactly the greatest weekend of my career!'

A couple of days after scoring that memorable goal against Marseille, McSwegan played his first full 90 minutes of the season. He relished the opportunity and reflects now, 'I was still on a high and was hoping for a run of games. It was unfortunate that Ally McCoist had picked up an injury but it gave me a chink of light. The only problem was we had quite a few injuries and the gaffer had drafted in three or four youngsters, which makes it that bit more difficult than if you were going into a team with ten regular first team players. I won't knock it, because it was a great experience and opportunity, but we weren't as strong as we could have been.

'I was back in the reserves for the New Year match against Celtic and scored both goals in a 2-0 win. I didn't see it as a massive drop down, as Old Firm games were always guaranteed to motivate you. I worked under John McGregor and he was very good. When he first arrived at the club, he didn't go to the Italian training camp, so he came on a pre-season tour of the Highlands with us. I came off in one game and sat down on the bench. One of the other guys said to me, "Why do they call John McGregor 'Mad Dog'?" Ten minutes later he answered by scything a boy across the chest. He was a hardy lad but also a really good player.'

McSwegan proved how much of a natural goalscorer he was in a reserve match at Dundee when he scored all five in an emphatic win. Each goal was different and the fact he had scored them against such an experienced goalkeeper as Jim Leighton was a bonus.

He said, 'I was really pleased with my performance that day. Ian Durrant was in the midfield and we had Pieter Huistra out wide. Three days later, I scored a hat-trick in a reserve match against Hibs. The following weekend I thought I had a really good chance of making the first team, but when I looked at the team sheet, both Durrant and Huistra were there and my name was absent. That was a defining moment in my Rangers career. I thought that if I've scored eight goals in four days and can't get a game, what's the point? I was still considered one of the younger boys but I was gutted.'

And there was further heartache to follow, as McSwegan explained, 'A game against Aberdeen was called off, and we were all sitting in the dressing room and the coach, Davie Dodds, said, "The gaffer has decided to take the first team squad away to St Andrews for the weekend," and I immediately asked if it included me. He went off to ask Walter and when he returned he said, "Aye, you can come if you want!" To be honest I was a bit pissed off at that response and I just got my gear together and left. Maybe they were testing me, I don't know, but I didn't go anyway.

'After that, I started to think, "It's not going to happen for me here, there isn't much more I can do." My contract was up at the end of the season so I decided to stay until then and see what kind of move I could get.

'An agency got in touch, obviously knowing that I wasn't playing regularly, and asked if I would consider going down south. It wasn't the right time, but I asked them to keep me in mind at the end of the season. Former Ranger Davie Wilson was one of the agents I spoke to. Agents weren't that big back then, and I didn't really know him too well, so part of me was wondering if he was perhaps working for the club!'

McSwegan's Ibrox swansong saw him included in the first team for a run of matches after Ally McCoist suffered a broken leg while playing for Scotland in Portugal. It was a bittersweet moment for Swiggy, as he knew exactly what it was like to be laid low with a plaster cast on his leg.

He said, 'My first match was at Tynecastle, when we beat Hearts, and we then beat Partick Thistle, but Aberdeen also won that day so the championship was put on hold. We went to Airdrie the following week knowing a win would give us the title. I was fortunate enough to score the only goal of the afternoon which meant we were champions, and that's something no one can ever take away from me. I have a great picture of me, Goughie and Bomber after the game, which brings back so many great memories.

'I played up front with Mark Hateley and he was brilliant with me. Obviously he was used to playing alongside experienced players but he took the time and trouble to talk me through the game and I'll always appreciate that. It was a new experience for me as well as I had been used to playing with someone like John Spencer in the reserves every week. Mark was different class and would win all the flick-ons. But for me to score a goal of such importance was just the stuff of dreams. It was my fifth goal of the season and it was Rangers' fifth successive title.

'After the match, I had a few thoughts for Coisty because he had missed out due to the broken leg. I had scored the goal which had clinched the league, but Coisty had been doing that week in, week out. I love him to bits, and it was just unfortunate that he missed out.'

McSwegan's goal at Broomfield paved the way for the small matter of a title party at Ibrox the following Saturday – with Dundee United the visitors, and once again Swiggy was involved.

He explained, 'I set up the only goal of the game for Pieter Huistra but one of the things I remember most about that afternoon was being wiped out by big John Clark. He took me from behind and I was up in the air for what seemed like an eternity. I didn't have a clue when I would come down! Defenders got away with things like that in those days. I liked Clarky, but he was rock solid.'

McSwegan added, 'A lot of the boys who were at the club at that time were Rangers supporters and knew the significance of becoming only the fifth team in the history of the club to win the treble. But when you look back at it now you appreciate it even more. It's such a difficult thing to achieve so we were rightly proud.

'We put so much into that season, and some of the lads were playing when they were only perhaps 75 or 80 per cent fit. When you look at guys like Bomber, we could certainly do with his type of character at the moment. Perhaps the only current player who would have fitted in with our ethos at that time would have been Andy Halliday. You can see how much it means to him. He reminds me of a mixture of Barry and Ian Ferguson. He's good on the ball but has the club in his heart.'

McSwegan admitted it was incredibly sweet to clinch the treble at Celtic Park in the Scottish Cup Final against Aberdeen. He said, 'I didn't play that day. I was on the bench, which was frustrating as I'd played loads of games in the run-up to the final, but I had to swallow the disappointment.

'With about five minutes to go, the boys seemed to be running on empty and Archie Knox said to me and Steven Pressley, "Right lads, karaoke time," and that meant we had to go out and get warmed up at the Rangers end and get the fans going to give the players a boost, and lift them for the last few minutes. It worked and we won the Scottish Cup.'

Rangers may have won the Scottish Cup – and clinched an historic treble – but McSwegan knew deep down he had taken part in his last match for the club. He said, 'If I'm being honest, I knew I would have to move if I wanted to improve. You can only learn so much on the training ground. You have to play first team football, and can't be playing for the reserves at 23 or 24. But at the back of your mind, you know you have a chance of winning medals, or playing in Europe. There was a lot to weigh up, but then you hear rumours that Gordon Durie and Duncan Ferguson are about to sign, and that helps make your mind up.

'Near the end of the '92/93 season, Walter Smith told me there would be another contract there for me to sign, as I was out of contract, but I was straight with him and said that I would be moving on.

'Rangers had to offer me a contract if they wanted a fee. Ally McCoist had broken his leg and I had played a good number of games, and scored a few goals. But my mind was made up, so I told Walter I wanted to leave because I needed regular first team football, and he didn't argue.

'I looked at boys I'd grown up with, like Eoin Jess, who were playing first team football and that's what I wanted. I might have been at the best club but I was getting left behind because they were developing more than me.

'I went to Notts County the following season and scored 17 goals in what was effectively the Championship. They had initially shown an interest in me without even seeing me play. County are a small club, and we finished seventh, so it was a good season. We had a lot of big games against teams who were geographically close. The matches against Forest were obviously the Nottingham derby, but games against Leicester City and Derby County were also huge. The [Nottingham] derby match, especially, meant a great deal to both sets of supporters, and was the bigger of the East Midlands games.

'I stayed in Nottingham for two years with the missus. We had already stayed in a flat in Glasgow but to move so far away was quite something for us, away from family, etc, but we enjoyed it, although we moved back up to Glasgow and got married, and I joined Dundee United.

'There are times when I look back and think that maybe I should have stayed down south a bit longer, perhaps even moved to another side. At the time, I scored home and away against Birmingham City and there was talk that they were interested, while there were others looking. Stevie Nicol was my manager and at one point he quizzed me about the press speculation linking me to Birmingham.

'If I had already been married, we would probably have stayed down there because the money had consistently gone up in England, while going down in Scotland! Financially we would have been better off, but for family reasons we came back to Scotland. My wife was an only child and was close to her mum, so that was the overriding factor.

'I had some good times at Dundee United, but strangely one of the things I remember most is a match against Rangers at Ibrox, which I missed due to injury. I watched the game from the stand, but next day I'm reading the match report in a paper, and it said, "McSwegan missed a good chance in 54 minutes!" And I thought, "Seriously?"

'Another part of the report insisted I'd set up an opportunity for one of my team-mates, which just proved to me you can't always believe what you read in the papers. The thing that bothers me about that is someone who wasn't at the game reading it and thinking I've missed a couple of sitters and had a shocker.'

Despite scoring goals for Notts County, Dundee United and then Hearts and Kilmarnock, McSwegan will always be remembered for his time at Ibrox, but he insists that the time was right for him to move on. He said, 'Perhaps I should have gone sooner, but no one can ever take away from me what we achieved in 1992/93. Once I left Rangers I grew as a person, but it's always going to be a step down when you go elsewhere, so you have to deal with that. When you leave, it's also easier to appreciate what you had, and you even think that you might like to go back at some point.

'While I was at Hearts, I was called into the Scotland squad and scored on my debut. Some of the papers gave me man of the match and I thought I would win a few more caps, but it didn't happen. It was frustrating because we played England home and away after that, and while I was injured for the home game, I was on the bench for the match at Wembley and I thought I would get the last ten or 15 minutes as we needed a goal, but the manager, Craig Brown, threw on Mark Burchill.

'It was frustrating for me because at that time I was scoring goals for Hearts, and Mark was only sporadically getting a run out with Celtic. I always found Craig Brown very diplomatic. He would say and do the right things and shy clear of controversy. It was as though he just tried to appease everyone.

'I played for about 23 years and the biggest disappointment for me was injuries; I think most players would say that. I had trouble with my hamstrings but not too many regrets. I looked after myself and played until I was 38. I enjoyed a night out, especially at Rangers, where the old motto "the team that drinks together wins together" was spot on.

'In fact, I was scouting for the first team when Ally McCoist was the manager and I've coached the youth team as well. My son has also been training with them so hopefully there is always going to be some sort of connection with the club. I also do some charity nights and bump into old team-mates, which is great, because you don't get that anywhere else. Rangers is an institution.

'Mind you, it must have been a joy for Walter and Archie to have such an amazing dressing room. No egos, no in-fighting, hard-working boys who would fight all day for each other. Nobody would cross Walter or Archie because we had too much respect for them.

'The team spirit was second to none. If you look round your dressing room and say, "He will fight all day for you, he will get you a goal, he will create something, he runs all day, he never gives up," then you have all the bases covered.

'We had a lot going for us that season. I'm sure many teams turned up at Ibrox thinking they couldn't win and that would help us psychologically. We could mix it, we could play; we had the lot. It's a rare thing and doesn't come along too often. After I left, the Italians and the Dutch came, but I don't think they achieved what we did in '92/93.

'And as a Rangers supporter, I was privileged to be involved in that.'

13

A Two-Horse Title Race

S ATURDAY, 2 January; the day that separated the men from the boys. Rangers may have beaten Celtic by just a solitary goal, scored by Trevor Steven, but the victory moved the Light Blues eight points clear of their cross-city rivals – and with two games in hand. In the days of just two points for a win, it effectively left Celtic requiring a six-game swing to make up the ground necessary to mount a genuine title challenge.

But the bottom line was that Celtic's challenge was over. Rangers were going great guns, in the middle of a 29-game unbeaten record and looked highly unlikely to drop anywhere close to 12 points in the run-in. Allied to the fact that the most credible challenge was now expected to come from Aberdeen or Hearts and you can see why it was easy to discount Celtic as a credible contender.

And Bomber Brown proved he was over his recent 'labour problems' by turning in a five-star display against Celtic. He said, 'I had a few days when I had quite a lot of pain in certain areas of the stomach and they thought it was my appendix, but when I went to hospital they didn't deem it serious enough to take it out. They tested a few other things but couldn't find anything wrong, so whether it was the appendix and it has now settled down, I don't know.

'Big "Elvis" [Steven] Pressley did very well in my absence so I was pleased to get back into the team for the Old Firm game. Our performance against Celtic could have been better. There were spells when we were knocking the ball about, but we let it go and Celtic came at us and gave us a few problems. But the important thing is we know we can improve and it's another two crucial points, so we can't complain too much.

'As long as we keep getting the results, I'm sure everyone will be happy come the end of the season, although we always like to put on a better show at home. And it's another New Year when we've got a result against Celtic so we're all chuffed to bits.'

Andy Goram backed up Bomber's mantra that sometimes points were more important than performance, and said, 'We've taken a bit of stick for our displays against Celtic, but we're still good enough to beat them even when we're struggling.

'The standards everyone expects from Rangers are so high and I must admit it's difficult to keep every performance at such a level. We've had so many games to play and some of the pitches we've played on haven't been great so it's unrealistic to expect great football all the time.

'Don't get me wrong, though, no one here simply wants to struggle through every match, even if we do keep on winning, but hopefully the Celtic game was a one-off and we can get back to playing well again and continue our successful run.

'The most pleasing aspect of Saturday's result was that we more or less finished off Celtic's title challenge, as their manager, Liam Brady, accepted after the match.'

And record-breaking Rangers were at it again as the attendance for the Old Firm match was the highest ever at the new-look Ibrox Stadium. A crowd of 46,039 turned up for the encounter and it was guaranteed to stand for quite some time. It couldn't be matched in Europe because of UEFA restrictions on the number of fans permitted in the enclosure for Champions League matches, and with the enclosure due to be seated in time to meet the Taylor Report deadline of August 1994, there would be few realistic opportunities to top the 46,000 mark again.

The crowd for the match against Celtic was the biggest at Ibrox since the league decider against Motherwell in April 1978, when 50,000 turned up. The capacity of the stadium before it was rebuilt was 65,000, and that was last achieved at John Greig's testimonial the same year when Rangers beat a Scotland select side 5-0.

Confusion still reigned over the official Ibrox capacity but Campbell Ogilvie said, 'It's around the 47,000 mark. However, we've had to remove a number of seats in the Main Stand because of sightlines and increase the size of the press box for the bigger matches, so Saturday's attendance is as close to capacity as we will probably get, although there is still a chance it could be topped.

'We aim to have the seated enclosure in operation for the 1994 deadline. We are still studying plans so we don't know for certain yet what the official capacity will be once work is complete, but it will be between 44,000 and 45,000.'

Two goals by Gary McSwegan made it a Ne'erday double as Rangers reserves beat their Parkhead counterparts 2-0 at Celtic Park, but while youngster McSwegan left the east end of Glasgow with a smile on his face there was agony for keeper Ally Maxwell. The former Motherwell stopper – a Scottish Cup Final hero for the Steel City men in 1991 when he played on against Dundee United despite breaking his ribs – was again in the wars, and the injury he sustained was a bad one.

With just 12 minutes remaining, Maxwell was hurt during an aerial collision, and even though he saw the game out, albeit in terrible pain, he missed the post-match celebrations to head straight for hospital. And there it was confirmed he had suffered a punctured lung.

He recalled, 'I went for a high cross and accidentally collided with a number of players on the goal line. At first I thought my ribs were damaged again because it was a similar kind of pain to the last time. I also felt pain when I kicked the ball out, but knew there wasn't much more than ten minutes to go and Celtic were putting us under a bit of pressure, so I decided to play on.'

Maxi, a £300,000 buy from Motherwell at the start of the season, was eventually released from hospital on the Tuesday and headed straight home to begin his lengthy recuperation. He was expected to be out for the best part of eight weeks.

Ironically the club's next match was against Motherwell in the Scottish Cup and gaffer Walter Smith issued a warning to his players ahead of the Fir Park tie. Motherwell – as cup holders – had visited Ibrox in the previous season's fourth round and it took a late double by Alexei Mikhailichenko to dump stubborn Well out. Smith said, 'Our players need only look back to that match to remind themselves how dangerous Motherwell can be.

'They had a great cup run the year before last and certainly didn't let it go easily last season. It took a tremendous performance from us, particularly in the last half hour, to secure our place in the next round.

'Motherwell came and attacked us that day and played very well and I expect this match to be another open encounter. Teams know they have to set out to win in the cup because a draw only gets you a replay – and no one wants that.

'Our ambition to retain the cup we won last term is as strong as ever. Last season's final win gave us an enjoyable end to the season and we want the same again this year.'

Ally McCoist ensured Motherwell's cup run hit the skids by scoring a double in a 2-0 win. The match was played in horrific conditions, although that didn't prevent Trevor Steven shining in midfield. But after the game, the Berwick-born star revealed he had an extra reason for wanting to win the game.

He said, 'I'm told that if we win the Tennent's Scottish Cup this season, and I'm involved, I will become only the fourth player in Rangers' history to win championship and FA Cup medals on both sides of the border. That would be quite something.'

The other three were Billy Stevenson, who played for Liverpool in the early 1960s, Alex Scott, who was at Everton at the same time, and Gary Stevens, who played alongside Trevor in the great Everton team of the mid-1980s. Indeed, when Stevens won his Scottish Cup medal in May 1992, he became the first Englishman of the 20th century to win Scottish and English badges. However, Steven missed out on the Gers' glory run the previous season, and was itching to succeed this time around.

He said, 'The fact I missed out on a medal last year makes me even keener to get one this time. The Scottish Cup is the only domestic medal I've missed out on. It would be nice to complete the set.'

At Fir Park, Rangers broke a record held previously by the Lisbon Lions, who went 30 games without defeat in 1966/67. Rangers' victory over Motherwell made it 31 games unbeaten, and Steven said, 'These are exciting times, with the commitments we also have in the league and European Cup. We are in a great situation and the only way we can cope is by having a big squad. If we had two or three players less I think we may have fallen by the wayside by now, but we are able to bring in players who aren't playing every week and they can still do a great job, which keeps us ticking along nicely.'

Prior to the Motherwell cup tie, goals by Hateley, McCall and McCoist had given Rangers a 3-2 win over Dundee United at Ibrox, and next up was a home game against Falkirk but before then there were fresh rumblings about the proposed new Scottish Super League set-up.

As Celtic decided to jump ship and throw their weight behind the Scottish League's 14-12-12 league proposal, Rangers chairman David Murray blasted, 'The Super League clubs will win the day – with or without the backing of Celtic!'

The ten member clubs were set to meet in Edinburgh to discuss Celtic's shock U-turn, while the Scottish League were due to hold a secret ballot to seek approval of their controversial set-up, even though they needed at least two other Super League clubs to back their proposal if their plans to restructure Scottish football were to succeed.

But Murray warned defiantly, 'The remaining nine Super League members WILL stick together. We will continue our policy of working against clubs who hang on to the coat tails of teams such as Rangers and Aberdeen – and indeed Celtic. I found their decision to favour the Scottish League unusual to say the least, especially when they appeared to back the rest of the Super League clubs all the way.'

If, as most observers expected, the Scottish League plans were defeated, Celtic would remain within the Super League as they were fully paid-up members but Murray reckoned it would leave them in a difficult position as they had lost a lot of the trust and confidence of fellow member clubs.

Under the league's proposals, clubs would play each other twice before splitting into two separate Premier Leagues. Premier A would feature the top six clubs, who would start from scratch again, effectively deciding the league title over ten games.

Murray said, 'Our fans cannot be expected to buy season tickets for 26 matches at the start of the season which, in effect, mean nothing. Under the Scottish League's proposals there would be far too many meaningless fixtures.'

Meanwhile, Gary Stevens was given the all-clear by medical experts to hit the comeback trail. The England international hadn't played since 1 December when he had fractured his knee in a bruising encounter with Airdrie.

He said, 'Last week I did a lot of work on my leg to compensate for the bulk of muscle which has been lost due to immobility. I also did a little ball work and although there were the usual little aches and pains, I'm pleased with the way things have gone. I expect to be playing some kind of football, probably for the reserves, within the next fortnight, depending on their fixtures.

'I'm a little ahead of schedule at this stage, but after being out for five months previously a little bit of panic set in when I found out I had fractured my knee. In retrospect, I probably came back sooner than expected last time, but I wanted to be fit for the match against Marseille. My comeback this time will depend on when the gaffer and myself feel I'm ready.'

When the draw for the fourth round of the Scottish Cup pitted Rangers against Ayr United there were screams of delight in the shower at East End Park! Confused? No wonder, but there's a simple explanation. Ayr had just beaten Dunfermline in the third round and the players were listening to the draw on United player Sam McGivern's portable radio – while taking a post-match shower.

When the crackly transmission mentioned Rangers and Ayr United in the same sentence, the players thought they had drawn COVE Rangers before they realised it was the more famous Gers, and that sparked off scenes of jubilation as almost the entire Ayr team of the time supported Rangers.

Former Rangers reserve player Nigel Howard said, 'We knew the big sides were still in the draw when it got down to picking the last few clubs, and when our name was drawn out, we were all shouting, "Come on, give us Rangers." True enough, Rangers were the next name out of the hat, but the reception was pretty poor and we all thought it was the Highland League Gers.

'Once we found out it was THE Rangers, everyone was delighted because it's such a good tie to be involved in. Most of the lads support the club anyway. We have a playing staff of about 24 and only one of the younger boys prefers Celtic. Guys such as myself, our striker Tommy Walker and goalie Cammy Duncan all follow Rangers and that's why we wanted to play them, rather than Celtic.

'It's a draw that has captured the imagination of the town. Even before we left Dunfermline it was all the players and fans were talking about. The place was buzzing last year when we drew Motherwell in the third round, so can you imagine how it will be when we play Rangers.'

Walter Smith admitted he was happy to have avoided a fellow Premier League side, and added, 'When you draw Premier opposition, it can be like just another league match as we play each other so often. However, this is the kind of tie the cup is really all about – a First Division side against one from the Premier League. Our players know the type of game they'll get down at Ayr, but it's one we are all looking forward to.'

Before that, though, there was the not-so-insignificant matter of a league match against closest rivals Aberdeen at Ibrox to negotiate.

Going into the fixture the Light Blues were five points ahead of the Dons, and with a game in hand. Aberdeen, in turn, were seven points clear of Celtic, so it appeared the title was a two-horse race. It would be a fortnight since Rangers had played as their league match at Fir Park against Motherwell had been postponed due to a waterlogged pitch.

And that frustration would be doubled as the match against Aberdeen suffered a similar fate – just 20 minutes before kick-off, and with 17,000 supporters already inside Ibrox. There was a double blow for fans as they missed out on an opportunity to see Olympic decathlon champion Daley Thompson in action. Not quite in sprint mode, or leaping over hurdles, though, as Thompson had agreed to take part in a special half-time penalty shoot-out, arranged by his sponsors adidas.

The double Olympic champion did admit he had been following Rangers' results in Europe that season, and added, 'I hear Ibrox is a beautiful stadium, so I'm looking forward to my half-time appearance.'

One man who was less frustrated than most was striker Mark Hateley, who had the Tartan Special Player of the Month trophy to help cushion the blow. He said, 'It's my birthday in November and it always seems to give me an extra lease of life. I won the same award this time last year!

'Seriously, when you pick up these awards it makes you realise people do see the role you perform in the team and you appreciate that. In saying that, I think everyone in our team is recognised anyway, not only myself and Alastair [McCoist].'

Hateley picked up the sponsor's bronze statuette and cheque for £250 for helping Rangers maintain their unbeaten run in December when they went five games without defeat, with the run including the 1-0 away win over CSKA Moscow. Allied to the 2-2 draw with Marseille, the win in Bochum had given Rangers cause for optimism in the Champions League. Hateley had also played a starring role against the French champions and had been voted man of the match, but was still to receive his award.

Rumours abounded that McCoist had mistakenly lifted the trophy, so when Hateley asked Coisty if he had seen the silverware, the hitman's sidekick, Ian Durrant, replied, quick as a flash, 'Too late big man, it's already in his trophy cabinet at home!'

Hateley had proved his worth to Rangers on many occasions since signing from Monaco a couple of years previously, but he revealed that when he left the French cracks in 1990 he had the option of joining four of the top sides in England.

Manchester United, Spurs, Arsenal and Everton were all interested in the striker – but he chose to continue his career in Scotland, and it's a decision he has never regretted. He said, 'Sure, those clubs are among the biggest in England, but I joined the biggest in Britain! I knew some of the lads who had played for Rangers before I joined such as Graeme Souness, Chris Woods, Ray Wilkins and Gary Stevens. They were always saying how good the place was, so I knew Rangers were a club heading in the right direction. We've got a good team, a nice stadium and a great support.

'I wouldn't have come here if I didn't think they were a club going places, but when you have all these ingredients, you're only going to go one way and that's the way we're heading.'

Rangers' incredible run, especially in Europe, had only reinforced Hateley's decision to head north, where it was generally accepted he was playing some of the best football of his career. The player agreed, and despite building a wealth of experience in England, Italy and France, he felt Rangers were up there with the rest of the European giants he had served.

He said, 'Rangers are one of the best teams I've ever played with and the most successful by a long chalk. When you play for successful sides you are more content on and off the park. Everyone in the squad is happy that we are winning week in, week out, confidence is high and that makes Ibrox a great place to be.'

Off the pitch, Campbell Ogilvie admitted confusion still reigned over the proposed Scottish Super League – especially after the previous week's Scottish League EGM, which failed to get the necessary two-thirds majority required to implement a 14-12-12 league structure in time for the 1993/94 season thanks largely to the voting power exercised by nine of the 12 Premier League clubs.

Ogilvie said, 'There is obviously some bad feeling in the aftermath of the EGM, but in truth there were no winners. Many of the smaller sides in the country now realise the top clubs must control their own destiny and if our wishes can be met within the Scottish League set-up, then fine.

'Hopefully both sides will get together imminently for discussions. My own opinion is that these talks would be best between two small groups, rather than having the top clubs sitting down in front of the 12-man League Management Committee. Yet even if we do sit down to talk, and changes could take place in time for next season, I would rather they didn't. We must make the correct changes and I don't think we have sufficient time between now and the end of the season.'

Ian Ferguson was relatively pleased when the matches against Motherwell and Aberdeen were postponed, as the midfield powerhouse had been out of action since breaking his left hand in the 3-2 win over Dundee United earlier in the month. Ferguson was due to have further x-rays to see if he was ready to re-join Walter Smith's squad for the second half of the season, and said, 'I really hope the bones have started to knit together. If they have, the doctor will be able to take my plaster cast off and replace it with a strapping, which I will be able to play with.

'Thankfully I haven't lost any mobility because of the injury – the only thing I haven't been able to do is weights in the gym. However, I've managed to join in with the rest of the lads in training, running and playing in games.

'When the doc took the original cast off, he prodded about with my fingers and I didn't feel a bit of pain, but subsequent x-rays showed it hadn't knitted together at all. This is a new injury. It's a spiral break at the back of my hand which I picked up with about ten minutes of the game against United remaining.

'I remember running after Jim McInally. I put in a sliding tackle but unfortunately I landed on my hand. Our physio came on and had a look, but it was too early to say what it was, although I knew it was broken shortly afterwards when I was chasing after Jim again and grabbed him by the waist, only to feel the pain shoot through me. That was that.'

The postponement of the match against Aberdeen left Pieter Huistra waiting to clock up a century of appearances for Rangers. He said, 'It would have been nice to make my 100th appearance against Aberdeen, especially as it was such a big match.

'To be honest, I have never kept exact details on how many matches I've played, even when I was with my former clubs Groningen and FC Twente. I spent three years with both, although in my first year at Groningen I was a 17-year-old apprentice, so in total I perhaps played between 60 and 70 games. With FC Twente, I played in most games, so I must have been involved in over 130.'

McCoist and Hateley were doing the business for Rangers. They were the most feared partnership in the country, but that didn't prevent Smith from looking to improve his options up front – although his latest move was to earn the club a verbal volley.

A bitter war of words broke out between Rangers and Dundee United over the former's proposed interest in 21-year-old striker Duncan Ferguson, and it led to United boss Jim McLean implying that Rangers had leaked their interest in Ferguson to 'stir up the situation'.

Chairman David Murray confirmed an offer of £2.5m had been made for the player, but insisted it was United and NOT Rangers who had leaked details of the proposed move. He said, 'I feel the story has been blown out of proportion by the media. I first spoke to Jim McLean about the player in the presence of Walter Smith two months ago and Jim told me he wasn't keen to sell him. I asked to be kept informed of any developments, but as the European signing deadline approached we had heard nothing.

'Walter again made it clear Duncan Ferguson was the player he wanted as back-up to Ally McCoist and Mark Hateley so on 7 January, eight days before the Euro deadline, I spoke to Jim again. We offered £2.5m, spread over three repayment terms, and Jim agreed it was a very good offer. He wanted to discuss it with his fellow directors at a board meeting the next day, but ONE HOUR later, after speaking with United director George Fox, he rejected our offer. He asked us to keep our discussions confidential and we agreed to this. I can categorically confirm that we did not speak to the player or his agent.'

However, newspapers and radio began to get wind of the offer and media men contacted Murray for a reaction. He said, 'I denied our interest, but speculation was becoming so widespread that it was obvious the confidentiality agreement had been breached. It was clear the story was coming out and because of this I confirmed our offer last weekend.

'I stress that only Walter Smith, Archie Knox and myself knew about our offer. The leak certainly didn't come from Ibrox. However, our reserve coach Billy Kirkwood was approached by a Dundee United player and asked about our bid. Apparently it was being openly spoken about by the players up at Tannadice.'

The players might have been lacking in match action but when they eventually got back on the pitch, there was no shortage of thrills for the thousands of Rangers supporters who made the journey through to Easter Road for the match against Hibs. The only incident of note in the opening two-thirds of play was a goal by Mark Hateley – and then all hell broke loose.

Pat McGinlay equalised in the 69th minute, Trevor Steven edged Rangers ahead just 60 seconds later and Hateley made it 3-1 on 72 minutes. Supporters hardly had time to draw breath before Darren Jackson reduced the leeway, and with McCoist and McGinlay scoring late on, the game ended 4-3 to Rangers.

Gary Stevens had mixed feelings about this encounter, and said, 'I was delighted to be back in the first team but not so happy with the way things worked out. Fitness-wise I felt okay and my knee was fine, but I was disappointed that we conceded three goals.

'I was suffering from a bit of staleness and was dragged into positions where I normally wouldn't have found myself. I got a bit of a telling-off after the game – which I deserved – and it wasn't really the start I wanted in my first game back. I've got to get my brain working again, geared up to first-team football, and hopefully the 90 minutes at Easter Road will have done that. But having said that, the most important thing was that we still got the two points.'

The win helped maintain Rangers' position at the top of the league – and the next goal was to reach the top of the hit parade! That was the aim of McCoist, Durrant, Ferguson and Smith as the Fab Four went into the St Clair Studios in Glasgow to add their voices to the new 90s version of 'Follow Follow'. The upbeat, rocky recording was put together by Glasgow producers the Treble Twins and Coisty said, 'It sounds sensational!'

It would be premiered in the new Rangers video the *Battle of Britain – Rule Britannia*, which featured highlights of the Bears' two European Cup victories over Leeds United. 'Follow Follow' also featured TV commentary of the goals at Elland Road as well as interviews with Durrant and McCoist on their roles in the famous wins.

Meanwhile, Rangers supporters faced an agonising wait to see if they would be able to Follow Follow their team to Bruges for the Champions League tie on 3 March after UEFA's shock decision to play the match behind closed doors. The governing body dropped the bombshell after crowd trouble between fans of the Belgian champions and Marseille when the sides met in France. Bruges lodged an appeal against the decision – but over 2,000 Rangers fans who planned to attend the game were told they would have to wait until 12 February before finding out if they would be allowed into the 18,000-capacity Olympic Stadium.

Campbell Ogilvie said, 'The announcement from UEFA came as a complete shock to both ourselves and Bruges. I spoke to club officials, the police and the British Embassy and no one had the slightest inkling that this would happen.'

Meanwhile, the following tale was recounted to me by a member of the backroom staff at Rangers. Let's just hope it's true. If not, it's quite a yarn!

'Before a game at Motherwell, I was chatting to Walter [Smith] at the side of the park when we noticed that one player was missing from the pre-match warm-up. He was busy watching the players being put through their paces, so I offered to nip into the dressing room to see if there was someone loitering about in there.

'Imagine my great surprise when I opened the door and spotted the incredibly laid-back Alexei Mikhailichenko sitting with his feet up reading a newspaper. I told him the rest of the players were outside on the pitch going through their pre-match routine, and that the manager had spotted that he was missing.

'"It's okay," he said in his broken-English accent, "I stay in here. It's too cold outside."

'Yes, we were in the grip of a particularly nasty winter, but I told him his place was out on the park with the others, and not sitting with his feet up in the changing room. He smiled, and repeated his mantra about the cold, etc, but I told him Walter would be furious about him missing the warm-up.

'He sighed, folded his newspaper slowly before laying it down on the bench and then standing up. "Great," I thought, "he's listening, it will save a confrontation with Walter." But he simply walked over to the other side of the room, picked up one of the hairdryers and sprayed the heat all over his skinny torso, switched it off and walked over and sat down again. He picked up his paper, looked up at me and said, "There, now I've warmed up!" and continued with his reading.

'I was flabbergasted and when I went back outside, Walter realised it was Miko who was missing and asked if I'd saw him. When I relayed the story, he stormed into the dressing room.

'I can only assume Miko received the hairdryer treatment, although this time for real!'

WHEN we reminisce about quality left-sided former Rangers, David Robertson is up there with the very best. Skilful, tenacious, athletic; the nine-in-a-row defender had the lot. Mind you, Robertson was familiar with flying up and down the left flank long before starting his six-year spell at Ibrox; a tenure that would bring honours beyond his wildest dreams, including six league titles, three Scottish Cups, and a similar number of League Cup medals.

Robertson recalled, 'As a youngster, my first position was on the left wing, and I enjoyed playing there. I was fast and could use my pace to get past defenders, but at that time I was still developing and hadn't really settled on a permanent position.

'When I eventually switched to playing left-back, it came as a complete accident. I was 14 and had been invited to a pre-season tournament in Rothes with the Aberdeen reserve team. After the first game we were left with just 11 fit players and as I was the only naturally left-footed player there, the manager Teddy Scott asked me to fill in at left-back. I won the man of the match award and ever since that day my fate was sealed – I was a left-back. To be honest, I was struggling as a left-winger at the time as I relied too much on my pace, so I was happy enough to drop back.'

And it was as a defender that Robertson eventually put pen to paper on a contract with the Pittodrie side, a day, he insists, that was very special.

He said, 'It was great to sign for Aberdeen as they were my home town club, and at that point they were very successful. I was just 13 at the time and, if the truth be told, the offer to sign schoolboy forms came completely out of the blue. It was something I simply hadn't been expecting.

'It was Sir Alex Ferguson who signed me and he was a remarkable man. I was just 13 years old but he came to all the youth games – even on a cold Monday night when we trained in the car park – and he knew every single player. His son Mark had played for the same Deeside team as me.

'Sir Alex was a perfectionist and one thing I really admired about him was even though we might just have won a game 5-0, he would still point out our mistakes. I was playing for the first team at 17, and I would walk off the pitch at half-time or full-time knowing he would have a go at me if I had made a mistake. But the next day he would always take you aside and calmly tell you what you did wrong. He was an amazing manager to play for.

'When I made my first-team debut, I didn't know until an hour before kick-off. I was fully expecting to be in the stand that afternoon as the manager was only allowed to name two substitutes then. Looking back, it was good that he handled it the way he did as I didn't have any time to think about what was just about to happen and, as a consequence, I played well that day.'

Robertson was 22 when he joined Rangers – after five years at Pittodrie – and insisted it was tough to leave his north-east base, 'It was hard to leave but I got the impression the club wanted to cash in on me and didn't really try all that hard to keep me. So in one way I had to leave. Like all players, you are ambitious and at that time a few English teams had been showing an interest in me. A couple of seasons beforehand, Sir Alex had tried to take me to Manchester United, and Liverpool manager Kenny Dalglish wanted me at Anfield, but Aberdeen turned both clubs down. I knew the size of these clubs, and that helped me set my sights on moving on.'

With Robertson eventually plumping for a move down the A90 to Glasgow, he was in for a bit of a culture shock when he arrived at Ibrox for his first day's work. He explained, 'I think the biggest differences between Aberdeen and Rangers are the fan base and the size of the stadiums. On my first day at Ibrox I was met at the front door by a commissionaire and shown into the dressing room. I took one look at all the big names sitting there and that showed me just how big a club Rangers actually were.

'On the pitch, there was also a big difference as the supporters more or less demanded you win every game. The expectations are so high at a club like Rangers, but it didn't take me too long to settle in, and I think that was because I was soon playing regularly. I was just 22, which is quite young to be at such a big club, and as I was also still quite immature I suppose I didn't really take it all in. Mind you, I started to receive death threats in the mail, but being young I didn't take any notice of them. I realise now that I should have told someone at the club, but when you're just 22...'

One of the most celebrated fixtures at Ibrox Stadium, and which still stands as a testament to the traditions of the famous old club, is the marble staircase, which has witnessed many an eminent footprint. Robertson recalled the first time he ever walked up it. He said, 'The day I signed for Rangers was unforgettable, although my first memory of the marble staircase was when I played for Aberdeen and Ray Wilkins was coming down the staircase just as I was going up. He stopped me, said hello and told me I had played well that day. That meant so much to me coming from a guy like Wilkins.'

Robertson was part of a title-winning team in his first season at Ibrox, 1991/92, and reckons it was the perfect start to a new chapter in his career. He said, 'It was a great feeling, although I missed the game the day we won the title as I was suspended, but it was still a great feeling. The league championships that followed were fantastic, but more of a relief than anything else.'

The 1992/93 season was the talented defender's second term at Ibrox, but one wonders if there were any early indications of just how good a campaign the team was going to have, and how good the squad was? He said, 'That season was incredible and I think I played in almost all of our games. It was also fantastic to win the treble against Aberdeen. We were strong all over the field and that must have been hard for the teams that came up against us.

'We also had a real desire to win and even when we were a goal or two down we knew we could still come back and win games. Having guys like Richard Gough, John Brown, Stuart McCall and "The Goalie" [Andy Goram] was massive as they were all real winners and leaders on the park. On a personal level, I was never really fully fit, but I kept playing because I knew that if I missed a game or two I might not get back into the team!'

Just a fortnight before flying out to the Italian training camp at Il Ciocco, on the eve of 1992/93, Robertson became a dad for the first time which meant he travelled to Italy on a real high. It was a fantastic time for the player and his wife, and he said, 'It was unbelievable, although it was touch and go whether or not Chelsea would be born in time, although thankfully she was. It was a great feeling to have your first born and to actually be present too, which really added to it. Throw in the fact I was playing for a big club like Rangers and I really was so fortunate.

'Mind you, I almost fainted at the birth! I'm not great with those things but I'm still glad I was there.'

Robertson made 58 appearances during the record-breaking season – bettered only by John Brown (57 plus two sub appearances) – but insisted he was happy with the number of games he played, 'I was delighted to be playing regularly and I soon got into a routine. Walter Smith was fantastic with me and gave me plenty of time to recover after games. I had quite a few fitness tests on the day of the game, but always played. It was frustrating because I was constantly fighting hamstring problems, which caused a lot of pain, but I would play on regardless.'

Robertson added, 'Old Firm games were very special. Mind you, there was so much noise you couldn't hear anything even from your own team-mates, so you were basically on your own out there.

'My best memory, albeit a funny one, happened during a game at Ibrox, when the Celtic physio had just treated one of his players and ran off the field without his medical kit bag. Next minute, John Brown ran over and gave it an almighty kick and it burst open. The physio spent the next few minutes running around the pitch picking up bandages and tape while the crowd gave him pelters!'

Robertson also enjoyed what would ultimately turn out to be a most impressive European campaign – and lapped up the matches against Leeds United, the side he would eventually move on to from Rangers. He said, 'It was a tremendous experience, particularly at Elland Road. For the best part of both legs we were under real pressure, but scored goals at exactly the right times. I'll never forget walking off the pitch at the end of the second leg and the Leeds fans applauding us.

'The stadium was really noisy, especially as Leeds attacked us a fair bit even after we got the early goal. Leeds fans are passionate so there was a great atmosphere inside the ground, but when we scored there was a deathly silence. After that, they ramped up the noise again.

'I must admit it was frustrating to get so far in the first ever Champions League and not win it, but we still enjoyed a great run and a great season. If we didn't have the treble to go for it may have been different, but it was still a great achievement to go so close. We did hear stories about Marseille after they had beaten AC Milan in the final, but at the time it wasn't a big issue for us.'

Robertson cemented his name in Rangers' history books by becoming part of just the fifth squad to win a treble. He explained, 'It was amazing, particularly for me as we beat Aberdeen to each of the three trophies, and to clinch the treble by winning the Scottish Cup at Parkhead made it even more special.

'We beat Aberdeen in both cup finals that season – and for the title – but there were no mixed feelings for me. I am a winner and wanted to win every single game I played in. It probably spurred me on even more because it was my old club. In fact, just imagine how I would have felt had my old club stopped us from winning the treble!

'If I'm being completely honest, it was quite tough to walk the streets of my home town after we won the league. I'm pretty sure my popularity dropped in Aberdeen after that.'

Robertson was part of a 1990s 'Iron Curtain'-type defence at Rangers, and played alongside the likes of Richard Gough, Dave McPherson and Bomber Brown regularly in defence. He admitted he found it easy to strike up a bond with these guys.

He said, 'They were great to play with and made my job a lot easier. They were all top level players and we developed a good understanding with one another. I genuinely feel that when you sign for Rangers, it's a club like no other. You instantly become a supporter and feel what the supporters are feeling and, in turn, give even more as you don't want to let them down.

'And I feel we did exactly that as Rangers had the best defensive record in the league during season 1992/93. We were hard to score against, but I think a lot of that was down to Andy Goram. He was without doubt the best goalkeeper I have played with. He was loud but we always knew if a team got in behind us he would save the day: Andy was an incredible keeper.'

Robertson won six league titles in his six seasons at Ibrox, which was beyond even his wildest dreams. He said, 'I went to Rangers to win honours, but six titles was unbelievable and was far more than even I expected. At the time you don't fully appreciate it, and it wasn't until I was moving home and started to pack up all my medals that I realised just how fortunate I was and what I had achieved during my time at Ibrox.

'Throughout my career I have accumulated six championships, four Scottish Cups and four League Cups. I also have a few runners-up medals, although I don't really count them!'

In his time at Ibrox, Robbo admitted he never once fell foul of the much-respected management team. He admitted, 'Walter Smith was first class and looked after me really well. He even made me feel I was better than I actually was. Mind you, he once had a go at me when we lost to Hibs in the League Cup, but I suppose once in six years wasn't too bad.

'I look back on my time at Rangers and realise how lucky I was to be a part of such a great era, and something so special. Like I said, at the time you don't take it all in, but when you look back it's hard to believe that a lad from Aberdeen was part of something so special.'

Following his success at Rangers and Leeds United, the Scotland international had a short spell at Montrose before taking over the managerial reins at Elgin City. He returned to Links Park to manage the Gable Endies in 2006 before moving to the US, where he ran a youth soccer club for a number of years and was also technical academy director at a club in Austin, Texas called Lonestar.

In January 2017, he took over as manager of Indian Second Division side Real Kashmir.

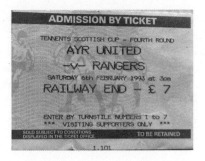

15

Gers are Top of the Hit Parade!

FEBRUARY started off with Rangers supporters down in the dumps when it was revealed that Ally McCoist and Mark Hateley wouldn't be going head-to-head with pop star Cher and supermodel Cindy Crawford in the wrestling ring! Instead, the quartet were ready to fight it out to see who would end the month at the top of the video charts.

McCoist and Hateley were just two of the stars of *Battle of Britain – Rule Britannia* and the video – which told the story of Rangers' stunning European Cup win over Leeds – was on course to become the first ever number one football video. But Cher, with her second fitness video, and top model Cindy, who was also breaking into the keep-fit market, were the biggest threat to the Ibrox stars.

'We're looking at the *Battle of Britain* as a possible number one,' said John Williams of producers Cameron/Williams. 'Rangers' last video, *Four in a Row*, sold well in excess of 25,000 copies. In fact, when it was released last May it was the top-selling sports video for over two months and was only pipped for the number one position by Cher's first keep-fit tape.

'No other football video has ever done as well as that before and in terms of sales, Rangers are easily the best of all the clubs in

Britain. We hope this video will do even better, but we face tough competition for the number one spot. Mind you, there is absolutely no reason why we can't achieve our goal because Rangers videos are definitely in the same league as Cher and Cindy Crawford.'

As well as action from the games at Ibrox and Elland Road, the hour-long video, with English commentary, was narrated by Scotsport's Jim White and featured exclusive interviews with the Rangers management team and most of the players involved in both matches.

Meanwhile, Pittodrie Stadium became the latest playground for the Andy Goram School of Goalkeeping Excellence as Rangers extended their lead at the top of the Premier League to seven points over Aberdeen with a game in hand.

Mark Hateley was on target just before the hour mark with a trademark header – and then Goram took over and showed just why he was the best in the UK. Rangers' number one produced a performance that left Dons boss Willie Miller gasping, both in frustration and admiration.

Goram pulled off stunning saves from Mixu Paatelainen, Scott Booth and Eoin Jess – and that was just in the first half. After the break, it was Goram's opposite number, Theo Snelders, who was called into action twice in a few minutes as Alexei Mikhailichenko went close, but it was Goram who took centre stage again late on as he defied Jess from a free kick.

We might only have been in February but Rangers' nine-point advantage over the Dons (assuming they won their game in hand) looked pretty much unassailable, especially as third-placed Hearts were 12 points behind, having played three games more. It would take a collapse of gargantuan proportions for Rangers to miss out on a fifth successive title.

Next up for the Light Blues was a Scottish Cup trip down the coast to meet Ayr United at Somerset Park – and a 'warm' welcome awaited from an old favourite. Just a few months before the tie, Bobby Russell was a football has-been whose career had been cruelly ended by injury. But a brief taste of Irish League action with Coleraine convinced the former Ranger he still had plenty to offer.

Russell said, 'Like all players who are forced out of the game through injury, the thought of a big-time comeback has never been far from my mind.

'And I could hardly ask for a bigger stage than a Scottish Cup tie against Rangers.

'This is Ayr United's big chance to grab a slice of glory and we are all determined to give it our best shot. Rangers have all the star name players and, on paper, it should be no contest – but when was the last time a football match was played on paper?'

The cut and thrust of Scottish Cup drama was a million miles away from the future – or lack of it – which stared Russell in the face in the summer of 1992. A troublesome knee injury convinced the silky midfielder, who won three Scottish Cup badges in his ten seasons at Ibrox, that it was time to hang up his boots – then former Motherwell team-mate Colin O'Neill convinced him otherwise.

Russell said, 'After leaving Rangers I spent five good years at Motherwell, but the knee was playing up. I was freed last summer and joined up with Jimmy Nicholl at Raith Rovers, but I didn't think my knee could take all the stresses of pre-season training so I decided to call it a day. But Coleraine manager Colin O'Neill talked me into making a comeback, and once I got a few games under my belt I felt fine. Unfortunately Colin and Coleraine parted company and I was out of the game.

'But now Ayr United have given me a chance to get back into the big time and I intend to grab it with both hands. I don't think I've looked forward to a game more than this week's match against Rangers. Believe me, Bobby Russell is alive and well and ready for the battle!'

The veteran midfielder was right – and he was wrong, because Ayr offered stubborn resistance for the entire 90 minutes and only goals by McCoist and Dale Gordon saw the Light Blues take their place in the draw for the quarter-finals.

Stuart McCall was a deserving man of the match, but his opposite number Russell showed that he had lost none of his dazzling skills, although maybe it was just age that caught up with the hero of Rangers' 3-2 win over PSV Eindhoven in Holland in 1978. Fifteen years on, though, and Russell had enjoyed his last shot at the big time.

One man who was overjoyed, though, was winger Gordon, who bagged his first goal in six months. It was his third of the season but he hadn't scored since August, and he said, 'I was well pleased with my goal but it was long overdue. Although I scored two earlier on in the season I wasn't playing as regularly as I am now, so it has been a bit of a drought.

'Over the years I've managed my fair share of goals. My main target, first and foremost, is always to get into the team, but once

I'm there and if I get the chance, it's nice to score on a regular basis. In saying that, I think I have quite a high ratio of creating chances for others, so that is pleasing.'

One of the main beneficiaries of Gordon's creativity was Ally McCoist, who bagged his 39th of the season at Somerset Park, but while he acknowledged the creative talents of those around him, he had a special word of praise for the man known simply as 'The Goalie'.

Coisty said, 'The whole team is taking so much confidence from Andy's displays. He has been outstanding this season and his performances are inspiring the rest of the team as we know it will take something special to beat him while he's in such great form.

'And we reckon if he keeps a clean sheet we will always have a fair chance of winning because we will get a goal somewhere along the line.'

And Goram clocked up shut-out number 19 in his 39th appearance by putting the blockers on a Falkirk side who had just knocked Celtic out of the Scottish Cup. That win saw the Brockville men applauded on to the Ibrox pitch before the match – before being ruthlessly taken apart by a rampant Rangers side.

The Light Blues welcomed back Richard Gough and Oleg Kuznetsov, and just over 34,000 fans watched Mark Hateley score his 19th and 20th goals of the season to add to strikes by David Robertson, Trevor Steven and Pieter Huistra. But one man who tried everything to get on the scoresheet was just out of luck, and his evening was probably best summed up at the end when Goram took off his shirt and handed it to Coisty before saying, 'You'd be better off between the sticks!' For once, Super Ally was speechless.

A couple of days later, though, Rangers welcomed bottom-of-the-table Airdrie to Govan, and even though Coisty was back on target with a double and Rangers extended their unbeaten run to 36 games, it was largely an afternoon to forget.

A point dropped in a 2-2 draw and the loss of captain Richard Gough to injury – where he joined Stuart McCall and Davie McPherson on the treatment table – saw the majority of the 40,000 crowd trundle out of the ground at full-time with a scowl on their faces. Despite scoring twice, McCoist also wore a post-match scowl due to two goals being ruled out for offside and another goalbound effort having been cleared off the line.

Archie Knox summed up the mood in the camp by saying, 'There was a slackness about us and we weren't as bright and eager as we were against Falkirk.' Still, the gap at the top between Rangers and Aberdeen was nine points, with both sides having played 28 games.

But there was a major boost for everyone at Ibrox when Ian Durrant skipped back through the front door, and straight into training before declaring, 'I'm raring to go again!'

The talented midfielder had been on a sunshine break in Florida on the orders of boss Walter Smith, who wanted him fighting fit to give the Light Blues a final push towards end-of-season glory. Rangers were still in with a great chance of landing the domestic treble and the Champions League.

Durrant's form had shaded at the turn of the year and he also had the added pressure of his court action against former Aberdeen player Neil Simpson hanging over him. However, his claim was settled out of court and he was back from the USA desperate to concentrate on the title run-in.

He said, 'The break gave me the ideal opportunity to recharge my batteries for the months ahead. After Christmas I felt a wee bit jaded, especially playing on the heavy pitches. The gaffer has known me a long time and he obviously spotted something, so he came and spoke to me about the break as an opportunity to get my mental attitude together.

'He has been really good to me and his idea came as a welcome surprise. I was only too happy to accept his offer and now I'm feeling fantastic. I've never done anything like this before, but hopefully it will work and I can come back and reproduce the form I was showing at the start of the season.'

Durrant headed for Orlando before the cup tie against Ayr United, and although he took in some of the tourist attractions it wasn't all sun and games. He explained, 'The break was great, but I also kept myself ticking over. I did a bit of jogging, other wee bits of training, and watched what I was eating. I generally looked after myself.'

And he joked, 'I also went to Disney World, but I thought I was seeing things as this giant mouse kept following me about!' The midfield ace was back to his old self and ready to play his part again.

But while Durrant's return was good news for Rangers it was bad for their rivals, as was Hateley's decision to sign a one-year extension to his contract. Even though Hateley had celebrated his 31st birthday in November, he was playing some of the best football of his career and had formed the most lethal partnership in British football with McCoist.

And he was hoping to finish his playing career in style at Ibrox. He said, 'I've got two more seasons left after this one, so hopefully by the end of the week it will be three. All the financial details have been ironed out and the club and Walter Smith seem happy. For me, it's just a case of signing on the dotted line.

'Obviously big strikers are at a premium, but I had no intention of leaving anyway. I just want to stay at Rangers and hopefully we can prove that we aren't only the best team in Britain this season, but also the best in Europe.'

Even though the globe-trotting Hateley family had spent the past decade in places as diverse as Portsmouth, Milan and Monaco, they had held on to the family 'home' in Nottingham, the town where Mark and his wife Bev grew up. But they were set to sell up and put down roots just outside Glasgow.

Hateley said, 'We love it in Glasgow and I can't see us moving away from the area. The house in Nottingham was our base for about ten years when we were abroad, but it's being sold and we will settle up in Scotland.

'And even when my career is over, I would love to be involved with the club in some way. I love the place and the people. But I've got a few more seasons left in me. Strikers don't mature until they're 35 anyway,' he joked.

Rangers number two Archie Knox insisted there would be no issues between his side and Dundee United ahead of the club's potential powderkeg fixture at Tannadice. The two sides were due to meet for the first time since a war of words erupted over the Duncan Ferguson transfer saga, but Knox said, 'What has been said previously will have no bearing on the match. Our sole purpose is to go there and get two points.'

The Light Blues had a number of injury worries going into the game with Gough, McCall, McCoist, Goram, Ian Ferguson and Davie McPherson all carrying a variety of knocks – and even manager Walter Smith was an injury doubt. The gaffer had just had stitches removed after an appendix operation but was expected to be back at his old Tannadice stomping ground for the tough fixture.

Meanwhile, thousands of copies of the new Rangers video, *Battle of Britain – Rule Britannia*, was delivered to stores nationwide at the beginning of February – and promptly sold out within a couple of days. High street stores struggled to keep up with demand and Rangers promised new stock would be available as soon as possible. Cher and Cindy Crawford were looking over their shoulders!

And so they should have been because the video went straight into the charts at number ten, while it was third in the sport and fitness section. It was on course to do even better than the *Four in a Row* and *Super Ally* videos.

Naturally, the video was on sale in the club shop, but supporters were asked not to worry that the store was about to close – because a newer, brighter and bigger branch was set to open next door on Edmiston Drive. And as a mark of how modern the store – three times the size of the one it was replacing – would be, the Royal Bank of Scotland asked if it could fit one of their new Cashline machines into the wall. The times they were a-changing!

And there was further good news when UEFA overturned its earlier decision to play the Bruges v Rangers Champions League tie behind closed doors. Instead, the Belgians were fined £100,000 and Marseille £17,000 and both warned as to their future conduct.

Operations chief Alistair Hood said, 'There will be the tightest security for fans in recent times because the authorities in Belgium are hyper-sensitive in the aftermath of the Heysel tragedy in 1985 and in light of the crowd trouble in Marseille.

'This match has always been regarded as a high risk tie by UEFA, but after the events in Marseille the emphasis on security is now even greater. For example, Rangers fans must carry their passports at all times, even to the match, and even if they have other identification to hand. Each Rangers fan travelling through the recognised tour operators will also be issued with a supporters' introductory card and this too must be carried at all times.'

Twenty-three coaches chartered through Parks of Hamilton were set to leave Scotland for the game, and four official flights arranged through Dixon Travel, made up the 2,500 tickets allocated to the Rangers fans in the Olympic Stadion.

Back to the domestic scene and Rangers maintained their incredible unbeaten record with a 0-0 draw at Tannadice, but supporters leaving the renamed 'windy city' would have been forgiven for feeling a little cheated as the entertainment value was zilch. Sub-zero conditions, made far worse by gales blowing in from the River Tay, meant good football was at a premium, and the result was the first 0-0 scoreline since a visit to Easter Road on 8 August. One downside was the booking picked up by skipper Gough which ruled the central defender out of the next two games.

And with the third of six Champions League ties looming, against Bruges in Belgium, gaffer Walter Smith warned his players not to look too far ahead – and to focus only on picking up two points in their next game, against Hearts at Ibrox. Only then would he turn his attention to Europe.

He said, 'With the number of high-profile fixtures we're facing it would be easy for players and coaches alike to let their minds stray from the job in hand. However, there's no way we can afford to take our eye off the ball. We have a good points cushion in the league, but that could disappear if we show any complacency.

'Football managers take a great deal of criticism from some sections of the media for mentioning terms such as "one game at a time", but that's what will carry us through. When you're involved in football you realise that's the only philosophy you can adopt.

'No one at Ibrox is under any illusions about the difficult games that lie ahead and we know we'll have to work as hard as we did in the early part of the season. We handled it then and hopefully we can handle it now.'

Meanwhile, Andy Goram spoke of how he owed much of his success to the coaching methods of goalkeeping guru Alan Hodgkinson – but revealed how an initial session with the revered coach almost sounded the end of their working relationship. In 1985, Goram walked into the office of Oldham boss Joe Royle and told him he couldn't stand working with the new goalkeeping coach.

Royle told Goram to give it a couple of weeks, and The Goalie took one of the best pieces of advice he had ever been given, even saying, 'If it wasn't for Alan Hodgkinson I wouldn't be at Rangers today!'

Hodgkinson had helped Goram collect more clean sheets than any other top-class British goalkeeper during 1992/93 and helped transform him into one of the leading stoppers in the world. Their relationship was as solid as Goram's recent displays, and built on a mutual respect which had grown despite those early days at Boundary Park when Goram, then a raw 20-year-old, was nicknamed a 'goalkeeping hooligan' by former Sheffield United man Hodgkinson.

Goram recalled, 'Hodgy was probably right in that description because I used to kick the balls away in frustration at training and he would send me straight off to fetch them again. However, it's not the spell you go through, but how you come through it which defines you and Alan gave me good technical ability at a young age which set me up for the rest of my career.

'I'll admit I couldn't stand working with him at first and I went to Joe Royle and told him so. I couldn't grasp what Hodgy was trying to get across to me. A lot of his exercises were new to me, I found them difficult and didn't enjoy them, and when I didn't enjoy them and didn't want to do them I found myself in a vicious circle.

'Thankfully I took Joe's advice and stuck it out for a couple of weeks and began to grasp what he was putting across. He taught me a lot and I have so much to thank him for.'

Goram was forced to call upon all his experience when Rangers made the short trip to Fir Park on league duty. With just 30 seconds on the clock, former Ibrox star Davie Cooper let fly and Goram tipped his rocket shot over the bar. Moments later, Ally Graham looked set to score from a shot before Goram sprung into action and pushed the effort on to the post.

It looked as though Rangers would again have to settle for a 0-0 draw, until a final 15 minutes that even the most imaginative Hollywood scriptwriter might have struggled to come up with. In fact, anyone who had slinked off early to the pub would have categorically refused to believe that Rangers won 4-0, but late goals by McCoist, Hateley (2) and Mikhailichenko had supporters wondering what all the fuss had been about.

Four days later, Hearts proved resilient midweek opponents at Ibrox, but first-half strikes by McCoist and David Robertson saw them edge this contest 2-1. The win helped open up an 11-point gap on Aberdeen – and sent Rangers off to prepare for Champions League duty in fine spirits.

DALE Gordon was born just 20 miles from Norwich, in the small seaside resort of Caister – a hop, skip and jump up the coast from its better-known neighbour, Great Yarmouth. The promising young winger made his senior debut for Norwich City when he was just 17 and would go on to play more than 200 times for the Carrow Road outfit.

A successful seven-year spell with the Canaries alerted a whole host of big-name suitors, and Rangers were among those with an interest in prising 24-year-old Gordon from the comfy confines of his Norfolk home.

Walter Smith made his intentions clear to Norwich and was invited to meet the player in London, a moment in his career that Gordon recalls with great fondness. He said, 'If I'm being totally honest, when I first heard about the proposed move, and travelled down to London, I didn't really know too much about Walter Smith. I knew Graeme Souness had gone to Liverpool, and taken Mark Walters with him, and I was bought primarily as a replacement for Wally, if you're making comparisons.

'My first impressions of Walter were that he was a charming man; a lovely fellow. There was no pretence about him, he was just very down to earth. As a manager, and I've always said this to people throughout my career, that of all the managers I've played under, Walter was the best man manager out there, without a doubt. He knew how to manage players properly, and he was very approachable.

'The gaffer would have no problems with you knocking on his door to talk about football or non-related football matters. His door was always open: he was a top, top manager. His knowledge of

Glasgow Rangers was incredible and I wouldn't be surprised if he was at the club in some sort of capacity for life.'

It's no over-exaggeration to say that 1992/93 remains arguably one of the most successful seasons, if not the most successful, in Rangers' history, but were the players aware at the time of just how good the team was?

Gordon answered, 'When I first joined the club, we had a squad the likes of which I had never come across in my career, with regards to the quality that was there. I had come from a small club like Norwich City, and even though we had a decent side, there weren't any what we would term superstars in that group of players, and we all knew that we had a solid base of 14 players.

'It was at Rangers that I first experienced squad rotation, which you obviously see much more in the game these days, so to have a group of perhaps 23 or 24 players travelling to every home and away game, with the quality of player that we had, was incredible.

'And we had all the different nationalities, with the likes of Oleg Kuznetsov and Alexei Mikhailichenko, Peter Huistra, myself and then all the home-grown boys. It was an incredible time and a fantastic season, but there was a great team spirit at Rangers and every one of the lads also wanted to play for the supporters, who were really passionate.

'One of the most important magical ingredients was the management team. They were also incredible, and it wasn't just all about Walter Smith. We also had Archie Knox, Walter's assistant, and while Walter would be the teacup-throwing boss, he didn't have to do it too many times because we used to win just about every week. Mind you, if there was a time when we let our standards drop, Walter would let us know and Archie would back him up, as would the other coach, Davie Dodds, so we had a great backroom team.'

But while the Ibrox dressing room was packed full of winners, and the management team instilled a winning mentality within their players, Gordon reckoned they had a potent weapon in the stands and on the terracing – the club's passionate supporters.

He explained, 'One of the things I liked about playing for Rangers was the level of support we received – home and away. Normally you go to a ground and the home support vastly outnumbers the travelling fans, but that wasn't the case with Rangers, it was quite often the other way round.

'Naturally that meant there was a high level of expectancy each week, and because the size of our squad was so big, the pressure to perform week in, week out was even greater. There were probably only three or four players who would be on the gaffer's team sheet every week, and Walter was fantastic at knowing when to rest players.

'I remember we played Ayr United in the Scottish Cup away from home. I scored and had a really good game, but I was left out the following week, but it was just something you had to accept. It was one of those situations and there was no point in moping around. To be honest, it's more or less the type of thing that happens in the modern game all the time.'

But if squad rotation, and being in and out of the team was the downside, then winning trophies certainly made up for that as far as Gordon was concerned. He said, 'People questioned my move and why I went to Rangers, because just as I was signing, a late bid came in from Tottenham, but I had spoken to people like Robert Fleck, who had come down from Glasgow to Norwich, and he said to me, "Look, you've got to go, you cannot turn this opportunity down. They are one of the biggest clubs in Europe and regardless of the opposition, you want to win trophies, and want to be able to share those experiences with your family and grandchildren." I have grandchildren now, and there is nothing better than sharing my experiences with them, or having medals or memorabilia which show you lifting trophies.

'I consider myself incredibly fortunate that I was given the opportunity to go to such a magnificent club as Glasgow Rangers and be able to play in some unbelievable matches, not just domestically, but also in Europe, such as the Battle of Britain against Leeds United. Games like that were very special indeed.

'And then there were the Old Firm games. I played in five of these matches and didn't lose one, and that is the stuff of dreams. They were incredible, but it's your job. What a job though!

'These days, we see a lot of young kids playing for the likes of France and Portugal, but I made my debut for Norwich when I was 17, and it was against Liverpool. I wasn't told until a quarter to two that I was playing, just over an hour before kick-off. I didn't have any nerves, just adrenaline, but it's what you're paid to do and you just have to go out there and do your best.

'You tend to find that as players get older, some of them can't sustain a certain level of performance, but the older you get, certainly the wiser you get and perhaps a little bit of nerves creep in, so maybe people like Wayne Rooney find it hard to maintain a level that he wants, whereas the youngsters just play with so much freedom.

'Every individual differs with regards to the fear factor, but as long as you're performing to a certain standard you will be okay. But supporters aren't all that forgetful when it comes to players dropping those standards. They will let you know, and the expectations are far higher at the big clubs.

'Rangers fans expect you to win every match, and I think now that Rangers are back in the big time, they need Celtic and Celtic need Rangers. I think Celtic suffered when the likes of Rangers, Hearts and Hibs were out the top league, because when you play at a higher level it shows if you aren't being tested week in, week out.'

In 1992/93, Rangers had goal threats throughout the team, although no one got anywhere near the heights achieved by Ally McCoist, but Gordon – who appeared four times for the England under-21 side – loved playing alongside the man they called Super Ally.

He said, 'Ally has never been shy at coming forward to say he is very natural and talented, but you have to remember that it wasn't just about Mr McCoist, but about Mr Hateley as well and those two had such a great partnership that would have rivalled any in that era, not just in Scotland but all over Europe as well. They had such a telepathic understanding. Hateley would know exactly where Coisty was with his flick-ons, and vice versa.

'I think Coisty got 49 goals that season, and he will still be gutted that he didn't reach the magical target of 50. And he will also tell you that every single goal he scored he made for himself, and that it was nothing to do with the rest of us boys, but you expect that from Coisty. In all seriousness though, he was a good lad.

'The last time I spoke about Coisty was a while back, when I was away in Hong Kong with the Rangers Legends, and guys like Ian Durrant, John Brown and Gordon Durie were there. He was the manager of Rangers at the time but there were murmurs that it was going to be his last season. I felt that when he took the job on, he was on a hiding to nothing. We all know how it turned out and if he wants to get back on the management ladder, he will have to rebuild his reputation.'

Gordon reckons Coisty could have done with even a slice of the team spirit that the Class of '92/93 had in the dressing room. He said, 'The spirit we had that season was just insane. Even training was mad. I think the club had sold their training ground just before my arrival, so we would meet at Ibrox, change and then jump on a minibus and go to the West of Scotland Cricket Club and we would get the goals out, and then have a little piggy in the middle – we used to call it Toro at the time – like the youngest would be in, the oldest, the baldest person, which would be Mark Hateley, as he was going a little bit bald at the time, and we would do piggy in the middle for about 15 minutes, and then half an hour at five-a-sides, and that would be us done, but the spirit we had was just so great.

'Sometimes we would have a day off and would all go for a bit of lunch, somewhere away from the football club. We didn't really play golf a lot, but we did stay at many championship courses while on our travels, but it was all for relaxation and fostering a good team spirit as there were a lot of big games coming up both home and abroad. It was an incredible period, absolutely unbelievable.'

But of course where there is joy, there is often heartache, and that came in the shape of a somewhat dodgy exit from the Champions League, just as the final of the inaugural competition beckoned. Did that bring pride or frustration?

Gordon said, 'At that time, Marseille had a cracking side, and we had two really tough matches against them, but the standout memory for me from that campaign was the infamous Battle of Britain against Leeds United, which we won to get through to the group stages.

'Overall, it was a fantastic journey and if you look back on it, possibly with regards to Walter's team selections and starting XIs, perhaps he might have tweaked it a little bit, but we had such a good side and Europe is a different animal as we all know. There are so many times that teams have threatened to do well, not just within Scottish football, and fallen at the last hurdle. But it's just another long line of good memories of when we played in many great places around Europe. Sadly we came up just a little short.'

Gordon is adamant that the squad that season were worthy of the success that came their way. There is no way, he insists, that it was merely a case of the team overachieving.

He added, 'Everything we achieved that season was well and truly justified, and well-earned without a doubt, because to go through the season with the success we had, both domestically and in Europe, was such a tough thing to do. Don't get me wrong, you always need a little luck along the way, and most good teams get that. And you must remember that when we were playing at home, the opposition would always raise their game 300 per cent, but I like to believe that quality almost always shines through in the end.'

Most players have regrets from their career. Sometimes, it's that they perhaps stayed too long at the same club – but Gordon's was the exact opposite. He explained, 'I should have stayed at Rangers longer. I definitely jumped far too quickly. If I'm ever asked about any regrets in my career, that is certainly one of them.

'I remember getting an injury to my medial ligament in the lead-up to the end of the season, but I was coming along nicely and was ready in plenty of time for the Scottish Cup Final, but the gaffer left me out and plumped for Neil Murray instead. I won't pretend that I wasn't really upset, because I was. My family, including my mum and dad, had come up for the game, and I was that upset that I didn't even go to Celtic Park that day. I just travelled straight back down to Norfolk.

'I got over my disappointment during the summer and was back up the road for the start of pre-season training fully fit and with a real spring in my step. I spoke to the manager and he told me I was part of his plans. I was made up, but at that time West Ham had just been promoted to the Premier League, and they had shown a bit of interest in me in the previous years because every time I had played against them for Norwich I always seemed to do really well. And then there was the little thing that my wife's family were from Dagenham, in the East End of London, and they were all West Ham supporters.

'Anyway, Walter told me Rangers had received an offer from West Ham and asked if I wanted to go and speak to them. I said I would, and he said that he was expecting to see me at Heathrow Airport to meet up with the rest of the squad as they were flying out to the training camp in Italy. So I spoke to West Ham and financially they offered me a better deal than I was on at Rangers.

'My wife had just had our second son, and we'd spent a bit of time away from the family, so at that moment in time it just seemed the right thing to do, although with the benefit of hindsight, it wasn't. I wish I had stayed at Rangers. I had just finished the second year of a four-year contract, and that will remain a regret for me.

'I still have a soft spot for Rangers, absolutely, I really do. I'm based in Dubai now and Derek Whyte, the ex-Celtic player, organises Rangers v Celtic Legends games over here, which I've played in, and they're great. And let's just say I've still not lost an Old Firm game, which is always good! I take any opportunity I get to pull on the blue jersey. That's what the club still means to me.

'I recently spent two weeks back in the UK, and within 24 hours of getting back to Dubai, I got a phone call from The Goalie, and he said, "What are you up to?" I told him I'd just got back from the UK and he asked me if I wanted to play for Rangers in the Hong Kong Sevens. Of course I did, so I asked him when it was. "Tomorrow," came the reply. I called my boss and told him that I had to go to Hong Kong for a Rangers reunion. He understood, because he knows that when the opportunity arises to go on a trip with my former Rangers team-mates, I like to take it.

'I've also been asked back to Ibrox a couple of times for some hospitality work and you just feel like you have to do it. That's the lure of Rangers Football Club. I like to treat it as a thank you from me for them allowing me to play for their football club.

'Whenever there is a Sky Masters football competition coming up, you always get a letter from the Professional Footballers' Association asking what team you would prefer to represent, as most ex-players have played for a number of teams during their career, and I would always put Rangers as my first preference, because as well as representing the club, and seeing all the boys, it's always a great night out in Glasgow!'

Gordon is still involved in football, and is currently coaching kids in his adopted home of Dubai. He said, 'I was director of football at the IFA, the largest grass roots football academy in the United Arab Emirates, but even though I am no longer with them, I am still coaching youngsters. I've got three youth teams which I'm coaching, and I'm also involved in radio work. I cover the Premier League for Dubai Eyes, which is great.

'I used to do a lot of media work back home with Norwich City, and my family are all still living there. My girlfriend has an events company, so we're always looking at different angles, and different sporting events. It keeps me busy and out of trouble!

'I'm also setting up lots of little satellite coaching centres to save parents, who are driving around all week, the hassle of getting their kids to the centre. I want to make sure it's on their doorstep. The centres each take between six and eight children for an hour at a time. If they can't get to the training schools, we will take the schools to them.'

17

Huistra Grabs Euro Point In Bruges

WALTER Smith reckoned it would take another 'Leeds-style performance' to beat Bruges. However, prior to the crunch tie, a volley of Scottish Cup and league matches had taken its toll on personnel and as a result Richard Gough (hamstring) and Gary Stevens (foot) were ruled out, while Ian Durrant, Trevor Steven, Ian Ferguson and John Brown all fell into the 'doubtful' category.

The 'doubtful' players travelled with the squad and all would receive treatment up to the last minute. Drafted in as cover were Brian Reid, Steven Pressley and Lee Robertson, with Neil Murray retaining his place after the win over Hearts.

Smith said, 'I still think we can get a result, but it will need a similar standard of performance to the one we gave at Elland Road earlier this season if we are to achieve it.'

And on his injury roll-call, he added, 'We've had injuries throughout the season and handled it, so hopefully we can do so again. Whether we're forced to put the younger players in or not is hard to say at the moment, but players such as Steven and Neil have come into the side and shown they can handle the big European nights when they both played against Marseille.'

And Englishman Dale Gordon was in no mood for beating about the bush when the squad travelled to Belgium. He said, 'Let's get one thing straight about tonight's Champions League clash in Bruges. Even though some people reckon a draw would suit us, we're going out there to win the game. Marseille must fancy themselves to beat CSKA Moscow in the other game, so we have to take that attitude if we want to stay at the top of the mini-league with them.

'We have a lot of experience in Europe now and have been able to adapt to every type of game we have faced and I'm sure we will get the right result. We've had a long break since our great result against CSKA in Germany and that set us up domestically for a good run while Europe remained on the back burner.

'Looking at our situation just now, we have a good unbeaten record, have won the Skol Cup and are still going strong in the three other competitions. At the start of the season, we obviously wanted to do well in Europe and win the three domestic trophies and we are right on track to do just that.'

Meanwhile, Mark Hateley was looking for a repeat of the scoreline the last time he faced Bruges – for the striker was part of the Monaco side which hammered them 6-1 in Monte Carlo. The astonishing score was achieved in the European Cup second round in 1989, even though the French cracks lost the first leg.

Hateley said, 'We created several chances in Belgium, including a shot which hit the post, so that gave us hope for the second leg. Sure enough, we raced into a 6-0 lead within the first 25 minutes of the game. The thing I remember most about Bruges is that they were a very workmanlike side and I think they have always been set up like that.

'I've heard they may be without their two first-choice centre-backs, but we will wait and see. Regardless of their team selection, our approach will remain the same – we will try to win. We have to win both matches against Bruges if we are serious about getting to the final, and everyone at Rangers is thinking along those lines.'

But as CSKA Moscow prepared to face Marseille in the other tie, Russian attacker Oleg Sergeyev insisted he was using the game to put himself in the shop window for a potentially lucrative move to western Europe. He said, 'A move to a big club in the west is every Russian player's dream, and playing against a glamorous team like Marseille allows me to show I can hold my own in the big time. After the euphoria of our victory in Barcelona, we all feel down after losing to Bruges and Rangers, but we feel we can have a huge say in who wins our group.'

Never a truer word was spoken, Oleg!

The final word in the build-up went to Leeds United midfielder David Batty, who was tipping Rangers to go all the way to the final. The 24-year-old Yorkshireman handed the Gers a timely boost by saying, 'One of the worst things that has happened to me this season was missing our home leg against Rangers. I had a knee injury and was forced to watch from the stand. However, I feel on the sort of display Rangers gave in Leeds they can beat anyone.

'The strike force of Mark Hateley and Ally McCoist is very impressive – you only have to look at their scoring record to see what they can do. Mark would be one of the top strikers in the English Premier League – and Ally has scored twice as many as him!

'The midfield speaks for itself in that the forwards have been well fed and the defence plugged whenever needed. On the last line you have Andy Goram, who just gets better and better. He was outstanding at Elland Road.

'Putting things into perspective, we have lost only one league match at Elland Road in the past two years, so no one should underestimate what Rangers achieved at our place. I don't know why, but there seems to be a belief in British football that if a team is Italian, Spanish or German they must automatically be better than us. Yet British clubs dominated European football for a number of years – and we can again.

'I don't see why Rangers shouldn't go all the way to the final where they will probably meet AC Milan and I don't see why Marseille should stop Rangers getting there either. All Rangers have to do is play to their best and they can match anything Europe has to offer.'

To the game, and the Belgians made the best start – which was probably expected given that Rangers were without Gough, Stevens, Ferguson, Gordon and Steven – and strike duo Daniel Amokachi and Foeke Booy had chances, although Dave McPherson and Andy Goram were alert.

With 14 minutes on the clock, Bruges skipper Frankie van der Elst latched on to a Goram clearance on the edge of the box and let fly. The ball whizzed past Goram but came crashing back off the bar and bounced off Goram's foot and away to safety.

It was clear early on that Bruges weren't just around to make up the numbers. And just seconds before the half-time whistle, a poor

Mikhailichenko clearance landed at the feet of Tomasz Dziubinski, and the Pole slotted home via the post.

The Rangers players reappeared for the second half with a flea in their ear and a determination to prove they were good enough to take something from the tie. For the first 30 minutes of the second period they were virtually camped in the Bruges half and had no less than ten attempts on goal.

But when Alex Querter and Lorenzo Staelens failed to properly clear a Mikhailichenko corner, Stuart McCall sent the ball back across goal, McCoist wrong-footed the home defence with a neat dummy and Pieter Huistra popped up at the back post to drill a right-footed shot high into the net.

It was no more than Rangers deserved and it sent their fans – camped behind that goal – into scenes of delirium. Sadly they couldn't find a winner, despite heroic performances from McCall and John Brown, who were outstanding.

After the game, McCall said, 'It's a measure of this Rangers side that we felt only one emotion on the full-time whistle – disappointment. The mood in our dressing room was pretty subdued, but then the result came through from the Marseille–CSKA tie [the match, played in Berlin, ended 1-1, and Marseille coach Raymond Goethals slammed his players for being "sloppy"] and helped cheer us up a bit. Ironically, at half-time we would have settled for a draw against the Belgians, but we dominated the second half, and if we had scored two minutes after the break, when first Mark and then Pieter forced their keeper into great saves, we may well have pulled off a win.

'I must confess that my involvement in Pieter's equaliser could not be called a shot by any manner of means. I simply took a swipe across goal and fortunately Pieter was there to finish it off.'

Huistra was delighted to get on the scoresheet, even though he was playing in an alien position on the right wing. The naturally left-sided Dutchman's equaliser, with the leg he normally used just for standing on, capped a fine all-round performance.

Huistra said, 'Playing on the right is still a relatively new position for me. I know exactly where to go when I'm on the left, but being on the other side gives new options and I'm still finding out about them. I hadn't played there before I came to Rangers and in the beginning I felt a bit awkward, but I'm finding it more comfortable playing there when it's required. Getting the goal was a big bonus for me and the team.'

One man who wasn't so happy, though, was operations chief Alistair Hood, who condemned a Sunday newspaper report for suggesting a hooligan link between Bruges and Celtic. The article, printed the weekend before the Champions League match, claimed a rowdy element of Bruges fans also followed the fortunes of Celtic and wore replica jerseys of the Parkhead club.

The story puzzled Hood, who said, 'The piece implied there could be possible involvement between Rangers fans and a section of Bruges-based "Celtic thugs". No intelligence or information of the nature of the "Celtic thugs" came to the notice of the club in our extensive pre-match preparatory work on operations with Bruges club officials, police or British Embassy staff.

'I publicly denounce this type of defamatory article which does nothing for the name of football, irrespective of the clubs involved. Where the journalist obtained his material from, no one knows but himself.'

Hood was also annoyed that Rangers lost their 'clean sheet' of arrests when a Torquay-based fan was detained following an incident at a hotel after the match. It was the only arrest of the trip, contrary to various media reports.

He said, 'It's disappointing to have one arrest in Belgium after the last 14 European games passed off without any. However, everyone at the club was delighted with the outcome of this particular trip. I received a call from the British Embassy in Brussels the morning after the game offering their compliments for the behaviour of the Rangers fans and I would second that.'

However, one theory behind the good behaviour of the supporters was that they had endeared themselves to the head of matchday operations at Bruges. Andre Ally was a superintendent in the local police and perhaps he thought the Light Blue legions were singing his praises when they burst into a chorus of 'Super Ally, Super Ally!'

From the nervy atmosphere of a Champions League battle in Bruges to the tight confines of Gayfield Park – and the notorious winds blowing off the adjacent North Sea. That was the poser Rangers faced just three days later.

Arbroath away in the Scottish Cup was an entirely different proposition, but there was a game of football to be won, and Walter Smith's men approached the tie in their usual professional manner.

Just under 6,500 crammed into the coldest ground in Scottish football and were rewarded with an all-action cup tie, and the visiting supporters were able to cheer goals by Hateley, McCoist and Neil Murray, the latter of which earned the youngster the man-of-the-match award – and helped steer Rangers into the semi-finals.

Meanwhile, forgotten man Chris Vinnicombe was just about ready to shake off the three-month injury misery that had made him a prisoner in his own home. In December, the reserve team skipper had been laid low by the same ear infection which had sidelined former Rangers goalkeeper Chris Woods. Then, a number of weeks later, Vinnicombe underwent an operation in a Harley Street clinic to clear up a niggling groin strain that developed into a hernia. That problem departed and with his ear virus rapidly on the mend, the 22-year-old began full training with his team-mates, but he said, 'Without a doubt it has been the worst three months of my career.

'My problems began back in November when I was suspended for three matches. Then, after serving the ban, two matches I should have played in were cancelled due to the weather. That's when the ear infection took hold, and it came on very suddenly. I was sitting watching television at home one Sunday evening and when I went to get up everything went dizzy. The doc explained it was the same inner ear infection that kept Chris Woods out and the most frustrating thing is that there is NO treatment for it, so I couldn't even take an antibiotic to clear it up.

'Throughout December and January I couldn't train, play golf or even drive much because every time I stood up to do something, I felt the whole room shaking. The only cure is rest and that's why I've been confined to the house, sitting around watching telly. It's very frustrating.'

Hibs arrived at Ibrox on 13 March, desperate to end Rangers' long unbeaten record, and were doing a pretty good job until five minutes before half-time – when youngster David Hagen took it upon himself to get the party started with a stunning individual goal.

The 41,000 crowd were starting to grow a little restless when Ally McCoist flicked on a John Brown cross, the ball fell to 19-year-old Hagen and, to the astonishment of the crowd, he coolly knocked it over Joe Tortolano with his left boot, chested it down and beat keeper John Burridge with a cracking right-footed shot. Hagen seemed to take the adulation in his stride as he was mobbed by team-mates, but the talented teenager had a more plausible explanation. He said, 'I couldn't believe I'd scored. After the ball went in, my legs were like jelly. Coisty and the rest of the lads grabbed me and they were basically holding me up.

'The ball had just arrived at my feet and I didn't really know what I was going to do, but I tried to flick it over his head and, luckily, it bounced back into me. I took a swipe and it went in. All I was trying to do was make sure I hit the target and I was stunned when I realised the keeper wasn't going to get it.' Further goals by Mark Hateley and Ally McCoist made sure Hibs went home empty-handed.

Next up for the Light Blues was a midweek trip to McDiarmid Park, Perth, and it took a McCoist goal ten minutes from time to salvage a point after Paul Wright had given St Johnstone the lead seven minutes into the second half. Ian Durrant showed unbelievable vision to drive forward and when he spotted Saints keeper Andy Rhodes off his line, a delicate chip almost found the back of the net, but McCoist was on hand to pick up the scraps and make it 42 games unbeaten.

One familiar name had been missing from the last three of these unbeaten games; that of Andy Goram. With the Scotland keeper out injured, it meant a rare opportunity for stand-in Ally Maxwell and he grabbed it with both gloves.

Maxwell had lost just a single goal in the three games, and even that was a stunning strike by St Johnstone's Wright. The former Motherwell keeper was happy to speak about the matches against Arbroath, St Johnstone and Hibs, but the only topic which remained off limits was the 4-3 defeat at Dens Park earlier in the season – and the catalyst for Rangers' impressive unbeaten run.

He recalled, 'To be honest, that match is one I don't like thinking about. The hardest thing when you come to a club the size of Rangers is trying to get the fans on your side. They expect nothing but the best, and that's only right.

'That day it simply didn't come off for me, so there was always going to be one or two this time who thought, "The last time Maxwell played, we lost!" However, I tend to let that sort of talk fly over my head and concentrate on the job in hand, which is to keep the shutters up at the back.'

Maxwell's home debut against Hibs was only his fifth first-team appearance after a £300,000 move from Motherwell. However, he recognised that Goram had been outstanding all season and kept his place in the first team entirely on merit.

He said, 'It's unfortunate that Andy has been injured because he has been doing so well, but at the same time it has given me the chance to show what I can do and – touch wood – things have gone reasonably well. When you don't play for the first team for a while you do become a little nervous and edgy. You have everything to prove, especially after something like the Dundee game, which still preys on my mind. But I know I have the ability to do well for the first team when Andy is injured, so hopefully I can maintain a high level of performance when I'm in there.'

Meanwhile, Rangers' vice-chairman Donald Findlay received a blow in his bid to have UEFA's controversial three-foreigner rule scrapped. Findlay was forced to re-think his approach after the SFA's Executive Committee decided not to support the case.

Clubs were only allowed to play three foreigners in European matches – a rule Rangers were keen to change as they felt it was contrary to EEC free-market guidelines. But the SFA refused to back the case because, in a letter to the club, they said it would give rise to too many possible damaging consequences.

Findlay said, 'The letter from SFA chief executive Jim Farry wasn't any more specific than that. I have now asked them to consider going back to UEFA to find out whether they might increase the number of foreigners allowed to four. Preferably, this would be the number of players allowed on the pitch at one time, so more foreigners could be on the bench. I believe this will be discussed by the SFA on 21 March, and I got the impression they might be more enthusiastic about taking this policy forward to UEFA.'

Goram was back for the Champions League tie against Bruges at Ibrox – and the 42,371 fans present witnessed one of the most bizarre goals in European history. Not only that, but supporters went through a whole gamut of emotions before Polish referee Ryszard Wojoik sounded the full-time whistle.

The Light Blues had performed heroics many times in an incredible campaign but they saved one of their best displays for the visit of the Belgian champions. Having started the game without five key players – and with captain Richard Gough struggling for match fitness – Rangers were further hampered by the first-half sending-off of Mark Hateley. The big Englishman became the first Rangers player to receive a red card that season when Wojoik insisted Hateley had shoved Rudi Cossey. The pair had tangled a couple of times before, but when Hateley pushed his marker away from his throat in the 44th minute, the Belgian went down as though he had just been shot by a sniper.

Ian Durrant had opened the scoring just three minutes before the red card, but five minutes after the break Lorenzo Staelens equalised for Bruges. Despite this setback, the home crowd continued to roar on their favourites and they were rewarded 20 minutes from time. The ball appeared to be going nowhere as Trevor Steven was crowded out on the right touchline, but it fell to Scott Nisbet five or six yards outside the Bruges box, and he thumped it goalwards.

It immediately spun off Stephane van der Heyden and the high bounce inside the box caught out keeper Dany Verlinden, and by the time he was able to backtrack and retrieve the ball, he was three yards over the line and Rangers had grabbed another famous victory.

Afterwards, it was suggested that as Bruges' goalscoring favourite was called Foeke Booy, then Rangers should rename Scott Nisbet 'Flukey Boy!' Big Nissy was ten-man Gers' hero with a 'fortuitous' strike which took Walter Smith's men one step closer to an appearance in the Champions League Final.

It was Nissy's first goal of the season, and he said, 'I thoroughly enjoyed it. When Bruges equalised, I thought "here we go again" as we were down to ten men, but all credit to the lads and the fans for lifting us.

'I actually didn't see the ball bounce into the net. I remember seeing it break to me and the Bruges player running towards me. However, he pulled out of the tackle, but luckily left his foot in and the ball came off it. There were so many players in front of me I couldn't see where the ball landed, but once I saw the fans in the Copland Road stand jumping up and down, I had a fair idea.'

However, Nissy revealed how he knew he was going to score in the match. He explained, 'I phoned my wife Anna a couple of hours before the match and she said that I would score.'

But while Nissy was enjoying his moment as Rangers' goal hero, Goram was spending his time getting to grips with the long arm of the law. As soon as Durrant opened the scoring, Goram ran straight behind his goal and jumped into the arms of an on-duty policeman! He put it down to over-exuberance and said, 'I didn't give it a thought, but he seemed a bit shocked – probably at how heavy I was!

'I simply got carried away because everyone knew how important it was to beat Bruges and the implications of the victory. The match was similar to our other European ties this season, with a degree of controversy and a slice of luck going our way. But it's wrong to say that we're a lucky side. Take a look at our injury list. That isn't very lucky, is it?'

Nisbet's freak goal brought no sympathy from Andy for Dany Verlinden, who watched in agony as the ball spun wickedly before bouncing high over him and into the net. Goram said, 'I wasn't surprised when the ball went in because it was always going to take a bad bounce off the surface because it was so solid. Ally Maxwell and I discussed the goalmouths before the game and they were like chalk and cheese. The Copland End was hard, while the Broomloan was soggy.

'But I was pleased for big Nissy that the ball went in. He has been in an unfortunate position because he has been in and out of the team. To his credit he hasn't complained and simply gets on with it and it's the same with the rest of the lads. In fact, that has been one of the keys to our success.'

But while Rangers were celebrating the win over Bruges, Marseille were running riot against CSKA Moscow in the French port. Hat-trick hero Franck Sauzee led the rout but the 6-0 win left many raised eyebrows as CSKA didn't look the type of side who would lose six goals to any team.

And there was further bad news when Rangers' incredible 44-game unbeaten run came to an end – at the home of their great rivals. Goals by John Collins and Andy Payton had Celtic 2-0 ahead, but even though Mark Hateley pulled one back the Parkhead side held out. Celtic may have put the brakes on a phenomenal run, but the Light Blues remained seven points clear of second-placed Aberdeen.

Defender John Brown should have been celebrating the signing of a new two-year contract but in the wake of the defeat against Celtic, he admitted he spent the Saturday night drowning his sorrows.

He said, 'I would only have been demented staying in the house, so I went out for a few drinks with some of the boys. We are all disappointed the run is over. We didn't want to lose it to anyone – especially Celtic. However, we have achieved a lot this season and the squad is in no mood to be misguided by one result.

'We had a couple of days off after the match at Celtic Park and we have returned to training focussed and ready to go again. The next stage of matches is all we are interested in.'

And Brown laughed off newspaper speculation that he was about to turn down the chance of a new deal at Ibrox in favour of a move to English champions Leeds United.

He said, 'That was simply newspapers picking up on the fact I'm out of contract at the end of the season and looking for a story. But the speculation never bothered me because there was never any truth in it. I spoke to the gaffer and he said he wanted me to sign on again and I was happy to do so.

'At my previous clubs, there were times I didn't look forward to going in to training, but at Rangers it's something I really enjoy – especially the bacon rolls! Seriously, the banter among the lads is great and there are so many characters in the dressing room that it's a great place to be every day.'

It was important Rangers bounced back in style from their first defeat in seven months, and they did exactly that when Dundee visited Ibrox. Pieter Huistra and Ian Ferguson made a triumphant return from injury, while fit-again Richard Gough was rock solid in the heart of defence. Trevor Steven was a class apart on the right-hand side of midfield – but turbo-charged Stuart McCall stole the show with another high-octane performance.

His work rate, tackling and distribution were of the usual high standard and he wasn't content with just taking on the role of the provider – as witnessed when he all but threw Hateley out of the way to net Rangers' opener. Gough started the move with a pass down the inside-right channel to Dave McPherson, who clipped the ball over Dee keeper Paul Mathers for McCall to dive in and nod home from six yards.

Further goals from McCoist and Ferguson had the Light Blues on Easy Street and manager Walter Smith said, 'We hardly did any training last week and the effects of that showed in the first half because we took a while to get into our stride. However, we achieved far more after the break.' With Aberdeen also winning, the gap at the top remained at seven points.

Stuart McCall was exactly the type of guy who played for the jersey – quite literally. During the 1992/93 season the midfield terrier had worn seven different shirts, with only 1, 3, 5 and 11 eluding him. He said, 'I used to be a bit superstitious about it and always wore 4 or 8, but I don't mind now what number I wear. There are players who like certain numbers but I just take what's left!'

However, McCall reckoned 2 was luckiest, as all five of his goals that season had come while wearing it, and he added, 'I don't know why that is, but I scored the first time I ever wore it, then I scored again the following week – and I'll never forget my goal in the Skol Cup Final.

'Even on Saturday against Dundee, Archie [Knox] was winding me up and saying, "We want a goal from you so take the number 2 shirt!" So when I scored I turned to the dug-out and gave him the thumbs-up.

'From the team on Saturday, Fergie likes to wear 8, Trevor Steven's preference is 7, Bomber likes 6, Big Slim [Dave McPherson] 5, Goughie 4, David Robertson 3, obviously Coisty likes 9, big Mark [Hateley] 10 and Pieter 11, so 2 was the only shirt left!'

Although the shirt had brought McCall a lot of luck, it had also brought him some grief – from his mother. He said, 'My mum watches on the telly from England but tells me she doesn't like me in number 2, because she thinks I'm playing full-back, so I have to explain to her that the numbers don't matter.

'As for stand-in goalie, I don't know. I probably would get shoved in there if anything happened to Andy [Goram] during a game. I don't think we've actually got a designated outfield replacement at the moment. It was Nigel Spackman, although I think Fergie might have gone in as cover before. But I don't think it would be too much of a problem for me. The size of the gloves Andy wears, I think I could stop everything as they're huge,' he grinned.

Meanwhile, a storm in a European cup was brewing after Rangers were fined £8,000 by UEFA, following alleged minor incidents of crowd disorder during the Champions League group match in Bruges. Rangers decided to appeal the fine, but in the interim pleaded with ticketless fans not to travel to Marseille for the forthcoming Euro match.

The club had received just 1,000 tickets for the game – a match that would ultimately decide who would qualify for the Champions League Final – after the French champions reneged on their original offer of 4,000 briefs. Director Campbell Ogilvie said, 'The fine imposed by UEFA was for a couple of relatively minor incidents, one of which was that our fans were in the wrong end of the Olympic Stadion in Bruges. It's evident there are going to be strong repercussions by UEFA if our fans get into any problems in Marseille, especially if they are in the wrong end of the ground.

'We are in a vulnerable position. It only needs one incident, no matter how minor, and we will be in trouble. Those fans who may be tempted to go to Marseille outwith the auspices of the club would be acting irresponsibly. We would urge them most strongly not to.'

McCoist may have been used to shooting from the lip – but against Dundee he was too busy shooting from the hip. The on-form striker killed off the Tayside men with Rangers' second goal of the afternoon and his 50th of the season.

And Super Ally said, 'It was one of the spawniest I've ever scored as the ball bounced off my hip before crossing the line, but I was delighted to get it. The thought of sitting on 49 goals for a while wasn't too pleasing. I was on that total for a couple of weeks and after a while you begin to wonder and worry, so it was pleasing to reach 50 and get it out of the road.'

Rangers' greatest ever season was now McCoist's most successful campaign in terms of goals. He had scored 33 in the Premier League, eight in the Skol Cup, four in the Scottish Cup, two in Europe and three for Scotland.

He said, 'At the start of the season, I honestly didn't expect to score anywhere near 50 goals. I'm really proud to have done so, but we're now entering the most vital stage of our season and I just hope there are a few more left in me.'

But while Rangers were on the verge of unprecedented success, one young lad had been having a miserable time of it. Sandy Robertson had been forced to sit idle for five months after a groin injury spread into his stomach and caused major complications.

He said, 'It was a great feeling being able to train again after so long idle. It has been a nightmare season, especially with the way things have turned out at the club. There have been a lot of injuries in the first team and a lot of youngsters have been given a chance. And until I can get myself playing again, I will be behind these guys in the queue for places. Then it will be up to me to show the gaffer that I'm ready to come back into contention and that I'm worth a place.'

With just nine Premier League games remaining, Rangers had a golden opportunity to race nine points clear of title contenders Aberdeen when the sides met in a midweek clash – and they grabbed it with both hands. A jam-packed Ibrox saw goals by Ian Ferguson and McCoist all but clinch a fifth successive league crown, and when man of the match McCall received a crystal tankard after the match, some wag suggested, 'Champagne glasses might have been more appropriate!'

Of course, Smith refused to accept any talk of titles in his post-match press conference, but even the most sceptical of Rangers men must have secretly admitted it was done and dusted.

During a pulsating 90 minutes, Rangers proved exactly why they were champions-elect by displaying guts, determination, skill and lethal finishing – as well as a unique will to win that marked them down as champions. The clock was ticking.

NOT many folk leave Manchester United to work for Rangers, but that's exactly what Archie Knox did – and he didn't regret it one bit. Mind you, the timing could have been a little better as he left Old Trafford the week before the European Cup Winners' Cup Final against Barcelona in Rotterdam.

United went on to win the cup by beating the Catalan side 2-1 and Knox was in the crowd that night in the Feyenoord Stadium.

He recalled, 'It is probably the biggest decision I have ever been asked to make in my life. It was the week before the Cup Winners' Cup Final; talk about timing! I thought I might be able to stay on for that game but Rangers only had a couple of games to go in the league and David Murray and Walter [Smith] wanted me up there straight away so I had to go, and Alex [Ferguson] knew all about it so it was a decision that just had to be made.'

Knox admits that when Smith and Rangers came calling, it was a job offer that appealed instantly, especially as the duo had played together at Dundee United. 'I knew Walter very well,' said Knox. 'We'd been together at Tannadice and when Graeme Souness left Rangers, and Walter was asked to succeed him, he called and asked me to come to Ibrox. Obviously I had a good position at Old Trafford, but after looking at everything involved in the move I decided to go for it. I'm the same as everyone else, I have a mortgage and wife and kids, so that was basically one of the most important aspects.

'Getting the chance to work in Scotland again wasn't in itself an attraction. I had enjoyed working at Old Trafford, even though we'd had a tough start. I was there about five years and we went through the mill, but we were starting to make the breakthrough. We had won the FA Cup and lost in the final of the League Cup to Sheffield Wednesday, so it was starting to happen for us.

'Everything was in place. We had a good scouting network and some fabulous kids coming through; something Alex prided himself on. We had been working with the likes of Beckham, Butt, Scholes and the Nevilles, while Ryan Giggs had already made his debut for the first team, and had scored the goal in the semi-final of the League Cup at Elland Road.'

Knox added, 'Rangers and Man U are both massive clubs but at that time Rangers were top of their league, while Man United were just starting out on the journey to becoming the top team in England. When Alex and I went to Old Trafford, United were in relegation trouble, while in our first full season we finished second in the league to Liverpool.

'At the end of that campaign, Alex decided it was time for a number of players to move on. It was a sacrifice because for the next two seasons we finished down the table a bit, although his decision started to bear fruit when the younger guys began to make the breakthrough into the top team.

'So the timing of the move to Rangers was terrible but Alex was absolutely fine with it. We sorted everything out amicably. Mind you, it was horrible missing out on a European final. When we were at Aberdeen together we had beaten Real Madrid in the same competition, and this time we were up against another massive Spanish side. But I made sure I was at the game, although it was a bit strange being there as a supporter after working with the guys for five years. It was a strange feeling.'

European final out the way, it was down to work with Rangers, and the opportunity to snatch the league title on the last day of the season – with, ironically, Aberdeen the visitors. Knox said, 'My first full season at Rangers was '91/92, and we did the double, but my first game was at Fir Park against Motherwell – at the tail-end of the '90/91 campaign – and we lost 3-0, which meant everything was riding on the last game of the season against Aberdeen at Ibrox. We won 2-0, so it was quite a start to my new career.

'You could feel the tension about the place, and we had loads of injuries going into the Aberdeen game. Quite a few played that day that clearly weren't 100 per cent fit, Bomber Brown being one of them. He took injections to get through the game, but snapped his Achilles during the match, which was awful for him.

'Mind you, I'll never forget coming into Ibrox on the Monday morning after we had lost at Fir Park, and at the time we were getting the Club Deck built at the back of the main stand, so the place was full of workmen. I was walking into the stadium and there was a squad of workies doing concrete shuttering and one of them shouts to me, "Aye, you've made a big fucking difference, eh?" You can't beat that humour!

'The game against Aberdeen was a nerve-wracking experience. The Dons were our main challengers at the time, and Alex Smith and Jocky Scott were doing a fantastic job up there, but we got the goals at just the right times that afternoon and were crowned champions.'

Fast forward to 1992/93, which would ultimately be one of the greatest ever campaigns by a Rangers side, and only three new signings – Trevor Steven, Dave McPherson and Ally Maxwell – were brought in. Knox said, 'We didn't feel we needed too many players, but when we knew Trevor was available, we made our move. Getting a quality player like him in was fantastic, because we were only really after players that would improve us, and he fitted the bill. That signing was a big boost for the club.'

Rangers headed for the hills – the Tuscany hills of Il Ciocco – to prepare for the new season. Knox insisted it was the perfect destination, and added, 'We loved it there. Graeme had known it from his time with Sampdoria, hence the reason we were introduced to Il Ciocco. I was at Ibrox for seven years and we went there to prepare at the start of each season. We were away up in the mountains for a week, well out the way.

'There was nothing round about, unless you were travelling by car. So part of the appeal was that there were very few distractions, nowhere for the players to have a night out! Our routine was, up early in the morning and straight into the outdoor swimming pool, before having breakfast and off to train at 9am, which ensured we got a good session in before it got really warm. The boys would be in bed for 2pm for a rest before training started again at 5pm, and in between we just kept them out of the heat. There was definitely no sunbathing allowed!'

At the start of the season, Richard Gough was quoted as saying that Graeme Souness had made a lot of enemies with his abrasive style. Teams wanted to beat Rangers that wee bit more, but Smith and Knox attempted to reverse that psychology. Was it a conscous decision to do that? Knox answered, 'It was just the type of person Walter was. He wasn't the same as Graeme in that respect. Don't get me wrong, he would show his teeth at times, but you can't do that all the time. Walter had been there a number of years and went about his job in a calm manner. He knew the job inside out.'

It was also the season Ian Durrant made a successful comeback from the terrible injury he had suffered at Aberdeen some four years previous, and Knox was delighted to see the influential midfielder back in a Rangers jersey.

He said, 'We were never too worried about Ian at the start of that season because we went on the advice of our medical folk, and we had a good backroom team at Ibrox. Being that amount of time out the comeback was obviously a big thing for Durrant, but what a talent he was. If he hadn't suffered that injury he could have been one of the best.

'The injury probably reduced his playing career as well. He had such a wonderful football brain and great energy. He also had a knack of scoring in the big games, with the one in Marseille a prime example. I don't think there was a better home-grown forward-thinking midfielder around at the time. He would have been a regular international and gone the whole road. He would have been right up there.

'And what a fantastic guy to have in the dressing room. Durrant and McCoist were a great double act. The one good thing about that group, even with all the changes that were taking place and foreign players coming in, was that they all bonded so well. It was unbelievable. Sometimes you think the foreigners might not embrace what's going on at the club, but they did.

'Under Walter, all players had to wear a collar and tie. It was the Rangers way, our tradition, and they all bought into it. There was never a problem. Guys like Mikhailichenko and Kuznetsov, the whole lot of them, turned up every morning in collar and tie. It was a great tradition and it's sad to see it gone.'

During a lengthy career, Knox experienced all types of derby matches, most notably in Manchester and Liverpool, but insisted the Old Firm takes a bit of beating. He said, 'I've experienced a lot of Old Firm games and as far as I'm concerned there isn't another one like it. I've had experience of the Manchester and Liverpool derbies, and even the likes of Millwall and West Ham, which is a serious game, but they just can't compare with the Old Firm.

'Take for example the match where we clinched nine in a row at Celtic Park. When it looked like we were going to win the game, a member of our staff – who shall remain nameless – came to me and said, "Why don't we do a huddle at the end?" I told him to tell all the players, and he did. The next minute the players formed a huddle quite near the tunnel and we were getting pelted with everything, but it was well worth it.

'I remember walking out of the tunnel that day and saying to Walter, "I don't know how long I can survive this." The atmosphere was electric, and he turned to me and said, "Archie, I'm the same." I honestly thought my heart was going to come bursting through my jersey that day, that's how wound up I was. I bet if I'd had a heart rate monitor on me it would have been through the roof. A specialist would probably wonder how we got through the day without keeling over.'

It wasn't just the intensity of individual matches that presented a health risk but the volume of games the top sides like Rangers were asked to play in that season too. By the end of September, Knox had complained that there were far too many domestic matches. He recalled, 'There was one point where we had four games in a row, including Champions League games, and it culminated with an Old Firm match and a League Cup Final. The big games were coming thick and fast, but it was a situation we just had to manage. We watched how hard we were training the players and tried to manage it that way.'

But when Knox was around, there was always time for a laugh and a joke – and on one occasion a French TV crew were at the centre of the gag. He explained, 'When we played Marseille at Ibrox the crew came across to watch our preparations. This was apparently common in France but I had my doubts about it. We were heading up to Bellahouston Park for a light training session and I spotted them about to follow us, so I made sure I had a wee surprise in store for them.

'I quite often drove the minibus and as we travelled the short distance to Bellahouston, I primed the players. When we arrived, we set up the cones and the crew set up their camera. Then I brought a rugby ball from the minibus and the TV crew looked on in complete confusion as the players started to kick and throw it about like rugby players. It was the day before the game so we were doing very little anyway. We'd had a game at the weekend and it was just a case of getting out to stretch the legs.

'After that, we packed up and headed over to the Place Cafe on Paisley Road West. Sure enough, the crew were right at our backs, so I said to the lads, "Okay, let's go in here and relax. Order what you want." And they did. Some of the players ordered bacon rolls while wee Durranty got his usual cream soda and ice cream drink. The Place Cafe was tiny, so we were all crammed in and munching away and I looked round and there's the TV crew, watching us open-mouthed and probably thinking, "Is this how they prepare for Champions League football in Glasgow?" All the usual punters would be in the cafe and they would by laughing and joking with McCoist and Durranty and the boys would be incredibly relaxed. It was a great way to prepare for a big match!'

Knox was a spy in the camp when Leeds United played Stuttgart for the right to face Rangers in the second round of the European Cup. He said, 'I remember going to watch Leeds play Stuttgart in the round before we played them and I was staying in the same hotel as them. After they got through, I could tell by the way they were talking that they thought they were home and dry against us. "Rangers? We will beat them."

'To be fair, Leeds had a great team at that time, with players like McAllister, Cantona, Chapman, Batty and Speed, so they thought they were more or less through to the group stages. Of course, I used this as motivation to wind the boys up, and we would also use newspaper cuttings. I would pin them up on the dressing room wall to let the players see what Leeds were going to do to us. It might have been their manager that was quoted, or a player, or even the English press. The staff at the *Rangers News* and others were keeping an eye on the press down south for me.'

Knox added, 'I was seven years at Ibrox and in all that time we didn't have our own training ground to work on. We used the West of Scotland cricket ground at Jordanhill, although that was usually in poor condition. We also used the cricket ground at Titwood. When I was at Manchester United we trained every day at The Cliff, so it was a shock that Rangers didn't have a dedicated facility.

'Walter and Campbell Ogilvie had been searching high and low for a place of our own. When we were at Titwood, we obviously weren't allowed on the actual cricket green, so the maximum size of pitch I had to train the lads on was about 70 yards by 45 yards at best. You had to work with what you had, but we would have to change things around when you wanted to make a penalty box and practise certain things.

'When you think of the calibre of player we had at that time and they weren't even getting to train on a full-size pitch, and having to travel to and from Ibrox, perhaps soaked to the skin, while sitting in a minibus. It wasn't ideal. Training on Ibrox was a no-no. It wasn't in the best of condition at that time, and with all the games we played that season – and the reserves playing on it every other Saturday – it was never going to happen. The only time we ever trained on Ibrox was on the eve of a big European match, or a cup final, and we had a session on it on the day before, but it was a very rare occasion.

'I remember we were training up at Anniesland prior to the match against Leeds, when this guy sidled up alongside me, and said, "You won't know me Archie, but I'm Stuarty Daniels, Kinning Park Loyal," so I said hello. He continued, "I've been watching my *Match of the Day* videos and you'll need to tell the boys to keep an eye on that Eric Cantona, touch him in the penalty box and he goes down so easily. I don't wanna interfere but I thought I would let you know."

'So, we're down at Leeds for the second leg, mindful that there won't be any of our fans there, and the bus draws up outside Elland Road, and just as we're getting off, there's this guy getting really close to the bus door; Leeds tammy, scarf, top, the lot. As I started walking down the steps, he lifted up his Leeds top and there's the Rangers jersey underneath and he saluted me. It was Stuarty Daniels from the Kinning Park Loyal. It was incredible.

'After that match, I remember phoning up old George, the night watchman at Ibrox, and saying to him, "Great result, eh George, knocking Leeds United out of the European Cup on their own patch," and he replied, "Aye, good result Archie, but don't forget the big one's this Saturday!" That sort of brought me back down to earth a bit and reminded me we were playing Celtic at the weekend!

'George really came alive in the lead-up to Old Firm games. You would walk through the front door in the morning and he'd say, "Did you see that Celtic game the other day? That Bonner was dropping everything," and it would be a different player getting it every day. He was a massive Rangers fan.'

By October 1992 McCoist had collected five hat-tricks, but was he the greatest goalscorer Knox had ever worked with? 'One word sums up McCoist – phenomenal. You couldn't teach Ally how to score goals, it was a natural instinct. Some players you can help improve different areas of their game. I remember wee Jim McLean working with the likes of Davie Dodds and Paul Sturrock and he helped turn them into real players; international players, but that was manufactured. McCoist wasn't manufactured. That was just what McCoist did.

'Even when Maurice Johnston was there, and he and McCoist were in the same team, you could guarantee that when the ball came into the box the two of them would be going for it. Anything between the posts and McCoist was there. See this running out wide and in behind full-backs and stuff like that, it wasn't McCoist, but when it came to anything in and around the box, when there was a chance to get a shot away, he was on to it in a flash. You would always find him between the posts, and he just had this instinct to get into space. He was clinical, and was the exact same at training. He loved scoring goals no matter the setting.

'Without a shadow of a doubt he is one of the best finishers I ever worked with. In fact, I would go as far as to say I haven't seen anyone better than him. And not just that, but what a guy to have in the dressing room. McCoist and Durranty were a great double act.

'The dressing room is vital. We would have new players coming in like, say Mikhailichenko and Kuznetsov, among others, and it was a bit of a tradition that before they went in for a shower, they had to stand in the doorway with a cup of water on their head, and McCoist, Durranty and co. would be taking off their socks, rolling them up and trying to knock the cup of water off! And these players, who had played for all sorts of top teams, and were usually internationals, all did it and stood there until this cup of water had been knocked off their head!'

It was a mixture of work and play which combined to foster the type of team spirit that more often than not saw Rangers over the line if a match was going down to the wire. That, and a little light lunch, as Knox revealed: 'Quite often if we didn't have a midweek match, which was perhaps once a month, Richard Gough would say on a Monday, "Okay lads, we've got Wednesday off, so after training tomorrow we will all go to the Parmigiana Restaurant for lunch." We would get there about 2pm, just as most people were leaving after lunch. On one occasion, we went up as normal and all the players and coaching staff were there, nobody dodged it, and we were having some food and a few glasses of wine.

'There was a couple sitting in the corner, and we're all thinking, "When will they leave?" but, no, they sat there the whole time and, of course, the players were a bit more subdued than normal, although the occasional bread roll would still bump off the top of your head – normally thrown by McCoist or Durrant. Just as we were getting ready to leave, the couple in the corner also stood up to leave, which was sod's law, but they came over and said to me, "We have to say, that's the best afternoon's entertainment we've ever had."

'And it turned out they were psychologists from Glasgow University. One of them said, "We can well understand why you have a successful football team because the camaraderie among the players is second to none."'

Knox added, 'I think Walter and I soon realised we had a special group of players. Mind you, it had probably just carried on from the previous season. We had a great mix of experience and youth, and a shining example was Neil Murray, who I thought was our man of the match over in Bruges. What a performance he turned in that night. We were criticised for not having a youth policy at that time but when you look at the number of kids who played, or were in and around the first team squad, it was amazing. We had boys like Davie Hagen, John Morrow, Gary McSwegan, John Spencer, Lee Robertson, Sandy Robertson and Steven Pressley. The lads proved more than adequate back-up for the top players and when they came in they never once let us down. And quite a few of the lads were sold on for decent money. Our squad wasn't just packed full of big stars, which many would have you believe.

'We had been forced to make a lot of changes when the three-foreigner rule was introduced. That was the reason the likes of Chris Woods had to move on, but I remember the day we signed Stuart McCall from Everton and I met him to take him to the Parmigiana for lunch. We jumped in a taxi and the driver, noticing Stuart was with me, said, "Welcome to Rangers Stuart, let me stick on some cultural music to welcome you to Glasgow," and next minute the Rangers tunes were blaring out! Stuart was a great player for us. He was a proven international at the time, which was the level we were targeting. He slotted in nicely alongside the likes of Mikhailichenko in the midfield.'

After Rangers knocked Leeds out of Europe, Dale Gordon insisted the Light Blues were good enough to win the English Premier League. Given Knox's knowledge of both leagues, did he think it was a fair comment?

He said, 'Whether or not we could have won the championship I don't know, but we would definitely have held our own. We would have been up there so I think it was a fair comment for him to make.

'After home and away wins in both European Cup qualifying games, we were in against the very best. The qualifiers are always the hardest of the lot, when you think of ties in other years like

Vladikavkaz and Famagusta. These places were tough to go to. Once you got into the group stages you could relax a bit and give it a good go, but when you get to that stage there aren't any easy games. These teams were all champions of their respective countries and had absolutely earned the right to be there.

'The likes of Marseille had an excellent side. They had players such as Barthez, Boli, Mendy, Desailly and Pele. I went to see them play a French league game beforehand and they were a big, strong powerful team. I remember even with the national side, people would say, "Aye, the Scots will get stuck into them and they won't be able to handle it," but all that fell by the wayside and Marseille not only had the brains, but also the brawn. That year in the Champions League, there was no way we would overpower teams because they all had good, physical attributes.

'My overriding emotion at not reaching the Champions League Final has to be one of disappointment, which just shows exactly where we were as a club at that time. From the outset, you know that the winners of the two groups are going to the final, and we were still in with a chance until that last game. The thing that bothered me was the 6-0 win for Marseille over CSKA Moscow, because every other game in the group had been tight. It was really disappointing the way it all ended but there was nothing we could do about it.

'Just to get into the group stages was a great achievement, because getting through qualifying is tough. You could be up against a side from, say, Scandinavia, who are in the middle of their season, and it makes a difference because when you're introducing new players to the team it takes time for them to bed in, and for the management team to work out the best way of playing. It's different at home when you're up against Scottish teams, because you know more about them than you do the foreign sides, even though you watch them as often as possible in the run-up to the ties.'

Knox added, 'At that particular time, Rangers were easily on a par with Manchester United, and there was all the talk of Rangers and Celtic joining the English league, but I don't think it was ever going to happen, and I certainly don't think it will happen now.

'I was at the England v Scotland game at Wembley last November, and I stayed down for England's match against Spain. I then travelled down to the south coast, where I watched Brighton v Aston Villa and Southampton v Liverpool. The day we arrived at Southampton, Rangers' under-18s were there. Southampton flew them down and back. I also went to the Rangers v Dundee match and there was almost 50,000 there, so Rangers can rival all these teams in terms of fan base, but the English game is awash with money, and even the gulf between the likes of Brighton, who were top of the Championship, and Southampton and Liverpool, was phenomenal, frightening even. If you watch the likes of West Brom and Burnley, the gulf to the top teams is miles long. It's night and day. There is quite a gap between the game in Scotland and down south at the moment.'

But no one can ever take away the achievements of Rangers' Class of '93 when Walter and Archie's side became only the fifth in the history of the club to win a coveted treble. Knox said, 'I was never one for looking back at achievements or history. For all the time I was in the game, I don't really have any memorabilia, photographs or anything else. For me it was always about getting the job done in the here and now; I wasn't one to keep medals or programmes or whatever. I enjoyed it at the time and that was satisfaction enough for me. I know I was very fortunate to achieve what I did in my career, and I enjoyed working at some fantastic clubs.

'My favourite part of the job was working with the players day-to-day on the training pitch. But you know what, I can't remember ever having a day off at Rangers. The players had days off, but we would go in and have a heady-tennis competition in the dressing room for the staff and even the likes of John Greig would come and join in. Everyone was involved, including the groundsman and we loved it. It was never about them and us when we were at Ibrox. We had a really close-knit environment, and when Christmas came round we would take the staff out for lunch.

'It was the same under Alex Ferguson at Manchester United. The first thing we did was get to know everyone who worked at Old Trafford. It was never a case of just a nod in the passing. We would pass the time of day with folk and it made for a very pleasant working environment.

'Up here, it's a tradition that when the players go out for a pre-match warm-up, the managers get together for a cup of tea, and perhaps a glass of wine at the end of the game. It's the norm in Scotland but it wasn't down south. Mind you, Alex and I encouraged it at United. Some would come in but many of the foreigners didn't. Once the game was over they would be on their way.'

And finally, was the 1992/93 side up there with the club's best ever? 'It's always difficult to answer something like that because of different styles and different eras. When you look at the team which had Henderson, McMillan, Miller, Brand and Wilson, how do you compare that with others? That was a fantastic Rangers side but it's nigh-on impossible to compare them with some of the good modern sides we've had. It's a totally different style of football now and how they go about it. It was working-class boys that played football at that time, whereas nowadays it's completely different.

'When I played football, I was a joiner to trade, and then a surveyor, and your mates were the same. I got paid a fiver a week at Forfar, and £2 for a win, and you could identify with your pals who weren't playing football. Nowadays, supporters can't identify with footballers, because many of them are living in mansions and are millionaires. I saw a bit in the paper recently that a Premier League [in England] player was being paid an average of £5.77m a year. It's frightening. A lot of players are so detached from the fans now.

'In my day, I remember agreeing to attend a supporters' function in Dumfries. It was on a Saturday night and guess who we were playing that day? That's right, Aberdeen – away. So I had to take my car up and drive from Aberdeen to Dumfries afterwards, and then back up the road again. It's a different world now.'

CHAMPIONS LEAGUE

OLYMPIQUE DE MARSEILLE
GLASGOW RANGERS F.C.

MERCREDI 7 AVRIL 1993
STADE VELODROME DE MARSEILLE

TICKET N° 03797
POPULAIRE

Ce billet ne peut être repris, ni échangé, ni revendu. Pour les places numérotées, il ne sera valable qu'accompagné du titre de réservation de sa catégori

19

French Farce
Ends Euro Dream

DESPITE Rangers having played more than 50 competitive games since the beginning of the season, suddenly April was shaping up as the most important month of the campaign and it started off with a Scottish Cup semi-final against Hearts – at Celtic Park.

At stake was an opportunity to keep the treble dream alive, although the Edinburgh side were having a fine season and had been in the top four since August. With just 20 minutes remaining, and Hearts 1-0 up thanks to an Allan Preston header, hopes of only a fifth treble seemed distant – until former Tynecastle skipper Dave McPherson took the matter into his own hands and slammed home an equaliser from a Trevor Steven corner.

Big Mac's goal merely enforced the message that this Rangers side never gave up.

And never was that better illustrated than when John Brown headed a Nicky Walker clearance back into the Hearts box and Ally McCoist reacted quickest to beat both Alan McLaren and Walker to the ball before knocking it over the advancing keeper and into the net. Cue the trademark celebrations for a dramatic 75th-minute winner.

Afterwards, McPherson said, 'Without a doubt, the two results over the past week – against Hearts at the weekend and Aberdeen a few days earlier – have given everyone at Rangers a massive boost going into the deciding Champions League tie against Marseille.

'It has been difficult not to think about that match, despite having other important games to play, because when people are phoning constantly looking for tickets it's always going to be on your mind.

'But I think if the players were being honest they would say they would prefer to beat Marseille more than these other two results. It would be a great achievement to play in the European Cup Final, and I think the lads have a belief that we can do it.

'We've done very well in the Champions League sections so far and I think Marseille, in the back of their minds, have a fear of us, so the cup final is definitely in our sights. Of course, we're disappointed Mark Hateley can't play, but we've shown before that we can adapt to losing our big-name players when youngsters have come into the side and performed well.'

Hateley was gutted at missing out on the chance to clinch a final spot, but told his mates, 'You can maul Marseille without me!' He added, 'We have a really good chance of making the final, especially as we have such depth in goalscoring. Ally McCoist can grab goals no matter the opposition and we have other players capable of scoring too. Pieter Huistra has already netted a couple in Europe this season and Ian Ferguson struck our winner against CSKA. We can get goals from midfield and that will help Ally because he won't be under so much pressure to find the net.

'When you play domestic football you've got to look for your midfielders to score over 20 in total over a league campaign. But that's even more important at this level in Europe and I feel we have the kind of players who can score for us in the Velodrome.'

Hateley's initial anger at missing out on the big match had given way to disappointment in the intervening weeks, and he said, 'Naturally, missing out on both our remaining European matches is a kick in the teeth, but it's not the be all and end all. I've tried not to think about it recently, instead concentrating fully on the big games I could play in. For a week or so after the incident I was still quite emotional about it and did a lot of moping and moaning, but the anger eventually subsided.'

Hateley decided to get away from it all in the build-up and spent three days in Monte Carlo, where he had earlier played for three seasons with Monaco. But he insisted on making the short trip north to Marseille for the match.

He said, 'The gaffer suggested I get away for a few days to forget about football, but I'll be in the Velodrome with the missus willing the lads to do it. I'm confident we can and, if I'm selected, I'll be back for the final later next month.'

Many years after the match, a newspaper would claim Hateley said he was earlier offered cash to not play in France. He is quoted as saying, 'A friend of a friend got in touch via certain routes and basically asked me not to play. "It would be financially rewarding for you," he said, "not to play in the Marseille game."

'He was not an agent I knew, but another agent had given him my number. It was a French-speaking person, offering me large sums of money not to play. It points the finger at a person, or persons, working within that club not wanting me to play.'

Hateley refused the bribe, but went on to miss the Marseille game after his controversial red card in the match against Bruges, a decision he suspected may have been influenced somewhere along the line by a certain Marseille official.

He said, 'As soon as that [the red card] came out, the phone call came straight to the front of my mind again. At the time, I didn't know if it was a hoax or if it was real. I'm now convinced it was real because of what followed. It was a once-in-a-lifetime chance for Rangers to get to the final of the Champions League, so of course I felt cheated.'

Marseille would go on to win their domestic league that season but would be stripped of the title following match-fixing allegations against their former owner, Bernard Tapie. Many felt that after their 'shock' 6-0 win over CSKA Moscow they should face a similar investigation in the Champions League, but no charges were ever brought.

Trevor Steven was in bullish mood as the Rangers squad left Glasgow and seemed more qualified than most to offer his opinion on the match on everyone's lips. He said, 'With the spirit and determination in this squad, we have a great chance of beating Marseille.

'Every good team must have spirit and determination and we have more than our fair share at Ibrox.

'We've already used it in a positive sense to record some good wins in the Champions League section, and although Marseille will be a tough obstacle, we can use it again in the Velodrome.'

It was Steven's first visit to the southern French port since leaving at the start of the season, but he insisted he wouldn't exactly have a lump in his throat when he walked out on to the pitch. He said, 'I wouldn't say the game is going to be any more emotional for me than it will be for the rest of the lads because it hardly evokes great memories.'

'And although I've only ever played there as a home player, I should imagine the atmosphere will be quite intimidating, with flares and fans chanting constantly. It creates a tremendous atmosphere when it's full, but it's actually a very disappointing stadium when you see it empty.

'Some of the things about the stadium may be an eye-opener for our fans who are across there for the game – it certainly was for me when I first arrived – but you must remember there's a different footballing culture in France.'

Marseille might have been the de facto capital of the French Foreign Legion but it was Rangers who showed true fighting spirit to emerge from the intimidating Velodrome with a point, and with their Champions League Final hopes still intact. The Light Blues were led superbly by Richard Gough and fought as if their lives depended on getting something from the game, while on the other side of the field many of Marseille's top players went AWOL.

The hosts led 1-0 at the break thanks to a Franck Sauzee effort from a Rudi Voller cross but Rangers hit back and Dave McPherson went close with a header. Ally McCoist was then unlucky with an effort after Gough and McPherson had created havoc in the Marseille box.

Marseille were clearly at odds with Rangers' set-piece prowess and it began to look as though that would be the Light Blues' best chance of a goal. And so it proved seven minutes into the second half. A Steven corner found its way to Ian Durrant, lurking on the far side of the box, and he took aim before rifling the ball beyond keeper Fabien Barthez.

Marseille tried hard to regroup but having worked so hard to get back into the match, Rangers were in no mood to surrender. Not even the loss of David Robertson and Pieter Huistra – replaced by Neil Murray and Gary McSwegan – could break their resolve. Indeed, they might even have snatched victory themselves twice in the last ten minutes, during which time the tension was almost unbearable for both sets of fans, but McSwegan and McCoist failed to take either of the chances.

Still, it was a remarkable performance by a remarkable group of players.

The Rangers party arrived home to discover they had made a clean sweep of the Scottish Football Writers' Player of the Year awards. Andy Goram was named top player in Scotland, with team-mates McCoist, Hateley and Stuart McCall finishing second, third and fourth.

Goram, who was celebrating his 29th birthday, was only the fourth keeper to win the award, following in the footsteps of Ronnie Simpson, Alan Rough and Hamish McAlpine. He said, 'This is the first major honour I've ever won and I'm delighted. It came as a nice birthday surprise. They say goalkeepers reach their peak between 29 and 31, so I'm looking forward to another few successful seasons.

'It's also a nice change to finish in front of Ally McCoist for once. I was at the awards last year when he picked up the prize and finished his speech by saying, "See you all same time, same place, next year." This time, stuff him. He's going to be the one looking on while I do all the talking!'

Mind you, it was proving hard to keep McCoist away from the limelight and the club announced that the prolific striker would kick off his testimonial year with a glamour game against Newcastle United. Super Ally had just been granted a testimonial for his services to striking, which had seen him net 288 goals in 441 appearances since joining Rangers from Sunderland in June 1983 for £185,000.

The match against Kevin Keegan's side, who were likely to be promoted to the English Premier League, was sure to be boosted by a handful of big-money signings by Newcastle and was just one of several events planned by McCoist's testimonial committee.

It was estimated that the testimonial would land McCoist a £500,000 windfall, which would be the richest testimonial pot ever in British football. However, he was set to give away a large chunk of the cash to deserving charities.

Walter Smith said, 'Ally has been our top scorer every season since he joined the club and that is a remarkable feat. He is also consistent in what is the most difficult position to play. He was a Rangers supporter as a boy, he loves playing for the club and anyone who has followed his career since he moved to Rangers must appreciate his contribution. I certainly have in my seven years here.'

But McCoist had a rare off-day when Rangers lined up against Motherwell, hoping to extend their lead at the top of the table.

Tommy McL1ean's side had been incredibly disciplined for 86 minutes but left Ibrox with nothing to show for their efforts when Bomber Brown popped up to fire home from just six yards.

It was Brown's fourth goal of the season, and three had come against the Fir Park side, but it was enough to ensure Rangers grabbed a virtually unassailable ten-point lead in the Premier League – with just seven games remaining.

With the 1992/93 season starting to resemble the longest campaign in the history of football, Rangers director Campbell Ogilvie revealed that UEFA was looking into having similarly-sized leagues throughout Europe with no more than 34 matches to be played per season.

At that point the Scots were playing ten games more and it was a hectic campaign that had been heavily criticised by the likes of Smith and Gough. Scottish football was in turmoil, with proposal and counter-proposal being put forward for league reconstruction, which would cut the number of games being played by the top players.

Ogilvie said, 'At this stage, only proposals have been put in front of UEFA's Executive Committee and they will consider them over the next few weeks. However, I believe they would like a standardised league set-up throughout Europe, which would allow windows to be built into the fixture calendar for regular European club matches and international games.'

Back to the domestic action and the latest stage of a fascinating title race moved on to the capital, where Rangers faced Hearts at a stadium most teams feared visiting. Rangers struggled that evening but the fact they got over the line at all was down to an abundance of spirit as they were minus a number of top-team stars, most notably 50-goal man McCoist. McSwegan took his place and there were also starting berths for Stephen Watson, Neil Murray and Steven Pressley, while David Hagen was on the bench. A first-half goal by McCall and a double from Hateley secured a well-deserved win.

A couple of days later, Smith's babes were back in action, this time against Partick Thistle when half the starting outfield players had been drafted in from the reserves. And the young guns didn't let anyone down with McSwegan grabbing a double and Hagen the other in a 3-1 win that put the Light Blues just one victory from the title. McCoist was on the bench but didn't make an appearance.

There was no rest for the wicked and Coisty was back in the starting line-up for the crunch Champions League fixture against

CSKA Moscow at Ibrox. It was a huge match, arguably Rangers' biggest of a terrific campaign, although the Light Blues would have to hope that Bruges could inflict pain on Marseille while taking care of the Russians in Govan.

Goram insisted he was only interested in how Rangers performed and didn't want to know of what was going on in Belgium until he was back in the Ibrox dressing room. He said, 'Everyone is talking about Bruges beating Marseille, but we've got to concentrate on beating CSKA first, because if we don't we could be in for a shock. It won't be difficult to concentrate solely on events at Ibrox because the lads know their minds must be 100 per cent fixed on our own game. After all, there's no point in anyone celebrating a Bruges goal if we're losing at home to CSKA.'

Smith added, 'When I came to the club seven seasons ago there was talk each year about how we should be progressing in Europe and this is the first year I believe we've actually come up with the type of performances people would expect on the European stage.

'Regardless of whether or not we qualify for the final we've had an excellent campaign and I hope our fans would agree the standard of football and excitement has been high. The Champions League format has been a winner.'

He added, 'Since the game in Marseille, every one of our players has been looking forward to this match as it's one which won't come up too often in their careers. Our players are all experienced campaigners who have shown a tremendous will to win all season, which I'm sure will again come to the fore against CSKA.

'Rangers play in a lot of big matches, but if you can sit back and look coldly from the outside, there's very few times we will play in a bigger match than this.'

Sadly, at the end of a hard-fought 90 minutes, the game finished goalless and Ibrox announcer Bill Smith played the Whitney Houston track 'Didn't We Almost Have It All'. As a backdrop to the chart hit, Rangers fans applauded their favourites as they went on an impromptu lap of honour. It was perhaps a fitting piece of music in light of the 0-0 draw – the first time Rangers had failed to score at home all season – but the overriding emotion was one of great pride.

The supporters were proud of their team's efforts throughout a lengthy European campaign; ten matches and not a single defeat, a feat unequalled by a British side. The players, many of them reduced to tears, were grateful for the tremendous backing they had received both home and away, and at that moment, players and supporters were together as one; an unbreakable bond had been sealed. In fact, the fans' appreciation of their side's efforts led to some of the most emotional scenes ever witnessed at the old ground.

Within the first few minutes of the simultaneous ties taking place in Glasgow and Bruges, CSKA keeper Evgeni Plotnikov had made the first of many fine saves, while news filtered through from the continent that Marseille had scored. Not that the Rangers players knew that. The fans were subdued for all of 60 seconds and then they never stopped singing until Danish referee Peter Mikkelsen had signalled the end of the game.

The fact Marseille had won in Bruges made the Ibrox result insignificant in terms of qualifying for the final in Munich, but Rangers came up just short in their efforts to secure a win on the night, despite creating more chances than in any other Euro tie that season.

Immediately after the final whistle, John Brown vowed to repay the supporters for their incredible backing by securing the treble. Bomber, who threw his shirt into the East Enclosure while on a lap of honour, promised to put smiles back on faces and said, 'The fans gave us a big boost by staying behind after the final whistle. It was such an emotional night because we put so much into the tournament and they were with us every step of the way.

'Throughout the season they have been magnificent. They've followed us everywhere and forked out a lot of cash to watch us play. That's why I threw my jersey into the crowd. Rather than swap it with a CSKA player I thought I'd give it to the fans as a gesture to show how much their support is appreciated. We are all disappointed we couldn't give them a European final to look forward to, so we're hoping to clinch the title at Airdrie. That's all we are focussing on now.'

Meanwhile, more than 10,000 supporters were present at Ibrox to see a young Rangers side beat Celtic 1-0 to win the Glasgow Cup. Charlie Miller scored the only goal of the game and when skipper Mark Fraser lifted the cup aloft, the cheers from the Govan Stand were deafening.

Before Rangers' title tilt at Broomfield, Scotland were on international duty against Portugal at the home of Benfica. The Scots were losing 5-0 and cruising to one of the worst defeats in their history when disaster struck in the 83rd minute. A Portuguese defender tackled McCoist and he went down in a heap. Moments later he was carried off on a stretcher with a broken leg. His season had ended in the cruellest of ways.

ESPITE being born in the Yorkshire city of Leeds, Stuart McCall's footballing future was being mapped out 200 miles away in Hamilton. For his extended family were all Rangers daft and every time the flame-haired youngster ventured north to visit relatives, the short trip to Ibrox ensured a lifelong affinity with the Light Blues. So you can imagine the joy felt by McCall when he discovered he was high up on the shopping lists of both Graeme Souness and Walter Smith.

The combative midfielder said, 'My mum and dad were born in Hamilton and my dad was a football fan in general, but my cousins and relatives are all big Rangers supporters.

'Dad enjoyed a good football career and played with the likes of Stanley Matthews and Stan Mortensen during his time with Blackpool. He was an old-style inside-forward; the number ten position, and was left-footed. He also played for the likes of Leeds United and West Brom.

'I was brought up with football so when other kids were getting an Action Man for their Christmas, it was always a ball for me. My mum and dad knew exactly what I wanted and I would be out kicking that ball from dawn until dusk. I was mad about football and I'm sure it was in my genes.

'When I was about 20, and a kid at Bradford City, Alex Ferguson and Archie Knox came down to Valley Parade to watch me when they were in charge of Aberdeen, and Davie Hay came to see me when he was manager of Celtic – which was never going to happen! That was the only interest in me from Scotland at that stage of my career.

'I went to Everton four years later and had three great seasons at Goodison Park, and then came a call completely out of the blue, about a month before the end of my final year [the season Rangers beat Aberdeen 2-0 in the last game at Ibrox to win the league]. It was from a reporter and, believe it or not, he asked what school I had gone to, and with me being born and brought up in Leeds I thought, "What the f*** does he want to know that for?" And then he goes on, "Eh, up in Scotland, do you sway any way when it comes to football teams?" And I'm thinking, again, "What is this all about?"

'I told him that since I was a kid, and any time I was up in Scotland, and among family, I would always go to see Rangers with my cousins and uncles, and that we would go on the Rangers supporters' bus from Hamilton, and that if I couldn't get a ticket I would go to watch Accies, and that's when I found out he was tapping me up on behalf of Graeme Souness, who was manager of Rangers at the time. He said, "Would you be interested in a move to Ibrox at the end of the season?"

'Eh, absolutely. But then everything went quiet, and Graeme left Rangers with three games of the season remaining, and Walter took over. When the initial call had come, I was completely happy at Everton, and I certainly wasn't looking to get away, but it eventually gets inside your head. Then, when I hadn't heard anything for a while, I started to think, "Was that a hoax call?"

'The end of the season came, and went, and I was still at Everton, which was fine. But then the manager brought in Peter Beardsley, and I was quite excited about playing alongside him. Graeme Souness had taken over at Liverpool, and I didn't think much more about Rangers. I couldn't, so I started to prepare for the new season with Everton.

'To be honest, I think the Everton manager Howard Kendall was looking to get rid of a couple of lads that he could get some money for as he had brought in quite a few midfielders, not just Peter, so he was willing to let me go. And then I got a call from my agent saying that Rangers were interested and could I be on a flight up to Glasgow that evening. It was the deadline day for signing in time to play in Europe. I said to him, "Can I be on a flight tonight? I'll just run up to Ibrox right now!"

'My situation was this: I had one manager, Howard, who was willing to let me go, and another, Walter, who I knew very little about, I've got to say. But obviously I knew the history of Rangers and everything about the club. So, on one hand it was a call completely out of the blue. During the summer someone had got in touch to say that if Trevor Steven was to move, then Rangers would come in for me, because originally Trevor's move to Marseille had fallen through, which was obviously a stumbling block for me. That had led to me putting a potential move to Rangers out of my mind – for a second time!

'Now, with Rangers showing an interest again, it was a complete no-brainer for me. I got on a flight at Manchester and met David Murray at Edinburgh. We had a chat and I was whisked through to Glasgow, picked up by Archie Knox and taken for a medical, and signed in the nick of time before the deadline. Meanwhile, in David Murray's big office in Edinburgh, they were doing the deal to take Trevor to Marseille. Thankfully the move went through and that enabled me to sign for Rangers. I don't think I would have got there otherwise.'

It was the days of the three-foreigner rule and having played for Scotland, McCall ticked all the boxes necessary to be a home-grown player. He added, 'It was a complete whirlwind: from three months previously, when it looked as though it was on, then it was off, with Graeme Souness leaving, and then it was back on again, but then Trevor didn't go to France, so it was on, off and so on. I missed the pre-season friendlies, but had completed pre-season training with Everton, so I was all but ready to go. Thankfully we got the green light, and I got my move.

'Last word on it, though. The Everton supporters were absolutely magnificent with me, and I had nothing but good memories of my time there, but Rangers had always been my team. I always had Rangers scarves and jerseys, even though I also liked Leeds, as my dad had played for them and I was born and brought up there. Had I got up to Glasgow only to discover Marseille had pulled out of the deal for Trevor, I would have been absolutely gutted, but thankfully it all went through okay.'

McCall was desperate to get started and made his debut against St Johnstone at Ibrox as an Ally McCoist goal got the new season off to the perfect start – and it wasn't long before he was 'fully accepted' at Ibrox.

He explained, 'I used to go into the kitman Jimmy Bell's wee room in the stadium and he would have pictures up on the walls of Graeme Souness, Terry Butcher and Chris Woods. Ian Durrant was his favourite, but even Durranty was pushed into a corner when the big English boys came up. The likes of Mark Walters, Gary Stevens and Trevor Steven started taking pride of place, but when we won the Scottish Cup at the end of the season, I said to him, "Never mind all the English lads like Butcher and Woods, where is the photograph of our cup winning team? I'm up here two minutes and we've won the league and cup double and I can't even get a picture up on your wall."

'The next day I went in and there was a big framed picture of me, right in the middle of the wall, and next to wee Durranty, so I had obviously tugged on his heartstrings and that was the moment I thought to myself, "I've finally made it!" Not because Rangers had just won the Scottish Cup for the first time in about ten years, but because I had made it on to the wall of fame in Jimmy's kit room. That was arguably my biggest achievement during my time at Ibrox!

'Seriously, though, it was great, because we didn't get off to the best of starts; knocked out of Europe early, and bundled out of the League Cup by Hibs. If I remember correctly, we had three damaging defeats in a week. But we came good and finished off the season with the double.

'Mind you, the game against Airdrie in the Scottish Cup Final was really disappointing. It was a really flat afternoon. It was a massive occasion but not the greatest of games, which was a shame, but I suppose that's irrelevant now as the history books will show we won the cup, although it would have been nice to do it in style. Mind you, the only great cup finals are the ones that you win, that's what we all remember.

'I always said that our Scottish Cup semi-final win over Celtic at Hampden was the night Walter Smith's team was born. There had been a lot of question marks prior to that game about whether or not he was the right man for the job. He had brought in a lot of new players, but that night at the national stadium we were reduced to ten men after just six minutes, when Davie Robertson was sent off, and to show the spirit we did, in the driving rain, was simply incredible.

'Don't get me wrong, we were under the cosh for long periods of the game, but all you had to do was look round at the players we had in our team and you soon realised we had a bit of everything out there. We had spirit and desire, two of the main ingredients for success, we played as a team and we also had a lot of quality. I had previously played in teams that had quality, but if you haven't also got the desire and spirit, then the quality isn't worth an awful lot.

'When you look back at certain games, and even certain moments in games, they can define what happens in the future. Perhaps if we had lost that night, and Celtic had gained the upper hand on us, certainly psychologically, would we have gone on and achieved nine in a row? It's certainly up for debate.

'After that game at Hampden, I looked round our dressing room and it was crammed full of leaders, something which is a dying breed in our game these days. But if you can look round and realise you have seven or eight leaders in the one team, then you know you always have a chance. Allied with the staff at Rangers and our incredible support, it was a great place to be.'

McCall's seven-year tenure at Rangers is crammed full of highlights, but he insists the 44-game unbeaten run in 1992/93 is up there with the best of them. He said, 'When we went on that incredible run, we were behind in so many games but always managed to turn it around and more often than not we got the win. With people like McCoist and Hateley up front, you knew you had goals in the team and, just as important, the opposition knew that, and it gave us an extra edge. We had the strength, mentality and character, but we also had a huge goal threat.

'The 1992/93 season was incredible; there isn't an awful lot more I can say about it, it was just amazing. But funnily enough, one game that sticks in the mind is the one up at Dens Park when we lost 4-3 to Dundee. It was early in the season and was memorable because it was one of the few times Walter had a real go at the players. I remember travelling back down the road on the bus with Walter's words ringing in my ears.

'I was angry, but not because of the bollocking, our mentality was more about "how do we bounce back from this" or "we can't afford to play like that again". We were also mindful that if we wanted to win the league again, which naturally we did, then we wouldn't win it playing like we did against Dundee that afternoon, so we were sort of self-policing in that way. We knew we had to buck our ideas up.

'We did just that – and in some style. We went on our incredible unbeaten run and the likes of Ally McCoist was on fire. He was knocking them in week in, week out, and we were playing really good, attacking football and putting teams to bed. The times we had to come from behind was down to the mentality of the players, because when you know your dressing room is rammed with people who have a never-say-die attitude then that's half the battle. We were also masters at noticing a chink in the armour of our opponents, which was something we would ruthlessly expose and go for the jugular.'

McCall was anything but a prolific scorer although he will never forget his strike in the Skol Cup Final against Aberdeen, which was down to the fact he was switched on for the entire 90 minutes.

He said, 'I thoroughly enjoyed the League Cup Final that season, and I was delighted to get a goal – and it was all down to a wee bit of anticipation. The back-pass rule had just been introduced, and when Roy Aitken played it back to Theo Snelders he wasn't able to catch it, like the old way, but it came off his chest and I followed it in and put it through his legs, although I have to say I didn't shout "meg" at the time!

'I don't know what I was doing that far up the park, but as soon as the ball hit the net I ran to the Rangers fans behind the goal. It was a dream come true. I think I might have had a tenner on myself at 25/1 that day, so that would have been a nice little earner for me and my family!

'Mind you, a few years later, when Theo signed for Rangers, I would enjoy reminding him of it, and when we were training I would say, "Remember now, whatever you do Theo, keep your legs shut!"'

McCall added, 'I didn't miss many games that season but I remember near the beginning of the campaign having a sore throat, and thinking, "There is no way I'm missing a European match [Lyngby at home] because of a sore throat." The Rangers doctor came out to see me and diagnosed tonsillitis, and I told him I still wasn't missing the game. He gave me a wry smile. When I awoke the next morning my throat had closed up and I couldn't speak – but I still made myself available for selection! That was when the doctor intervened and told me I wasn't to come within a mile of Ibrox as I would spread it around the place, so I had to listen to him and I wasn't even allowed to go and watch it.'

With Lyngby safely despatched, the draw for the second round of the European Cup pitted Rangers with McCall's boyhood favourites, Leeds United. Surely not a conflict of interests? The popular Yorkshireman answered, 'I was happy with the draw because there was so much negativity towards Scottish football from down south and I thought this game was the perfect platform to show people that we could actually play football up in Glasgow.

'It also represented a hell of a challenge for me personally, because of the position I played. They had a real special four in midfield, with Gordon Strachan, Gary McAllister, David Batty and Gary Speed. When Leeds won the league, those four were seen as unstoppable. They had everything; skill, power, drive, energy, experience. So it was always going to be a huge test, although a bigger test arrived in the shape of tickets.

'There was a ban on away supporters for both games, and with me being born and brought up in Leeds, I had a lot of people who wanted to come and support me. Gary McAllister was in a similar situation to myself, only in role reversal, as his family were Rangers supporters, so we got Gary tickets and he came up trumps for us for the return match. Two of the tickets were for my brother-in-law and his mate, but unfortunately he couldn't sit quietly when we scored our second goal and he got kicked out!

'One thing that will live with me forever is the wall of noise that hit us when we walked out of the tunnel in the first leg at Ibrox. Forty-odd thousand Rangers fans created an incredible atmosphere, and I even spoke to Gordon Strachan and Gary McAllister in the tunnel about it, and they were relishing it, but they had a few lads in their team who had never heard anything like it and I think it put them on the back foot, so the idea was to get right at them and make full use of the crowd, but inside 60 seconds Gary Mac hit a peach of a volley and it went from bedlam to silence with a flash of his boot.

'It was as though someone had pulled the plug out of the juke box and the music had stopped. Mind you, by the time the ball was back on the centre circle, that wall of noise had returned and the fans were right with us again. That was magnificent and helped us so much.

'We went in 2-1 up at half-time and dominated the second half, which was magnificent, but it was quite flat when the full-time whistle sounded because we had created some good chances without finding a third goal, and I think our fans were disappointed. They probably thought our fine margin of victory wouldn't be enough to see us through.

'We were also disappointed, but with hindsight, going behind so early in the match and coming back to beat a top team 2-1 was a decent effort, and while we knew the second leg would be tough for us, we also knew it would be tough for them. But I think what helped spur us on was the interviews and press articles coming out down south. I had great respect for ex-Leeds players such as Eddie Gray, Billy Bremner and Peter Lorimer, but when they were being interviewed for the English papers, it wasn't really a case of who would win, but just how many Leeds would win by.

'And the day after the first leg, we had a journalist from *The Sun* saying that even though Leeds had lost 2-1, the return leg would be a walk in the park. Straight away, Archie Knox had it pinned up on our noticeboard.

'We stayed down in Leeds the night before the game, and had a training session at Elland Road. My dad didn't go to the game, as it would have been too much for him, but came along to watch us train and we were talking about some of the articles in the English press, which we both thought were a bit disrespectful. It would have been fine had the papers down there talked about Leeds winning, but it was a bit naughty the way they went on about embarrassing score lines.

'That definitely got our back up, so we were well up for the match that night, and when we walked out the dressing room and "Eye of the Tiger" was blaring out, we were ready to give them a game. We were talking in the dressing room beforehand about how Leeds had a good team, but also spoke about how we had the right type of characters for the job, as they were reliable and would have done anything for each other. One quick look and you would see Gough, Goram, Ferguson, Brown, Hateley, McCoist sitting beside you; everyone really. And then to get the start we did, with big Mark scoring after just three minutes, was a dream beginning for us.

'When we went 2-0 up, I was standing in front of the Kop, the terracing I'd stood on as a lad supporting United, and they were giving me a chorus of "United reject". I could picture the pals that I'd gone to the games with joining in with the abuse and so I put a couple of fingers up to remind them of the score, which they might actually have taken to mean something different!

'Eric Cantona got a goal back for Leeds but they still needed another three to knock us out, and found Andy Goram in unbelievable form, with Bomber clearing up everything he could. And I remember at the end of the game Andy being gutted that he'd lost a goal, so I reckon he must've had a wee bet on keeping a clean sheet! We had just won both legs of the Battle of Britain and Andy wasn't happy, but that's how much of a perfectionist he was.

'There were two things that stood out for me at the end of the game. The first was when the final whistle sounded and I looked at the terracing, there was a good percentage of Leeds fans still in the stadium and we did a small lap of honour and they were very gracious towards us in their applause. They were incredibly sporting and that's something I will never forget. They also gave their own players a round of applause as they had played very well and thrown absolutely everything at us.

'Secondly, the first person, outwith our own staff, to come into our dressing room to congratulate us was Sir Alex Ferguson. He went round every player and shook hands and said well done. He seemed so pleased with the score and proud of the team, obviously with his past Rangers connections, as well as his friendship with Walter and Archie. In fact it might even have been the first time him and Archie had spoken since Archie had left Manchester United to join Rangers.

'Probably the best part of the night was going back to Manchester, as we were flying back to Glasgow from there the next morning, where we met up with some of the guys from United's Class of '92 – Beckham, Scholes, etc – and they had arranged to get us into the VIP section of a top club – and if you are ever going to go to any city in the country after beating Leeds, it just has to be Manchester, as United and Leeds have arguably the biggest rivalry in the country. We were treated like kings; drinks all round, and it flowed all night.

'I recall chatting to this Man United fan; a decent bloke and we were enjoying a couple of beers when he decided to sing a Man United song. And then he said, in a nice manner, you might have beaten Leeds but we're a bigger club than Rangers and we have more songs than you, and we have better fans. I listened for a wee while and then started to stick up for my team and have a proper debate. And then I told him that we definitely had better songs than his lot, and he looked at me and said, "Like what?" So I sang him one. He then sang another Man United song and then it was my turn again, and we did this until we had exhausted the songbooks of both clubs, and he finally said, "Fair enough, you f*****' won the singing!" It was hilarious, and a great night in general.

'But it was eventually time to head back to the hotel and I think I was rooming with Dale Gordon. It was about three or four in the morning, and even though I knew I'd had a few drinks, I struggled to work out how I couldn't get into my room. And then I realised it was because there were bodies stacked up against the door. When I eventually got in, there was the whole of Bomber's family, all of Durranty's mates and god knows how many other people in there. There were bodies slumped everywhere.

'The beds had long been taken but there wasn't even any room on the floor, so I went back down to the hotel foyer where the bold Davie Dodds was sitting with a king-sized cigar and a bottle of ice-cold champagne and a beer. I said to him, "Doddsie, you look as though you could do with a bit of company." I sat down, we chatted, we drank and I must've fallen asleep. Next thing I know it's 7.30am and the lift door opens with a loud "ping" and out walks Walter Smith, looking immaculate in his suit and ready to catch the flight up the road.

'My eyes were barely open and I didn't have a clue where I was. I looked over and there was Doddsie, slumped on his chair, beer spilt all over him and looking a proper picture. Walter looked at me, then looked at Doddsie, then back at me. I said, "Morning gaffer!" He said, "F*****' morning? Come on, we're f*****' leaving in an hour. And more importantly, we've got a huge game on Saturday, and this is Thursday." I looked at him again and answered, "It's okay gaffer, it's only Celtic!"

'We got up the road and the gaffer had us in on Friday for some light training, and then we walked over to our usual wee cafe on Paisley Road West. The Saturday game had a 12.30pm kick-off and I reckon we were still filled with booze when we took to the pitch at Celtic Park. But we were ready for the game as we always were, although we were under the cosh for large parts, and I thought to myself, "I can't believe I said to the gaffer that it was only Celtic, they are absolutely pummelling us!"

'Once again, Goram was brilliant and wee Durranty popped up with the only goal of the game to give us another precious two points. We had a bit of luck that day, but I'm also a firm believer that you make your own luck, especially when you're throwing your body in front of everything and defending for your life. We came off the pitch knowing that victory was all about our spirit – perhaps even the spirits that were still in us from the Wednesday!

'But I was just so proud to be involved with such a special group of players, staff and supporters and that afternoon at Celtic Park epitomised just how strong we all were together. It was a great time to be at Ibrox and playing for the team you supported: it didn't get any better.'

Celtic would get revenge of sorts the next time the sides met at Parkhead – but McCall remembered how he and his team-mates received a standing ovation at the end of that one. He said, 'That game ended our amazing 44-game unbeaten run but our supporters realised what a great achievement it had been and stood as one at the end to cheer us off the park. We were gutted, but that applause really lifted us and, of course, we were a load of points in front of Celtic anyway so it didn't have a bearing on the destination of the title.'

McCall was also disappointed to see such a great European run end in disappointment, although he insisted it was still a fantastic campaign to be involved in, despite ending on something of a sour note due to the controversy surrounding Marseille. He said, 'Of course there will always be frustration there, but when you look back at how we came back from 2-0 down against Marseille, a real top side, and also losing to Bruges but finding a way to win the game, then these are definitely positive memories. We should also have won in Belgium, but one of the best memories of that Champions League run is the atmosphere our fans created game after game. It was unbelievable.

'But I'll also remember the final whistle going in our last match of the campaign, a 0-0 draw at home to CSKA Moscow, and looking at the reactions of their players and thinking, "Have they just won the Champions League?" I had never ever seen a team, with nothing to play for, celebrate a 0-0 draw the way they did. They had also lost 6-0 to Marseille, so we were all thinking it was a bit strange. But after that game we walked round the track at Ibrox to say thanks to the supporters for the backing they had given us and I think we were both very proud of what we had achieved together.

'We all know that we carried a wee bit of luck during the European campaign, like Nissy's goal, but we needed that because we didn't have the outstanding individual players of AC Milan and Marseille, but we had a collective spirit that was hard to beat. I know Walter later had world-class individuals such as Paul Gascoigne and Brian Laudrup, but would find it difficult to fit them into his team-building plans and still keep the tight defensive and midfield units that he liked.

'And perhaps when supporters are reminiscing about the nine in a row era, they will automatically think of guys such as Gazza, Laudrup and Albertz, but the most successful season out of nine in a row was definitely 1992/93. We went into games never contemplating losing; the thought never entered our heads. And if we lost a goal, we rolled up our sleeves and got stuck in, that was the way we approached things.

'Celtic were going through a transitional period at the time so Aberdeen were our main challengers. They were tough opponents but for any supporter, if you can go and clinch a treble at the home of your rivals, it doesn't get any better, so we were delighted to win the Scottish Cup at Parkhead.

'We were only the fifth ever Rangers team to win the treble, but one of the things I remember most is the following season when we could have repeated the feat. Back-to-back trebles would have been incredible. We had won the League Cup and league, and got to the Scottish Cup Final where we lost 1-0 to Dundee United. It was so flat that day, and when you look back and think we missed out on becoming the first ever double treble winners, it was very disappointing. But that's one of the few negatives from that period.'

Despite having a career spanning an incredible 23 years, McCall is in no doubt as to his most successful season in the game – although there are a couple which run 1992/93 pretty close. He said, 'I suppose 1992/93 must go down as the most successful season of my career. It has to when you come out of it with big trophies. I won two promotions during my time with Bradford City, and they were really special, especially as we got them into the Premier League and that was something no one could ever have predicted. It was the first time in 70-odd years that the club had been there, so that was special.

'I then went to Sheffield United as a 38-year-old, played over 40 games in the Championship and got to the semi-finals of the FA Cup, where we lost 1-0 to Arsenal. We also got to the semi-finals of the League Cup, where we played Liverpool. We beat them 2-1 at home, and lost 2-0 after extra time at Anfield, and we also lost in the play-off final. I believe that goes down as one of Sheffield United's best ever seasons and I was proud to play a part in it, especially as people thought I'd just moved to United to wind down and retire.

'I've been really lucky to have played for four great clubs in my career, but the 1992/93 season certainly eclipses everything I achieved elsewhere, and even during my six other seasons at Ibrox.'

McCall concluded, 'Rangers have been through such a ropey time of it these last few years so I just hope the memories we managed to make 25 years ago provide a grain of comfort. I remember when I moved back up to Scotland to manage Motherwell, and we were in the process of moving into our new house, and my wife asked me to go through six or seven of my boxes of "things" and I said, "No problem, I'll only be a couple of hours."

'Two weeks later, I was still sorting it out, because every time I came across a DVD I would be sticking it on and saying, "Oh, I remember that game against Bruges," etc. And you know what, if you're ever at a low point, there is no better cure than sticking on a tape and having a "those were the days" moment.

'It's great to have memories, but this was something a little bit more than that, it was friendships, or bonds, and I used to love going round the supporters' clubs – sometimes three a night – in the days before social media when players could visit their supporters' clubs, and I became great friends with many supporters as a result.

'It was just a great time to be a Rangers player or supporter. It was a magnificent campaign and one I will never forget.'

21

McSwegan Seals Title Glory

SATURDAY, 1 May was the day of reckoning and Rangers knew victory at Broomfield would seal the Premier League crown, regardless of how Aberdeen fared in their match. Almost 12,000 packed into Airdrie's ground – the majority decked out in red, white and blue – and, as expected, the Light Blues certainly didn't have things all their own way, but when Gary McSwegan scored just a couple of minutes after the break, the terraces came alive.

Aberdeen were losing but Bears knew the only way they could be sure of a fifth successive title was for their favourites to take care of business, and when the full-time whistle blew, McSwegan's strike remained the only goal of the game. The Maryhill man's fifth of the season meant the celebrations could start in earnest – with the noise reaching fever pitch when the players returned to the park for a well-deserved lap of honour.

Ally McCoist had missed the game through injury but his team-mates ensured their buddy didn't miss out on the celebrations – and they had a little help from two supporters who had taken along a life-size cardboard cut-out of Coisty. When the players asked if they could take 'Ally' on the lap of honour, the supporters duly obliged.

Fan George Allen, from Kirkintilloch, said, 'We know Ally is a real Bluenose and that he would be sick at missing out, so we thought the cut-out was the next best thing. We chipped in with a couple of pals and bought it from the Rangers Shop the day before the game and we were delighted with the reaction we received from the crowd and the players.

'Andy Goram spotted it first when the ball went out for a corner near where we were standing and he burst out laughing. Then, on the lap of honour, big Davie McPherson asked for it to be passed down to the front through the crowd.

'Unfortunately, after the celebrations, Ally is now lying in the back of my car in a bit of a state, but we've decided to clean him up in time for the Scottish Cup Final.'

Meanwhile, it was announced that Richard Gough would be presented with the championship trophy before the match against Dundee United, the only remaining home game – and Walter Smith paid tribute to the players who helped set a new post-war club record of five successive titles. Only the great Rangers side of 1927–31 had matched that achievement.

Smith insisted that losing just twice in 40 league matches surpassed even his expectations. He added, 'At the start of the league campaign I reckoned on us losing just one league match in each quarter of the season, yet only Dundee and Celtic have beaten us. That's a remarkable achievement and the players deserve full credit for the work they've put in.'

And the bad news for the rest of the Premier League was that Smith expected his side to be even stronger the following season. He admitted he was in the hunt for a top-class striker to take the weight off Mark Hateley and McCoist – as well as a few other tweaks here and there.

Apart from a few remaining – and all but meaningless – league fixtures, all eyes were now focussed on winning the treble, and if Smith's men could see off Aberdeen in the Scottish Cup Final at Celtic Park, they would be the first Rangers side since 1978 to achieve such a feat.

Gough revealed how he had been asked if Rangers were bored with winning the championship, and his reply, 'I tell them I want to be as bored as this for the next FIVE seasons.' And that was no random figure plucked glibly from the air, because another five titles would see Rangers eclipse rivals Celtic's great achievement of winning nine successive titles. The halfway stage had been reached, and it was beginning to form as a viable thought in the minds of many Gers supporters.

But Gough was also worried about complacency – and rustiness – setting in before the cup final. He explained, 'I recall my season at Spurs in 1987 when we reached the FA Cup Final against Coventry. We had a match scheduled for the Monday night before the final and our manager David Pleat asked who wanted to play. Not many did, to avoid injury which would have kept them out of the final. However, the end result was that many of our players went into that final not having played a match for a fortnight and it definitely had an effect on us as we lost 3-2.'

Stuart McCall, on the other hand, shocked everyone when he revealed that the 1992/93 season wasn't his most successful in the game. He grinned, 'I think I had a better year when I was playing for my under-nine team and I scored 60 goals in one season!'

It was McCall's second successive championship badge and he added, 'Seriously, it has been a phenomenal season and I have enjoyed every single moment of it. There are always ups and downs in football and you've got to make the most of the ups when they come.'

It was becoming harder and harder to get to see Rangers in action – especially at Ibrox, as the waiting list for season tickets for the 1993/94 campaign soared to 3,500. The success of the team in getting so far in Europe – and still in the hunt for the domestic treble – meant interest in the club was at a modern high.

But despite Rangers' increasing popularity, supporters still didn't know what type of league set-up they would be watching the following season. The club was set to back plans for a radical shake-up of Scottish football, which would see four leagues of ten introduced for the start of the 1994/95 campaign. The proposal was set to go to a vote at the Scottish League's AGM. Ibrox director Campbell Ogilvie revealed the club's intention to go with the new shape, with two teams coming into the Scottish League, probably from the East of Scotland and Highland Leagues.

But he stressed the principles endorsed by the Scottish Super League would still apply if the new set-up were given the go-ahead. He added, 'The major clubs are together in our support of the 4x10 set-up and it's a proposal which is gathering momentum, but the number of teams in the league is only one of many important factors to be considered.

'If the 4x10 set-up is approved, the next stage is to make sure the League Management Committee take on the responsibility of improving stadia, facilities, standards of play and the structure of youth football. We must stand firm on that, but we won't be hard and fast on bringing in criteria.

'For example, next season it looks as if the 12-12-14 system will still be in place and that will give us a good platform to push the criteria into effect. However, we will also be realistic and fair to clubs promoted into the Premier League. Government guidelines give five years to get stadia up to scratch once promotion to the top division has been achieved, so clubs have plenty of time to measure up.'

As is often the case, the game immediately after the title-clinching win at Airdrie proved to be a damp squib. Rangers rolled up at Firhill for a midweek match against Partick Thistle – and promptly lost 3-0. As defeats go, it was up there with the most disappointing, and the least said the better.

But better times lay ahead and when Dundee United visited Ibrox the following Saturday, the atmosphere inside the stadium was electric. Mind you, after the 90 minutes was over, and the supporters were still buzzing, it wasn't because of the contest they had just witnessed. No, the fans were there to see the Premier League trophy being handed over to Richard Gough, something that was becoming an annual ritual on Edmiston Drive. The stadium was packed and the Light Blues had managed to preserve their unbeaten home record thanks to a deflected Pieter Huistra effort – and then the party started.

It was Rangers' 61st game of the season and, as Walter Smith said, it was no time to start out on a winless run, especially with the Scottish Cup Final looming. He added, 'Even though we have won the championship, the last thing we want is to start getting into a habit of losing. The cup final is at the end of the month and we are all looking forward to that, but there is business to take care of before that. And after losing at Firhill, getting a win was more important than a good performance.'

Midfield ace Ian Ferguson was delighted to get his hands on the trophy and said, 'What a fantastic afternoon. We wrote ourselves into the history books and joined the Ibrox elite. I am very proud to be involved with the current team, who will go into the history books as only the second team since the great days of the '20s and '30s to win five titles in a row.

'Those famous sides featured players such as Alan Morton and Bob McPhail and it's a huge honour to go down alongside great names like that. Winning the championship was a good feeling. I've now picked up five medals on the trot, but to me this latest one is every bit as special as the first.

'You never know what lies ahead – next season or beyond – so it's important to enjoy it while you can. From my own perspective, it's fantastic because compared to the last two or three seasons, this one has been amazing. On Saturday, I started my 40th match of the season, which I think is greater than my appearances from the previous two years put together. I've also had the backing of the fans and that has helped me too. They've realised now that I am, hopefully, doing the business on the park and it's good to have them off my back!

'Now, we have our minds set on a glorious treble. We're up for it, although I feel we've hit a little lull over the last couple of games. Certainly that appeared to be the case against Partick Thistle, but the gaffer has been quick to remind us that we're playing for our places in the cup final – and that will help us buck our ideas up.'

One man who made sure he didn't miss out on the title celebrations was the irrepressible Ally McCoist. Sidelined through injury, McCoist didn't allow something as trivial as a broken leg to keep him away from Ibrox and he joined the post-match celebrations on crutches and with that life-sized cardboard cut-out of himself strapped to his back, with his face replaced by that of film star Oliver Reed.

And as the celebrations died down to a crescendo, McCoist revealed how he had received more than 2,000 get-well cards from Rangers supporters – and fans of Hearts, Hibs, Aberdeen and even Celtic!

He grinned, 'I don't know if that was a compliment or not, as they all seem to want me back playing as quickly as possible!'

Fellow pros such as Gordon Strachan and Alex McLeish had been in touch, as well as ex-Sunderland team-mates. During his stay at Ross Hall Hospital, Ally also received a fax from officials at Celtic wishing him a speedy recovery. He said, 'All the cards, flowers and messages have been very much appreciated. I'd like to thank everyone but unfortunately there have been so many messages it won't be possible.'

McCoist admitted the first couple of days following the accidental collision in the Stadium of Light were among the worst of his career, but it was clear the messages of goodwill had cheered him up, even though a season which had promised to be his best ever in football had ended in such a horrific way.

He said, 'Hey, I'm not the first guy who has ever broken his leg. You should see my X-rays – the break is as clean as you can get. It's as if someone has cracked a ruler along my shinbone. I won't even need a plate and I know I'll be back again at the start of next season, so what's the point in moaning?

'When I see guys like Ian Durrant and Gary Stevens, I realise I don't really have any problems. What these guys have gone through is far worse and puts my situation into perspective.'

Meanwhile, the ground staff couldn't be accused of letting the grass grow under their feet – as they ripped up the Ibrox playing surface straight after the match against Dundee United. The pitch was to be replaced in a £400,000 operation as part of a series of renovation works aimed at giving the club one of the best surfaces in Britain.

Over 30 dumper trucks and bulldozers moved in on Saturday evening and Sunday morning to begin the work, which was expected to last six weeks. The complete overhaul meant dropping the pitch by an extra 12 inches and moving it 14 inches towards the Govan Stand to give a clearer view of the match action. There were also plans to improve the surface by digging down an extra 18 inches and adding a new drainage system, soil mix and undersoil heating pipes. In addition, the maintenance team would oversee work around the playing surface, including the laying of a mini synthetic running surface to replace the existing red ash track.

Staff would also add two new rows of seats to both the Copland and Broomloan Road stands and three to the front of the Govan Stand, increasing capacity by 1,300. The work was set to continue throughout the summer and be finished in time for McCoist's testimonial match against Newcastle United on 3 August.

Pitch superintendent Alan Ferguson admitted he had been forced to act by the poor condition of the park, and added, 'Throughout the season we've had awful problems. We've had the wettest winter for 25 years and it has highlighted just how incapable we are of coping with heavy rain.'

Four matches had been cancelled that season, which had led to the purchase of rain covers in February to protect the pitch. And Alan reckoned the covers had prevented the loss of another four games. The main problem was not so much the rain, but poor drainage under the playing surface.

It was a win-win situation all round as Rangers struck on the novel idea of selling off the turf at a fiver per square metre. Profits, estimated at £6,500, went straight to the Ibrox Charity Fund to be donated to a number of worthy causes at the end of the season.

Supporters queued from 4am to make sure they got their hands on such a novel souvenir. By 10am, queues were snaking around the Copland, Govan and Broomloan stands as fans turned up in cars, vans and trailers to collect their turf.

There was the small matter of two league matches remaining, and the first, a trip to Pittodrie to face second-top Aberdeen, saw Walter Smith field virtually a full team of fringe players. There were starts for Ally Maxwell, Neil Murray, Oleg Kuznetsov, Brian Reid, Lee Robertson and David Hagen, but the players put up a sterling performance and could still hold their heads high despite a 1-0 loss. Both sides had a man sent off with Oleg Kuznetsov seeing red for clipping the heels of Duncan Shearer.

The final match of the season saw Rangers travel through to Falkirk, and the Light Blues signed off by winning 2-1 and setting a new Premier League points tally of 73 – one more than their total for the previous season, which had matched the figure reached by Celtic on their way to winning the title in 1988.

And while Rangers had already been crowned champs, and the Bairns were officially relegated the week previous, the match was still one of the better adverts for the Premier League. Goals by Mark Hateley and Alexei Mikhailichenko proved sufficient to cancel out Tommy McQueen's effort and ensure Rangers ended the league season on a high.

Meanwhile, Gary Stevens looked back on 12 months of injury misery and confessed, 'I thought I would have to quit football.'

The 30-year-old full-back was only starting to see light at the end of a disastrous season in which he had managed to play just ten times. His injury woes began at the end of the 1991/92 season when he fractured his foot playing for England against Brazil at Wembley. He was able to make a comeback in November, but played only three and a half matches before fracturing his knee against Airdrie. That ruled him out for a further two months, but his return to the top team lasted only three weeks before complications set in and he was forced to undergo another operation on his original foot injury.

He said, 'You have to be philosophical about these things, but there were times I worried if I would ever play again. When you spend four months out with a foot fracture, you expect it to heal, yet mine didn't. And I think because it was a re-occurring injury a series of worrying thoughts went through my mind.

'The worst times came at Christmas when I was back in the side for four matches and then fractured my knee at Broomfield, and also at the end of February when I found out I would have to go in for a second operation on my foot.'

Another Englishman who was less than happy was Mark Hateley, but the big man's anger was directed at Scotland's soccer chiefs over the delayed date of the Scottish Cup Final. The former England striker was bemused that the game was being held over until 29 May despite no matches being planned for the weekend before.

He said, 'It's hard to come away from Saturday's game at Falkirk knowing you won't be playing for another two weeks. It's a crazy situation. In an ideal world it would be nice to play the cup final this weekend, therefore giving players from both sides the chance of an extra week's summer holiday.

'When you're forced to play over 60 games each season it would be nice to have as many weeks' rest as possible over the close season. The players would be fresher, and therefore the product better.'

But Hateley was thrilled to have bagged his 28th goal of the season against the Bairns, and said, 'It's my best Ibrox tally yet – and there is one game left, but my total doesn't surprise me because my striking partnership with Alistair is thriving beyond my wildest dreams. We've scored more goals together this season than we did last, and even then we had scored more than the previous campaign, so it just seems to be getting better and better.'

One player on cloud nine was Brian Reid, who had just enjoyed the busiest spell of his Rangers career – and his best. The cultured central defender was delighted after getting back into the first team following a knee injury sustained in the Campbell Money testimonial match in 1991.

That came just two months after he was the last signing made by Graeme Souness, and Brian's performances in the recent matches at Aberdeen and Falkirk hinted that he may be well on the way to recapturing the form that persuaded the former Ibrox boss to pay Morton £300,000 for his services.

In addition, Reid also captained the Light Blues to victory in the Reserve League Cup Final at Hamilton the previous Thursday – after extra time. But there is no way he was complaining about playing five hours of football in such a short space of time.

He said, 'When you've missed so much of your career, you play as often as you can and you don't complain. This is the best I've felt since the injury. It took Ian Durrant a while to fully get his fitness back and hopefully the year I've spent in the reserves will do it for me. It has been a year of ups and downs, but the last week has been great and hopefully we can see a few more ups now.'

Rangers supporters missed out on a weekend in London when the English FA banned the club from taking part in the Makita Tournament, which was being hosted by Tottenham Hotspur over the weekend of 31 July and 1 August.

The FA insisted that it was worried about thousands of Scots converging on the capital for the two-day event, and rather than risk the possibility of trouble between fans of the clubs involved – Spurs, Arsenal and Ajax – the association, after discussions with Metropolitan Police chiefs, decided to sanction the tournament only if Rangers were not involved.

The decision was criticised by Campbell Ogilvie, who said, 'There is no longer a Wembley weekend for Scotland fans and the authorities felt if they allowed Rangers fans to travel, it could turn into a similar kind of two days. However, we regard this as a slight on both Rangers and Scottish football fans, particularly given the good disciplinary record of our supporters at home and abroad in recent years. We're also very disappointed because we've been in official contact with the English FA since early February, yet we've been forced to wait until May for a definite answer.'

P IETER Huistra's move to Rangers might have come about through coincidence but the passion and love he would come to feel for the club was heartfelt and genuine, and the former Dutch international still retains that affection – 22 years after leaving his adopted home on the south side of Glasgow.

Speaking of how the transfer came about, he said, 'I got a move from FC Twente to Rangers through more or less a coincidence. My agent met Graeme Souness at the draw for the European Cup and within a few moments they had struck up a conversation. My agent asked Graeme if he was looking for any type of player in particular and he said he was searching for a winger. My agent said he had a Dutch international winger and Graeme asked if I could come to the pre-season training camp – and that's how it started.

'I went to the training camp at Il Ciocco in Italy and I seemed to do quite well. Graeme then said to me, "I like you but I have to see you playing in a game. Would you be willing to come back to Glasgow with us?" Naturally I was and while in Glasgow I played a match against Queens Park at Lesser Hampden and after that game he spoke to me and said, "Okay, we can offer you a contract." And that was how I ended up at Ibrox.'

Huistra had other options at the time, with one being to remain in Holland with a top club, but he admits he quite fancied the idea of taking a little bit of a gamble. He added, 'At that time I was thinking the moment was right to leave FC Twente, but I was supposed to go to PSV Eindhoven. There was no Bosman then, and Twente didn't want me to go because I was an international player, and so they made it difficult for me to leave.

'PSV offered a good amount of money, much more than Rangers did. In fact, PSV offered around two million guilders, which was about £800,000, while Rangers offered £300,000. Due to the contract situation in Holland back then, it was much easier for me to go abroad, so Rangers got me quite cheaply I think at that moment.

'But since the day and hour I joined Rangers, I never regretted the decision to come to Glasgow one bit. Many Dutch players have signed for Rangers in the last couple of decades, but I am still very proud that I was the first Dutchman to sign for the club. It was very easy for me to settle in because I had good help at the club and communication wasn't a problem as I spoke English.

'Mind you, Scottish was quite a bit different! It really did take me quite a while before I was able to understand some of our players, but once I could understand Ian Durrant and Ian Ferguson I was fine. Seriously, though, I felt at home right from the beginning and knew I had made a good choice.'

The tail-end of Huistra's second season – 1991/92 – was about as low as it got for the talented left-sided player. He missed out on both the Scottish Cup Final and the Dutch squad for the European Championships and admits that he felt a real sense of frustration.

He explained, 'It wasn't a good time for me as I missed out with both Rangers and Holland. I realise it was difficult for the Rangers manager back then because the rules only permitted 13 players to be stripped for action. Two substitutes wasn't a lot so it was a tough call for the manager, and having been a coach myself I know that it isn't easy. Normally, these days, you have a good idea of your one to 11, and then there are one or two subs that you know must be in there, but I struggle with naming the rest of the substitutes as it's really difficult for players to miss out altogether.

'For the Scottish Cup Final it was difficult, because we had a big squad and we had good players so that's how it was and it is always going to be a big disappointment if you're not in the squad for a cup final. I certainly wasn't happy about it, but that was not a reflection on the manager or the club, just me, but I renewed my contract, so I was obviously happy with Rangers.

'As far as the Dutch team was concerned I was in the initial squad of 25 for the European Championships, but unfortunately I was one of the three who dropped out when the final 22 was announced. To be honest, one of the main reasons I missed out on the Dutch squad was because I had a problem with my groin. I had an operation in the February, so I didn't play in March or April and I made my comeback right at the end of the season. I wasn't at my best as I still had to build up my match fitness, which is also the reason the manager left me out.'

As Rangers chased glory on the European front, Huistra revealed how the club's foreign legion would all wait patiently to see who was in and who was out. He said, 'The three-foreigner rule applied only to Europe so every time a match came around we would all wait to see who was in the team. We all knew the rule beforehand but we would all be trying everything we could to be one of the three, so it was like a little contest within the squad. I still managed to play my fair share of European games so it was okay for me.

'I always liked to think of myself as a wide-playing midfielder, but I liked to get up the park as much as possible and get good crosses into the box and, let's be honest, when you had players like Mark Hateley and Ally McCoist in the box you always had a chance of scoring. Hateley had the ability to turn a bad cross into a good looking one, and whatever the big man missed, McCoist was there to clean up. McCoist was a very good goalscorer but I think he got more chances because Mark was there to distract the opponents. He was very good at disrupting the organisation of the opposition.'

Huistra has no doubts that the 1992/93 season was the most successful of his playing days; a career which has included stints in Holland, Belgium, Japan and, of course, Scotland. He said, 'Yes, it was my most successful by far – definitely the best ever. Maybe we didn't have the best ever Rangers players that season but we had the best team. That team was unbelievable and many times I tell people that we simply refused to lose football matches. Our side wasn't even content with a draw, and losing wasn't an option.

'We went on a fantastic 44-game unbeaten run that season, and on many occasions we were behind in these matches, but you could physically see the players getting a little bit angry and then we would switch gear; perhaps move two gears up, and we wouldn't stop when it was 1-1, or even 2-1. When we got a third goal then everybody would say okay, and switch back a gear and suddenly think about the next game. It was quite unique.

'The games were coming thick and fast so that is why we had to peak in such a short space of time; turn the game back in our favour and then relax a little, because we had so many matches to play. After you switch back down the gears, often what happens is you get a bit more space. You relax more and tend to keep the ball and pass it around a bit better and longer.

'I certainly think the best way to peak as often as possible is to play as many games as you can. Okay, sometimes you can have too many games – possibly like that season – but you are calling on your adrenaline, and also the games against the bigger teams tend to bring out the best in you. If you're playing against the smaller Scottish teams, games that you're expected to win comfortably, then we are only human and sometimes you relax just a little too much.

'Aberdeen were definitely the second best team in Scotland that season. We beat them in both cup finals and they finished just behind us in the race for the championship, so they were our main contenders. They had a very good team at that time; they were a good unit. They stuck together very well and gave us a few problems. They were a tough team to play against but we ultimately did very well against them, especially when it mattered most.

'The thing that made us such a difficult team to beat that season was our incredible team spirit, there is no doubt about that. I can't successful just how important that is in football. We played an incredible amount of games, so therefore team spirit became that bit more important as we had to rely very heavily on each other.

'If you take the number of games for Rangers and add in matches for the various international teams, then we were more or less playing weekends and midweek for the entire season. Playing all the time takes its toll on your body, while travelling and not getting to see your family so much can also be emotionally tough. Guys like David Robertson played just about every game that season, so he must have been very tired at the end. If my memory serves me right, he pulled his hamstring just through sheer fatigue. But it would be worse if it was a long season and you had nothing to show for it at the end.

'One of the most important things was that you walked on to that pitch knowing you had a great chance of winning, and also knowing that the team would support you whatever you did. That makes you feel almost invincible, and it was something that I never had to such a high degree in any other season. And with your body language, the other team knows that you think you are invincible, so it maybe has twice the impact. You could see it when you were in the tunnel waiting to go out. Perhaps it was a little bit of arrogance, but you could certainly feel it.'

Huistra will never forget the incredible European campaign as long as he lives. It seemed like Rangers made a new memory with each passing tie, but it wasn't all a bed of roses. He said, 'To be unbeaten in all ten matches was very pleasing, but there was a sense of both pride and frustration at the way it all ended. First and foremost we were very proud of what we had achieved. In the run-up we played Lyngby and Leeds – and won both home and away legs – which was very pleasing.

'Up to the last game it was all about goal difference, as we had drawn both games against Marseille, and then they had this crazy score against CSKA Moscow, and against a very good Moscow team, I should add. To this day people still talk suspiciously about that result.

'And of course we were a little bit disappointed that we drew the last game against Moscow. They had good players but we were very keen to finish up with a win, and we tried so hard and had so much pressure in the game at Ibrox but they just didn't give in.

'It was a pity we didn't qualify to meet Milan in the final but we could still take a lot of pride in what we achieved in Europe that season. We came very close to being in the final. In fact, after the final match was over I was speaking to a few of the AC Milan guys when we met up with the Dutch national squad and they were saying they were happy not to be playing us. The likes of Marco van Basten and Frank Rijkaard knew how we played and said they didn't like our style. They didn't like our fight and determination, but they also couldn't cope too well with our direct approach in games.'

Huistra insisted he will never have anything but good memories of his time at Ibrox, and said, 'For me, my time at Rangers was the best part of my career. It really was a great place to play football and whenever I look back at it I do so with real fondness.

'When it was time for me to move on from FC Twente, I didn't see the move to Rangers as too much of a gamble, as they already had a very good name on the continent. Scottish football in the late 1980s was doing okay in Europe. We had the likes of Aberdeen and Dundee United, and obviously Rangers. So, for me it was not a big gamble as Rangers were a big club, and I knew of them.

'I suppose when you move anywhere you always have to wait and see how it will turn out, and that was as much up to me as I was going to a new place and I had to make the best of it. You have to adapt and you have to work on making yourself a better footballer. I definitely improved as a player because of my time at Rangers.

'I had a good relationship with Graeme Souness, the man who took me to Rangers, and I always felt appreciated by him, and when Walter Smith took over it was more or less much of the same. I think Walter and Archie Knox were definitely the right management team at the right club. They knew all the players very well, especially Walter, as he had been the assistant to Graeme Souness, so there were no real problems when he took over as manager. Archie then came in and he gave the players energy with his banter and enthusiasm, so that was a big positive.'

Huistra is now involved in management, and he concluded, 'I just finished with a team in Japan and had a very nice year there and then I came back to Europe to take a bit of time off before getting back into football again. Japan is a lovely country and I thoroughly enjoyed it, but now it's time for a new chapter.'

But with a final reflection on his time at Ibrox he said, 'One of the main legacies I will carry with me from my time at Rangers is the fact that we were only the fifth Rangers team in the club's history to win the treble. To be honest, that was very special. It was definitely one to cherish as it hasn't happened so much, therefore it means an awful lot to me.'

23

Make Mine a Treble!

FROM the moment Walter Smith threw down the gauntlet to his players, urging them to prove they deserved their place at the table reserved for the greatest ever Rangers, to the Scottish Cup Final itself, the spotlight on the Ibrox squad was as intense as ever.

Aberdeen, led by former Ibrox captain Willie Miller, had lived in the shadow of the Light Blues the entire season. Beaten finalists in the Skol Cup and runners-up in the Premier League, they had regained a shred of integrity by edging Rangers 1-0 in the penultimate league match at Pittodrie, although the champions had fielded a shadow 11 that evening.

Rangers had won the other three league meetings but there was never much between the sides, and the Skol Cup Final had gone all the way. There was no question that Aberdeen had emerged as the main contenders in 1992/93. Celtic may have finished third in the table but had never seriously threatened Rangers' domination. The Light Blues had been on a different level to the Parkhead side and the eventual 13-point gap between the clubs was a poor reflection of the actual gulf in class.

If they say football is cyclical, and I believe there is merit in that theory, then Celtic – a once-dominant force – were in among the also-rans. So it was fitting that the season's grand finale should see the top two teams go head-to-head for the final piece of silverware in the showpiece event, which was ironically being held at Celtic Park, and both had valid reasons for wanting to be victorious.

It was three years since the Dons had lifted a trophy, namely the Scottish Cup, and they were still smarting from losing the league title on the final day of the season to Rangers one year later. Miller was also keen to land his first trophy as Dons boss.

Richard Gough, on the other hand, was well aware that success at Parkhead would see him and his mates join an elite band of blues brothers; those who had won a treble at the most successful club side in the country. As I alluded to in the opening sentence, Smith demanded that his current crop join the elite and become only the fifth Rangers side in history to win a treble.

Also, victory in the final would be a fitting end to a season that was rapidly gaining the title of the best in the history of the club, and it was hard to argue. A fifth successive league title, the Skol Cup, a tremendous European run and a 44-match unbeaten sequence, including ten in the European Cup, was the main reason the Scottish Cup would be the icing on the perfectly baked cake.

Smith said, 'I think we have shown this season that we have the right to be counted among the best ever Rangers sides and I hope our players cement that reputation by beating Aberdeen. The chance to win the first treble in 15 years is a great motivation for everyone at the club. It has been achieved by other Rangers sides in the past and we want to follow in those footsteps. That would put us alongside the best this club has produced.'

However, Smith was aware of the pitfalls of losing, and said, 'It's important to end the season with a bang rather than a whimper because there's always big disappointment if you lose the Scottish Cup Final. It's the last game of the season which means you have to mope around for the rest of the summer. Along with the chance of a treble, we also want to win for that reason.

'The players are aware of what's at stake, we don't need one last push. They know they have to be up for this match and they will be.'

Both sides had faced a rather unnecessary break in the fortnight leading up to the showpiece match, due to fixture scheduling, and Smith had whisked his first team squad off to Monaco for a few days before returning four days before the final to prepare in earnest.

He admitted, 'I don't think anyone would have wanted that break. We would have preferred to finish the league season and go right into the Scottish Cup Final as normal. However, it hasn't been too much of a problem. The boys had a relaxing few days away and they have been buzzing again in recent training sessions. The anticipation and awareness is back and I can sense just how much they're looking forward to this game.'

Rather interestingly, Bomber Brown suggested that by winning the Scottish Cup, Rangers could realistically become the final Scottish side to win the recognised treble.

He explained, 'Recent talk about league reconstruction has led to hints that the League Cup could be removed from our football calendar within the next couple of years, so this could very well be our last opportunity to grab all three trophies in one season – a feat which we were also the first club to achieve!

'Aberdeen will be desperate to win the cup, to rescue something from their season, but the chance of a treble is by far a bigger carrot dangling in front of our eyes. And, if any extra incentive were needed, there are still quite a few of the lads at Ibrox who were involved the last time we blew our chances of the treble in 1989.

'Even though we won the Skol Cup and league championship that season, our whole summer was ruined because we let the Scottish Cup slip away. We will be transferring that memory across to the rest of the lads who weren't at the club at that time just to let them know we can't have a repeat this time around.'

But if there was one player who had an extra incentive to get his hands on the national trophy it was Ian Ferguson – and that was so the midfield powerhouse could finally get to see inside the hallowed Ibrox trophy room. Superstitious Fergie had never been inside the treasure trove housed at the top of the marble staircase after vowing to look inside only when the Light Blues won the treble. It was a promise he made when joining from St Mirren in February 1988 and he had stuck to his promise.

He said, 'I've had plenty of chances to look inside. Some of our fans and even the tea ladies at Ibrox have asked me into the trophy room for photographs, but each time I've declined and stood at the door instead.

'When I first signed for Rangers I wanted to go up there and have a look at the Skol Cup, which we'd won that season, and the league championship trophy, which we'd collected the year before, but I stopped short and decided I would wait until we'd won the treble, and I've stuck to that decision ever since. I haven't even been tempted to have a peek round the door!'

The 26-year-old Glaswegian was easily the most superstitious player at Ibrox, and he revealed how he was adding even more rituals to his routine the older he got. While most players were content to stick to the same pre-match meal, wear the same clothes each matchday or put their kit on in the same order, Fergie went a few steps further.

He said, 'My mother is also superstitious and I think I take it from her. Even in my early days working for the soft drinks company Dunn and Moore, or in the hospitals as a porter, I refused to walk under ladders or do anything that was supposed to bring bad luck. But now I'm desperate to get rid of one of my superstitions, and that is to be able to go into the trophy room for a look around – and if we win the Scottish Cup, that will be sorted!'

On the eve of the big match, Mark Hateley warned Aberdeen, 'Watch out for Super Swiggy!'

The message for the Dons was aimed at dispelling any notion that Rangers' firepower had been diluted since Ally McCoist's season-ending injury in Lisbon. Far from it, because Gary McSwegan had stepped into Super Ally's boots alongside the big Englishman and the goals had just kept on coming.

Hateley joked, 'Of course I miss Ally up front, but I no longer suffer from earache as I normally do when he's playing.'

He added, 'Seriously, Ally is a great character and a great player, but Gary has come into the side in his absence and played really well. We both scored goals when we played together in the run-in to the end of the league season and I have no doubts we can do the same again at Celtic Park.'

Another youngster hoping to grab a slice of the action in the showpiece final was central defender Steven Pressley. And when he discovered his pre-season break would extend to just three weeks, he couldn't have been happier.

'Elvis' was named along with team-mate Lee Robertson in the Scotland under-21 squad, which was set to travel to the prestigious Toulon Tournament in France on 5 June. The Scots were drawn against the host nation, Bulgaria and Mexico. And with the tournament scheduled to run until 15 June, and pre-season training starting at Ibrox on 7 July, there wasn't a great deal of time for both Pressley and Robertson to rest and recuperate.

But Pressley said, 'You do need a holiday over the summer, but this tournament will give me a lot of experience, so it won't be bad for me. It's a great opportunity to play with and against a lot of good players in front of a lot of important people and I'm really looking forward to the trip.'

But talking about domestic matters, he added, 'I had hoped to be involved in a few matches for Rangers this season, so to have played in ten so far and to be in with a chance of making the squad for the cup final has been a dream come true.'

On to the east end of Glasgow for the big game and Smith named the following side to take on Aberdeen: Goram, McCall, Robertson, Gough, McPherson, Brown, Murray, Ferguson, Durrant, Hateley and Huistra. The substitutes were Pressley and McSwegan.

Aberdeen lined up with Snelders, McKimmie, Wright, Grant, Irvine, McLeish, Richardson, Mason, Booth, Shearer and Paatelainen, with Smith and Jess on the bench.

Referee Jim McCluskey of Stewarton got the game under way at 3pm and it was the men from Pittodrie who appeared to settle quicker, soon enjoying the lion's share of possession. With just 90 seconds on the clock Brian Grant broke free from the middle of the park and unleashed a cracking shot that smacked off the outside of Andy Goram's post. Three minutes later, Goram had to look lively to punch clear a dangerous Paul Mason cross.

It was an early warning for the Light Blues and 14 minutes had passed before they managed to carve out anything of great significance. Stuart McCall crossed the ball into the box and Mark Hateley nodded it down for Ian Durrant, but the midfielder was under pressure from two defenders and failed to get his header on target.

But eight minutes later, Rangers took the lead. Pieter Huistra waltzed down the left but found himself crowded out on the edge of the box. He prodded the ball back to McCall, who swept it first time into the box. Brian Irvine failed to cut out the danger, leaving Neil Murray in acres of space at the back post. He looked as though he had lost the chance with a clumsy first touch, but he managed to get a shot in and looked on with unbridled joy as it deflected in off Irvine, leaving Theo Snelders helpless.

Durrant was by this time running the show and was at the heart of everything good about Rangers' play. Suddenly, Smith's decision to allow him time off to holiday in the USA was paying dividends. He created chances for Murray and Ian Ferguson but both were missed.

And it was Durrant's vision and precise passing ability that led to Rangers' second goal just before half-time. Durrant, Huistra and Hateley worked a triangle on the left, before Durrant threaded the ball through and Hateley's left-footed shot beat Snelders at his near post.

After the break, Aberdeen stepped up the pace again but despite Lee Richardson pulling a goal back, Rangers defended well and, superbly marshalled by Richard Gough, held on comfortably to win the Scottish Cup for the 26th time and secure their place in the Ibrox history books.

For Aberdeen, it was the third time of the season they had played the role of bridesmaid to the all-conquering Rangers, but Smith – who became just the fourth Rangers manager to win the treble – refused to believe that his club's dominance of the domestic game was a bad thing for Scottish football.

He said, 'I don't think we should concern ourselves with the reaction of others to our treble win and what it might mean for Scottish football. As long as we are acquitting ourselves well in Europe, people will actually look in on Scottish football and say that at least the team that is winning everything there is also doing well on the European scene. In fact, I would hope we've actually lifted a lot of people's estimations of the game up here with our displays at home and in the European Cup this season.'

Since taking over the Ibrox hot seat in April 1991, the only domestic trophy Smith and his assistant Archie Knox had failed to win was the Skol Cup in 1991/92 when they were knocked out by Hibs in the semi-finals.

However, Smith was only interested in paying tribute to his players for their latest efforts, and said, 'Winning the treble is a terrific achievement. We have been building towards it for a couple of years now and I think the players thoroughly deserve it for their efforts this season.

'The cup final was always going to be difficult as it came a fortnight after our last league match and a month after we won the title, so our competitive edge had been blunted somewhat. However, to come back into the match and play as we did is a tremendous credit to our players. We have lived up to the traditions of the great Rangers teams this season!'

The Rangers supporters present at Celtic Park also received praise for their performance as they turned the terraces into a Union Jack paradise. Smith said, 'I think our fans are enjoying the success at the moment and you can see that on the terraces. After all, they are the reason football clubs exist in the first place. We want our fans to come, enjoy their football and hopefully see their team winning things and it's evident that they are having a great time. I can't speak highly enough of them and I think any supporter who has followed our team home and abroad will take a great deal of pleasure from this season.'

McCall also praised the supporters – and insisted they had inspired him to his greatest ever campaign. The Scotland midfielder also said the manner in which they had backed the team both home and away was nothing short of phenomenal.

He added, 'The fans at Parkhead were amazing with all their flags and streamers, and the lap of honour afterwards was certainly one to remember. But for me the bus journey back from Celtic Park after the game was an absolute highlight. It took us three-quarters of an hour to get past the District Bar on Paisley Road West! The fans poured out of the pub when they heard the team was coming and their reaction was just unbelievable.

'Usually, we like the driver, Jimmy Bell, to drive as quickly as possible, but Andy Goram was spot on when he told him to get the handbrake on when he saw all the supporters. We wanted to savour the moment.

'It hit home that our season is all about giving our supporters something to celebrate, and I'm so glad we could do that against Aberdeen. We never once contemplated defeat.'

Ian Ferguson revealed after the final whistle that he was just 24 hours away from missing out on the big match. The midfielder was confined to bed for two days at the team's pre-match retreat at Turnberry – and it was touch and go as to whether he would make it or not as he was suffering from a high temperature and swollen glands.

He said, 'Had I been the same on Friday morning I think the gaffer would have ruled me out there and then. Fortunately, I felt a little better that morning, did some training with the rest of the boys, and that seemed to clear my head.

'I had a good night's sleep on Friday and sweated the flu out of me by the morning of the game. But I felt very tired as the match went on, although I thoroughly enjoyed the game, as well as the party atmosphere created by our fans.

'I thought it would go to the wire, and that's the way it turned out, although I must confess I was very surprised we had a 2-0 lead at half-time. Often teams can get complacent with a cushion like that but we continued to battle to get the result we deserved.

'The feeling that we've won the treble hasn't sunk in yet, but I'm sure it will over the summer, and I can now end my self-imposed exile from the trophy room – as we've won the lot!'

Meanwhile, goal hero Hateley insisted his dad Tony was his lucky mascot. The former Liverpool, Chelsea and Coventry hitman was in the stand to watch his son carry on the family tradition of scoring big goals in important games.

Hateley junior said, 'I was confident before the game that we would win and that I would score. My dad was there, so we couldn't fail. He's a big game man and comes to all the cup finals and definitely brings me luck.

'Parkhead is a good place for me. I enjoy playing there and I also happen to enjoy playing against Aberdeen. The atmosphere was brilliant as well, so I had a great day. I just remember a little flick-on from Ian Durrant. I ran between the two defenders as I knew he was going to knock it through the gap. I made my mind up early to have a go and my shot went straight through the keeper's legs.

'You should never score from there really, but I was fortunate enough to manage it. I can't think of too many times I've nutmegged a keeper, but a cup final is probably as good a game as any to do it.'

Hateley thoroughly enjoyed playing up front with temporary strike partner, Durrant, and the injured McCoist was overheard passing on some tips to the makeshift striker, who joked, 'You're history McCoist. After a performance like that I'll be keeping the number nine jersey next season!'

But McCoist countered with, 'Yes Durranty, but when you're wearing it you're supposed to score!'

And it was exactly this type of dressing-room humour that illustrated the bond which quite clearly existed between the players at Ibrox. 'The team that drinks together, wins together' etc, and there was certainly more than an element of truth in it.

So many of the players interviewed for this book insisted they had never before been part of anything so special as Rangers' Class of '92/93, where an indomitable team spirit seemed equally as important as the agility of Goram, the creativeness in midfield of Durrant or McCoist's goals. So often had the team come back from the dead in matches, or resembled a pride of lions when having to dig deep against the best the continent had to offer.

For us supporters, it was the ride of a lifetime. From that narrow opening day league win at home to St Johnstone, when David Murray unfurled a fourth successive league flag, to the Scottish Cup Final victory over Aberdeen at Celtic Park, it was something that will forever have its own special place in our memories.

One of the eight stars on the Champions League flag is reserved for Glasgow Rangers – as one of the eight teams to have taken part in the original competition – and that can never be taken away. It's there for keeps and is just one fantastic remnant from an unforgettable campaign.

All that's left to say is, 'Thanks for the memories. It was a blast.'

1992/93:

Date	Opponent	Result	Competition	Venue	Scorers	Attendance
August						
1	St Johnstone	1-0	League	Home	McCoist	38,036
4	Airdrie	2-0	League	Home	Gordon, Hateley	34,613
8	Hibs	0-0	League	Away		17,044
11	Dumbarton	5-0	Skol Cup	Hamp	Durr, Gord, McCoist, Hate, Miko	11,091
15	Dundee	3-4	League	Away	McCoist 2, Ferguson	12,807
19	Stranraer	5-0	Skol Cup	Away	McCoist 3, Hateley 2	4,500
22	Celtic	1-1	League	Home	Durrant	43,239
26	Dundee Utd	3-2	Skol Cup	Away	Gough, McCoist, Huistra	15,716
29	Aberdeen	3-1	League	Home	Durrant, McCoist, Miko	41,636
September						
2	Motherwell	4-1	League	Away	McCoist 3, Brown	10,074
12	Partick Th	4-1	League	Away	McCall, Gough, McPh, Hateley	10,460
16	Lyngby	2-0	European Cup	Home	Hateley, Huistra	40,036
19	Hearts	2-0	League	Home	McCall, McCoist	41,888

Date	Opponent	Result	Competition	Venue	Scorers	Attendance
22	St Johnstone	3-1	Skol Cup	Hamp	McCoist 3	30,062
26	Dundee Utd	4-0	League	Away	Steven, McCoist, Huistra 2	13,515
30	Lyngby	1-0	European Cup	Away	Durrant	4,273
October						
3	Falkirk	4-0	League	Home	McCoist 4	40,691
7	St Johnstone	5-1	League	Home	McCoist 2, Hateley 2, Ferguson	9,532
17	Hibs	1-0	League	Home	McCoist	40,978
21	Leeds United	2-1	European Cup	Home	Own goal, McCoist	43,251
25	Aberdeen	2-1	Skol Cup Final	Hamp	McCall, Own goal	45,298
31	Motherwell	4-2	League	Home	McCoist 3, Brown	38,719
November						
4	Leeds United	2-1	European Cup	Away	Hateley, McCoist	25,118
7	Celtic	1-0	League	Away	Durrant	51,958
11	Dundee	3-1	League	Home	McCoist 2, Hateley	33,497
21	Hearts	1-1	League	Away	McCoist	20,831
25	Marseille	2-2	Champs Lg	Home	McSwegan, Hateley	41,624
28	Partick Th	3-0	League	Home	McSwegan, Steven, McPherson	40,939

248

Date	Opponent	Result	Competition	Venue	Scorers	Attendance
December						
1	Airdrie	1-1	League	Away	Brown	8,000
9	CSKA	1-0	Champs Lg	Away	Ferguson	9,000
12	Falkirk	2-1	League	Away	McCoist, Hateley	12,000
19	St Johnstone	2-0	League	Home	D Robertson, Gough	35,369
26	Dundee	3-1	League	Away	McCoist, Hateley 2	13,983
January						
2	Celtic	1-0	League	Home	Steven	46,039
5	Dundee Utd	3-2	League	Home	McCall, McCoist, Hateley	40,239
9	Motherwell	2-0	Scottish Cup	Away	McCoist 2	14,314
30	Hibs	4-3	League	Away	Hateley 2, Steven, McCoist	17,444
February						
2	Aberdeen	1-0	League	Away	Hateley	15,500
6	Ayr United	2-0	Scottish Cup	Away	Gordon, McCoist	13,176
9	Falkirk	5-0	League	Home	Steven, Huistra, Hateley 2, Rob	34,780
13	Airdrie	2-2	League	Home	McCoist 2	39,816
20	Dundee Utd	0-0	League	Away		13,234

249

Date	Opponent	Result	Competition	Venue	Scorers	Attendance
23	Motherwell	4-0	League	Away	McCoist, Hateley 2, Miko	14,006
27	Hearts	2-1	League	Home	McCoist, D Robertson	42,128
March						
3	Bruges	1-1	Champs Lg	Away	Huistra	19,000
6	Arbroath	3-0	Scottish Cup	Away	McCoist, Hateley, Murray	6,488
10	St Johnstone	1-1	League	Away	McCoist	9,210
13	Hibs	3-0	League	Home	McCoist, Hateley, Hagen	41,076
17	Bruges	2-1	Champs Lg	Home	Durrant, Nisbet	42,731
20	Celtic	1-2	League	Away	Hateley	53,241
27	Dundee	3-0	League	Home	McCall, McCoist, Ferguson	40,294
30	Aberdeen	2-0	League	Home	Ferguson, McCoist	44,570
April						
3	Hearts	2-1	Scottish Cup	P'head	McPherson, McCoist	41,738
7	Marseille	1-1	Champs Lg	Away	Durrant	40,000
10	Motherwell	1-0	League	Home	Brown	41,353
14	Hearts	3-2	League	Away	McCall, Hateley 2	14,622
17	Partick Th	3-1	League	Home	McSwegan 2, Hagen	42,636
21	CSKA	0-0	Champs Lg	Home		43,142

Date May	Opponent	Result	Competition	Venue	Scorers	Attendance
1	Airdrie	1-0	League	Away	McSwegan	11,830
4	Partick Th	0-3	League	Away		9,834
8	Dundee Utd	1-0	League	Home	Huistra	42,917
12	Aberdeen	0-1	League	Away		13,500
15	Falkirk	2-1	League	Away	Hateley, Miko	8,517
29	Aberdeen	2-1	Scot Cup Final	P'head	Murray, Hateley	50,715

Appearances and Goals

Player	Starts	Subs	Goals
David Robertson	58	0	3
John Brown	57	2	4
Mark Hateley	53	1	29
Stuart McCall	53	1	6
Dave McPherson	53	0	3
Andy Goram	52	0	0
Ally McCoist	50	2	49
Ian Ferguson	42	1	5
Richard Gough	39	0	3
Pieter Huistra	37	5	7
Trevor Steven	35	1	5
Ian Durrant	34	13	7
Alexei Mikhailichenko	24	15	4
Dale Gordon	22	5	3
Neil Murray	17	6	2
Scott Nisbet	16	1	2
Ally Maxwell	12	0	0
Gary Stevens	10	0	0
Gary McSwegan	9	5	5
Steven Pressley	8	3	0
Oleg Kuznetsov	7	1	0
David Hagen	6	4	2
Nigel Spackman	3	0	0
Steven Watson	3	0	0
Brian Reid	2	0	0
Lee Robertson	1	0	0
Paul Rideout	0	2	0
Sandy Robertson	0	2	0